Beyond the
Mommy Years

Beyond
THE
Mommy Years

How to Live Happily Ever After ...
After the Kids Leave Home

Carin Rubenstein, PhD

SPRINGBOARD PRESS

NEW YORK BOSTON

Springboard Press
Hachette Book Group USA
237 Park Avenue, New York, NY 10017
Visit our Web site at www.HachetteBookGroupUSA.com

Springboard Press is an imprint of Grand Central Publishing. The Springboard name and logo is a trademark of Hachette Book Group USA, Inc.

FIRST EDITION: AUGUST 2007

Library of Congress Cataloging-in-Publication Data

Rubenstein, Carin.
    Beyond the mommy years : how to live happily ever after . . . after the kids
    leave home / Carin Rubenstein. — 1st ed.
        p. cm.
    ISBN-13: 978-0-446-58080-9
    ISBN-10: 0-446-58080-5
  1. Middle-aged mothers. 2. Middle-aged women—Life skills guides.
3. Empty nesters—Life skills guides. I. Title.

HQ1059.4.R83   2007
306.874'30844—dc22   2007000339

10 9 8 7 6 5 4 3 2 1

Book design by Fearn Cutler de Vicq

Printed in the United States of America

Contents

Introduction

I wrote this book to convince myself that my life wasn't over after my children left home. Here's what I discovered: most of us will learn not only to live with our children's absence but to love it.

As I began this book, I was living through the very early stages of adjustment to my newly empty, newly child-free house. Even with my husband around, it felt very empty, very quiet, and very, very clean.

In fact, it felt completely unnatural, like an unhaunted house on Halloween, an undecorated home on the holidays. It was disorienting and upsetting, but also strangely wonderful.

I was living my life feeling a mysterious mixture of both loss and gratification, a stage of life that has no real name. Indeed, "empty nest" hardly describes the magnitude of the changes I was undergoing and seems inadequate to explain what this stage of life is about. A close friend told me recently that she doesn't like the phrase "because it sounds too much like 'emptiness.'"

And, pardon me, but the nest is far from empty just because the kids are gone. After all, my husband and I are still here, and we're the ones who started the nest, built and feathered it, and paid to fix the water heater and the boiler and everything else in the nest. So to call it empty is grossly inaccurate.

I'm still here, so please don't call my nest empty. My wallet is certainly empty, but not my house!

Still, during the first few weeks after my son left home, I felt a sense of loss as I looked at both of my children's empty bedrooms. I missed them, I missed their physical presence, I missed their "being-hereness."

I grieved for their absence, but also for the loss of my role as a full-time mother. A friend says that since her three children moved out, she feels a kind of phantom-limb pain, a persistent ache at their absence. She can't get over the realization that she made career decisions based on the fact that she was a mother and wanted to be available for her children. But, it turns out, her situation wasn't permanent, she says. "I thought this was for keeps, but no, this is a rental," she explains, referring to her children's presence in her life.

That expresses the problem, exactly. At the time it was happening, **we felt as if it would last forever, but everyday motherhood does not last**. Our time with our children is borrowed, leased, rented out to us, and there comes a point at which we have to realize that it's mostly over. And, as a sociologist pointed out to me recently, mothers will know their children for much longer as independent adults than they will have known them as dependent children.

Think about that. Your child is a child for barely eighteen years; but your grown child is an adult for decades. So we have to prepare ourselves to be mothers of adult children for the rest of our lives.

This is the reason that the children's departure signals a new stage in life for moms, a transition from the intensive-mothering stage to the occasional-mothering stage. It's the official end of the mommy years. But while it signals a conclusion of one stage, it's the beginning of another very important one.

It's the beginning of a time of life that is not about the children; it's about us.

It is about facing life as more than mother, as after mother, as beyond mother. It's about what we do with ourselves and the next part of our lives, the emancipated stage of motherhood, the third adulthood.

First there was adult life with no children, which began on our eighteenth or twenty-first birthday. Next came parenthood. Finally, once again, there is life with no children at home.

It's déjà vu all over again.

Only this time, we're not the ones doing the leaving—we're the ones being left. But make no mistake, watching our children leave home is one of the most important turning points in our life. It is also the fulcrum on which the remainder of our life rests.

Some of us may look back with longing to the good old days of being in college or of day-to-day motherhood. But others will face the future as women with decades of a new and different kind of life ahead of us. It's a life that includes our growing and grown children, but one that also goes beyond motherhood. This is a life starring us, written by us, and directed by us. If our lives were a movie, it would be called *Mom, Emancipated.* Or maybe *Motherhood, Unplugged.*

This new postmommyhood life is a luxury endowed to baby-boom women because we've had fewer children and will live longer than mothers have ever lived before, so we have more good years left after our children leave for college or jobs. There are millions of us, and our numbers are growing each year, as more and more of the youngest children of baby-boom parents leave home. Census figures indicate that about seventy-seven million Americans are baby boomers, born between 1946 and 1964. Of them, at least thirty million no longer have children younger than eighteen.

As members of a huge cohort, the giant generation known as the baby boom, we're moving toward this turning point with a lot of company. Right now, around half of married-couple families do not include any children. And every year for the next decade that proportion will continue to rise.

As more mothers join the no-children-at-home brigade, we will also be reinventing ourselves. We are a generation with a unique mind-set, one that values honesty and independence, one that endorses feminism and shared parenting. We would never say that a woman's place is only in the home—to be a wife, to stay at home, to defer to her mate. Instead, we embrace the notion that women have choices. It's acceptable for women to marry or not, to have children or not, to be highly educated or not, to work full-time or not. We love the idea of giving ourselves choices as we make our way through life. We question authority, we are irreverent, we are idealists, and we are obsessed with youth, even as we ourselves grow older.

All of us in the baby boom are traversing the same path through this half of adult life. Some of us are already there; others will be there soon enough. But eventually we all will be in the same postmommyhood boat together.

The question is this: will we chart a new course for ourselves and our new lives, or will we paddle around in circles, never getting anywhere we haven't already been?

The answer is the subject of this book.

My focus here is mostly on the intense five- or ten-year period when all of these changes take place. I'll offer women examples of how to be thrivers and survivors, rather than stuck and out of luck. Thrivers and survivors embrace life's many changes, not just biological ones, like menopause, but those that are psychological, like giving up the full-time mother role and replacing it with something equally exciting and rewarding.

Perhaps most important, however, **this book is not about how children change as they are launched**. And it is not about fathers, either. It is about the mothers who are initiating the launch countdown. It is about the women who emerge on the other side of motherhood, while also propelling themselves into motherhood's second half. The feeling is remarkably similar to breaking from our own parents, only now it's the mirror image. It is a time of intense self-reflection, self-examination, and a new setting of priorities. It is a time for undoing regrets, for exploring all possible selves, for finding hidden identities that have been squelched under the enormous pressure of Being Mom.

Fathers deal with their own sense of loss when their children leave home, but theirs is a different story, and one that I am not going to touch upon here. Quite frankly, the issue often matters more to mothers, and they are more likely to experience some anguish and soul-searching about what happens next. I would guess, however, that much of what I say here will apply to fathers, especially those who had primary responsibility for child rearing.

For most women, the MotherLaunch stage is triggered when children leave home. That's when the mother mode is in the "off" position, and the "me" mode is turned back on. Millions of baby-boom mothers have devoted enormous energy and affection and attention to their children for at least eighteen years. And, although it shouldn't come as a surprise to them, many are completely unprepared for what comes next, for defining themselves as someone who is other than mother.

How will mothers adjust to having no children at home? How will we fill our time, and our hearts? How will we manage to have adult children who are, nevertheless, still dependent? How will we cope with having adult children who sometimes disappoint or hurt or irritate us?

These are questions for all empty-nest mothers, and they are also my own.

But just because our children are gone doesn't mean we've vanished from our parenting lives in a puff of smoke. Actually, many of us are stealth parents, because we are in disguise. We still live in the child-centric neighborhoods and towns in which we raised our children, only our children aren't home anymore. We look pretty much like everybody else, maybe a little worn around the edges, but we certainly haven't turned into graying grannies rocking on our front porches. Actually, we could probably pass as mothers of school-age children, because so many other boomers postponed having children into their thirties and forties.

And even after our children leave home, they tend to come back, usually several times. Mine, for instance, have returned temporarily.

They were gone while I wrote most of this book, but now they're home again, and I'm juggling the needs of two almost-adult children. Both of my children are in college, but it's summer now, so they are both back home. My son returned from his freshman year in May, and it took him almost four weeks to find a job. Finally, he was hired as a busboy at a snooty country club a few towns away. He was working six days a week, for low wages and to the point of exhaustion. But five weeks later, he was fired. So he's home again.

My daughter has been studying in the Dominican Republic and Argentina for a year, but now she's back home for a few weeks, trying to catch up on a year's worth of sleep deprivation. At the end of the summer, she will need a ride back to school, three hundred miles south, to move into an unfurnished apartment in Washington, D.C. The same week, my son will need a ride back to school, three hundred miles north, to Boston.

Finally, in September, my husband and I will be on our own again, along with our dog, Kippy.

In case you haven't noticed, the process of emptying the nest of children takes years. In fact, it's like a five- or seven-year labor and delivery period. The children leave and return, leave and return, many times over. Eventually, the yo-yoing of the empty nest, full nest, empty nest, full nest will be over, but there's no way of knowing in advance how long that process will take.

That's why this time of life requires a whole new way of thinking about ourselves, as mothers, as wives, and as women. We have to unthink our sense of ourselves as full-time mothers and rethink ourselves as other than mothers, as postmothers.

This is actually much easier to do than it may first appear.

I discovered this, and much more, in the original research I conducted for this book, a Web survey answered by one thousand women across the country who told me exactly how they felt when their children left home. I interviewed many by telephone, and dozens more in person. Once I overcame their compulsion to talk about their grown children instead of themselves, I found I had hit a mother lode of motherhood information. They love their children, they will always think of themselves as mothers, but now they want more. And they are discovering what that "more" is.

I also interviewed many experts by telephone—psychologists, sociologists, doctors, and economists—who are at the forefront of research on issues related to midlife. In this way, my discussions helped to expand on and enrich the statistics and conclusions in their published research papers.

The stories I tell, and the women I quote, are drawn from personal interviews and Web survey responses. They are all real, although I have changed all of their names and most of the identifying details to ensure the anonymity of my sources.

Among the hundreds of women I have interviewed, most return to a recurring theme about this stage of a woman's life. It is this: the postmotherhood life is not only not so bad, it's actually wonderful. If these moms had a theme song, it might be "Leave Already" or maybe "Change the Locks, I Want Some Privacy."

My research shows that the so-called empty-nest syndrome, in which mothers become miserable and maladjusted when children leave, just doesn't exist. Our own mothers, the neighbors, and even some so-called experts expect us to fall apart when our last child leaves home.

But guess what? For many, many mothers, the postparenthood phase is simply and absolutely fabulous.

That theme was reflected in my "Name This Book" contest, which I held to search for the best book title among those who answered my survey or visited my Web site, www.drcarin.com. (I continue to collect data, and I invite you to take my Web survey.) The results were sometimes humorous, often poignant, and always quite telling.

Mary, from Syracuse, New York, for example, suggested *Motherhood Rocked, Now Me-Hood Rules,* which is not half bad. She also offered *My Journey from Motherhood to Me-Hood* and *It's Okay to Be Happy They're Gone.*

Emie, from Chappaqua, New York, suggested *When Mothers Spread Their Wings,* which has a nice ring to it, but sounds as if it would be a primer on postdeath behavior.

Linda of Long Island, in New York, sent in a list of twelve possibilities, including, oddly, *Is This the Face of a Stupid Person?* I have no idea what that book would be about, but I love the sassy attitude.

Sybil, a therapist in Rockville, Maryland, gave a long and not quite lucid explanation for her proposal, *Song of Motherhood: The Remix.*

One father even offered *Cutting the Cord* and *Mom's Separation Anxiety.* His wife could be having issues, unless, of course, he's projecting!

A few women focused on the negative, including the one who suggested that this book should be called *A Hole in My Heart,* and another who threw out *Life in the Lonely Lane,* but they were definitely in the minority.

My sister, Joann, suggested *Grown, Flown, Alone,* which has a nice ring to it, and she even used Photoshop to insert the title atop a picture of a slightly ratty, vacant bird's nest.

A few of my other favorites, in no particular order: *Mothership, Stage Two, Mom in Late Bloom, M-Other, Loving Life at Fifty and After, The Nest Is Empty: Did the Egg Crack or Did I? Waves of Sorrow, Ripples of Joy, Flapping My Wings Again,* and *Free at Last.*

The reality is that, as mothers, we have practiced for this moment for years, in saying hundreds of little good-byes to our children: when they left home to go to nursery school or kindergarten, when they left home to ride bikes or go on playdates, when they left home to drive, when they left home to spend time with friends. Once they leave for college, we can speak by cell phone, e-mail them, and instant-message them, but it's not the same. At this point, our time with our children is brief, and the good-byes are longer and more definitive. Most of them have already left home, emotionally if not physically, and they are all too eager to grow up and away from us.

Still, happy good-byes are what most of us want for our children. We want to send them out into the world, confident and secure and joyful. We're all in the business of parenting to work ourselves out of a job.

Think about mothers who have children who are unable to leave home, like one I interviewed recently. Her child has a congenital neurological disorder, does not speak or move, and spends all day in a wheelchair. She has devoted her life to becoming his advocate, raising money to help prevent and cure his rare disease. Meanwhile, though, the boy is dependent on her for everything. She dresses him, bathes him, connects his feeding tubes, secures him to his chair. She is thrilled when a doctor mistakes him for a victim of cerebral palsy, a higher-functioning disease than the one he has. She would give anything to be able to launch her child into the world as an independent young man, out on his own.

Remember that it is a blessing to have children who are able to leave home. Be grateful and proud that they can do so.

My delight in my own children's departure is, quite frankly, tinged with envy. My children are at their beginning; they do not yet know great disappointment, failure, or rejection. They live communal lives, among their closest friends. In fact, they live a Club Med life, a year-round, all-inclusive vacation, with food, lodging, entertainment, and education paid for in advance by me and my husband. My daughter goes to school in Washington, D.C., but travels constantly, to study and to work. My son goes to school near Boston, at the center of the known college-student universe.

"What's not to like about that?" as one of my friends asks. She's the one who says that paying college tuition is like paying for a fantastic cruise every month, only you never get to go anywhere. It's like emptying your savings account in front of a fan, and watching it blow child-ward.

It's not that I'd want to be young again, but I wouldn't mind a trip back to my younger self, as in Francis Ford Coppola's 1986 movie *Peggy Sue Got Married.* The middle-aged mom travels back in time to become her high-school self, only she knows about everything that has happened in the decades since, including the invention of panty-hose and computer chips. I'd love to be equipped with my much wiser, middle-aged brain, plunked into my much better, and younger, body. I'd appreciate what I had a lot more, and I wouldn't take any of it as seriously.

It's too bad there's no such thing as Fantasy on Demand, like HBO, only customized. I'd take a few months of time travel back to my younger self, if I could afford it.

Back to my real life. Here, in the no-time-travel zone, I'm nervous, but pleased to launch myself into the postmotherhood phase. Life without children at home is drastically different for me, certainly. Although I work full-time, my own daily routine used to revolve around an axis of children that no longer exists. Even with teenage children, I had a schedule of forcing breakfast, packing lunches, planning evening activities and dinnertimes. I had a car-borrowing schedule and permission slips to sign and proms and school concerts to prepare for. I had baseball games and ballet performances to attend.

That carefully planned, child-centric calendar is gone, replaced by my own life, and my husband's.

Gone is the mealtime pressure. Gone is the car borrowing and stay-up-until-he-gets-home pressure. But gone, too, are the good-night kisses and head pats accepted by teenagers, gone are the minor and elusive details of what's going on in my children's lives, day by day, night by night.

Friends tell me that they miss the commotion of having teenagers at home. They miss the noise of bad rap music. They miss the endless telephoning and texting and IMing. My friend Teri says that she has begun to miss what she hasn't seen for at least fifteen years, when her son was a toddler. "I miss his toothless grin. Every once in a while, I look at that picture of him, and I miss that little boy," she says. "When he started to walk, I'd put out my foot to trip him, so he wouldn't run away from me so fast," she adds.

Still, he ran, all the way to freshman year in college. And this time she let him go, without sticking her foot out.

Our daily duty of mothering little children, and big ones, is over and done with. Sometimes it seems so completely vanished it's as if it never existed at all.

But then I remember all the work, the many years of meal planning, for instance.

I prepared three meals a day, five days a week, minimum, for, let's say, fifteen years. That's at least 11,700 meals cooked for two children, not including my husband's food. That's a lot of planning and shopping and cooking and cleaning up.

But I don't have to do that anymore. My husband and I eat easily prepared food, and we don't complain if we eat the same thing three nights in a row.

Then there's our marriage. We're all alone again, just the way we were before we struggled with serious fertility problems, before I had surgery, before I got pregnant, before I bore and raised two children.

So what do we do now? He's still here, and so I am, but nothing else is the same. We're older and heavier; he's got a lot less hair, while mine is graying rapidly. We have decades of child rearing between us that seem to have lasted forever, but also seem to have lasted no longer than a millisecond.

Some days, I feel as if I am desperate for a system reboot, as if I were a faulty computer. I long to restore my family system to the way it was ten or fifteen years ago, so I can do it all over again, only·better.

But if I think about it carefully, that's not really what I want. I'm pretty sure I don't have the energy, or the motivation, to make that enormous effort all over again.

I'm finished with the intensity of daily mothering. My mother-mode days are over, and my me-mode days are back.

There is a definite upside to this transformation.

Not only don't I have to worry about what I'm serving for dinner, I also don't have to worry about being at home at a certain time or having the car back or doing errands for time-pressured teenagers. I am first on my list of priorities again, in a way I haven't been for twenty years.

One of my friends, a mother of two, sees many advantages in having sent her youngest son off to college in Virginia. She is sad, she says, but "my husband is thrilled. There's not another man to get into pissing matches with." Not only that, she adds, but "we can go into New York City without worrying if a party's going on at our house!"

Another woman I know, a mother of three whose twins just left for college in upstate New York, is giddy with the notion that she's on her own during the day.

She can play tennis, go to meetings, meet friends, work on charity events, all without worrying about being home to pick up the kids or to make dinner, she says. The sense of complete freedom, she reports, is invigorating, and even a little scary.

She feels guilty about not feeling bad that they're gone!

Mothers agree, however, that they are never "free" of their children, nor would they want to be. It's just that, as another mom tells me, "I have time now to relax, and to take more of an adult role. It's another stage of life."

This stage of life—liberation from children—is both exhilarating and terrifying, all at once.

It's a launching platform from which mothers send themselves into a new kind of motherhood, one that includes generativity, the desire to extend yourself beyond family. The transition period, though, can take at least several years, or even a decade. When my children first left, I was in Stage One, Grief. (The stages of what I call MotherLaunch are discussed in detail in chapter 3.)

I cried at vaguely sad television shows and movies, for example. Anything heartfelt made me weep. A few years ago, when my daughter left for college, I removed her place mat, number four, from the table. Then there were three left, one for me, another for my husband, the third for my son. For the next two years, there were three mats, except during holidays and parts of summer vacation, when we were again, briefly, four. When my son left for college, though, I wasn't able to put away place mat number three for months.

Also, I wasn't used to all the enforced intimacy, all of this odd, uninterrupted time with my husband. So I watched TiVo while he watched sports on another television. (And I started a blog, called TiVoLady .com.) We both realized that we could walk around the house naked if we wanted to. One mom told me that she realized recently that her whole house was now available for sexual encounters. "We could have sex on the kitchen floor if we wanted, but who wants to?" She laughed.

The truth is that it takes time to get used to this newfound sense of liberation. Here's a short quiz to help you decide how well you've adjusted to having no children at home. Try to answer quickly. And be honest.

THE MISSING MOTHERHOOD QUIZ
True or False?

1. On some days, you catch yourself at three o'clock or three-thirty wondering if there's something you forgot to do or someone you forgot to pick up from school.
2. You drive by the high school occasionally, or you still belong to school-related committees.
3. You call your children several times a week.
4. You check your e-mail, or your instant messaging service, to see if your children have sent you anything or are online at that moment.
5. Your child has banned you from sending instant messages.
6. You send care packages to distant children, several times a month, or more often.
7. You avert your eyes when you walk past your children's bedrooms.

8. You find yourself looking at babies and toddlers with uncon-cealed longing.
9. You consider it a good day when you have spoken to all of your children.
10. You dream of being pregnant again, or of carrying babies in your arms, or both.

If you answered "true" to at least six of these questions, you may be suffering from major mother disorientation, the mother of all mother shocks of disbelief that come when all of your children have left home.

This book is probably for you.

Don't fret, though. There are definite advantages to being child free. Now take this alternate test, to see how unplugged from motherhood you are.

THE REJOICING AT POSTMOTHERHOOD QUIZ
True or False?

1. You work late whenever you want.
2. You rarely feel guilty.
3. You don't bother shopping for groceries unless you feel like it.
4. You traded in the van, or the large car, for a smaller one.
5. You revel in how quiet and clean your house or apartment feels.
6. You spend more than fifteen minutes a day talking to your partner.
7. You watch what you want on television, for as long as you want.
8. You talk to your dog or cat, at length, and it doesn't seem strange.
9. You refuse to do laundry for returning children.
10. You've thrown away, or given away, most of your children's toys and books.

If you answered "true" to at least six of these questions, then your adjustment time may be much faster than you might have thought. That's because you've already learned to celebrate the pluses of life without children. You can work late and not feel guilty about it. You sense freedom, that your days are yours, your weekends are yours, you can do what you want, when you want. The house is clean and neat and quiet. The telephone is always available, and so are the television and the computer.

There's no more setting-of-example pressure. You can eat cereal and marshmallows for dinner; you can watch television for twelve straight hours on a Saturday; you can *not* make the bed. Nobody else will learn bad habits from you, except you.

A close friend says that when she had two boys at home, she was always aware of maintaining her privacy. Now that the boys are gone, though, she doesn't have to worry about what they see. Her husband walks downstairs naked to make breakfast, and she walks to and from the shower without a towel. "All my doors are open," she says happily.

And that is the point.

We did the best we could as mothers. We are thrilled that our children are ready and able to grow up and move out. And we are also delighted to let them go. At this point in our lives, all our doors are open.

How we live these postparenting years is entirely up to us.

If we treat this stage of life as a disaster, as a major loss that derails our sense of purpose as neatly as if we were a train running off a lifetime track, we are in for more than a little misery. If we are unwilling to fashion a newfangled self, then we may be trapped in a frustrating, and ultimately harmful, frozen mother mode for years to come.

But, if we view this time of life as a challenge, as an opportunity to chart a new course through life, it's possible that we'll accomplish more than we ever thought possible. Deciding that this new phase of life is a gift will require a near-complete reevaluation of ourselves, our roles in life, and our goals and priorities. But if we do, we will ultimately be rewarded.

The choice is ours.

CHAPTER ONE

There Is No Empty-Nest Syndrome

L et's get this out of the way right now.

There is no "empty-nest syndrome." It does not exist. Period.

The vast majority of mothers do not sit at home weeping about the loss of their precious progeny, the children who have left their home and family to go to college or to work or to get married or to serve in the military.

Most mothers do not experience a deep personal crisis when their children leave home, as many psychiatrists and so-called experts have said. They do not scramble to "fill the void" left by absent children, as some insist. They do not have the "forty-year-old jitters," as one anthropologist asserted. Even so-called overinvolved and overprotective mothers, as they are known among certain psychologists, women who tend to live through and for their offspring, are not in great danger of becoming depressed, demoralized, alienated, or alcoholic.

Americans hold a strong belief that motherhood should be intensive, that mothers must be child centered and emotionally involved with their children, wholly devoted to their children's care. Good mothers, the rule goes, are those who have subsumed their own needs and goals to those of family. And so, the parallel expectation goes, those mothers will surely be devastated when their children no longer need them.

But a funny thing happens on the way to children's independence. When women lose their full-time role as mothers, they do not despair, they are not racked with self-pity, they do not long to have their babies back again. Instead, a vast majority of mothers thrive and prosper when their children grow up. They are thrilled to have finally grown past the mommy years.

At first, of course, mothers admit to feeling some sadness when their children leave home. It is certainly natural to mourn the loss of a former life, a way of being that no longer applies. But most mothers do not grieve for more than a year or so. Instead, they celebrate their new lives. They're more likely to sing a hallelujah chorus than a song of desolation when the youngest child walks out the door.

When that door slams shut, many mothers feel great. Here are a few of the words they use to describe what it is they are feeling at that moment: excited, curious, happy, proud, relieved, relaxed, liberated, free. Add exclamation points after each word, and you get the idea: excited! liberated! free!

Take Tara, fifty, an office manager who lives in a New York suburb. She just sent her second son off to Colgate University, in upstate New York. She feels completely liberated, she says, because she has relinquished the sense that she must always be available to control and guide her boys. "I have no fears. I did the best I could as a mother and I saw that they were ready to move on. And I was more than ready to let them go," Tara says.

You can almost picture her wiping her hands, hitching up her chic jeans, and moving on.

Dina, fifty-two, is a close friend of Tara's who lives on Long Island. She has three children, including twin daughters who are freshmen at a state school in Albany, New York. She doesn't work for pay, since her children were her work, but she doesn't feel as if she's been fired without notice. Not at all. Instead, she says with a laugh, she's noticed that when she's puttering around the house now, "I'm actually whistling!"

"All of a sudden, I have my own time," Dina says. "For the past twenty-one years, my life has been my children. I did everything for them. I took care of them and I took care of their friends whose moms worked, but I have my life back again. I'm doing projects around the house. My mind has never been clear enough to read a book, but now

I'm reading constantly. And I can play tennis without rushing home to pick up one of the kids or to make dinner."

It is only now, she says, that she realizes that she has been striving to reach this goal for the past two decades. "For twenty-one years, I did for my kids. Now I deserve this freedom. I worked for this freedom," she says, with a fierce resolve that would surprise her children.

Freedom is the buzzword for mothers whose children have left.

In fact, freedom's just another word for no kids left at home, which is what Janis Joplin might have sung if she'd lived long enough.

Having no children at home feels sublimely and deliciously liberating for many women.

How much freedom do they feel? Let us count the ways.

They feel freedom from daily responsibility for children.

They feel freedom from anxiety when they hear nearby police sirens.

They feel freedom from worrying about what other people think.

They feel freedom to do new things.

They feel freedom to reinvent themselves.

They feel freedom to get to know their own husbands again, in a new way.

They feel freedom to make their own decisions.

They feel freedom to open themselves to a sense of possibility.

Finally, they feel freedom to focus all of the energy and emotion and time that went into child raising somewhere else, somewhere of their own choosing.

How Many Freedoms Are There?

Mothers express their sense of freedom in endless ways, but here are some examples, taken from among the responses given by the hundreds of women I interviewed.

- ❖ Mothers of means buy a second home, on a lake, near a beach, or on the Upper West Side of Manhattan.
- ❖ Mothers trade in the stodgy old van for a brand-new sports car.

- ❖ Mothers move to Florida, just for the month of March.
- ❖ Mothers take dance classes with their husbands.
- ❖ Mothers go back to school, to become counselors or nurses or Realtors.
- ❖ Mothers work longer hours or take more challenging jobs.
- ❖ Single mothers use vacation time to drive to states and cities they've never seen.
- ❖ Single mothers bring dates home for guilt-free sleepovers.
- ❖ Mothers renovate guest rooms.
- ❖ Mothers join health clubs, run half-marathons, and climb Mount Kilimanjaro, in Tanzania (as one woman at the gym tells me, while she works on machines to strengthen her leg muscles for her upcoming trip to Africa).

One mother even started a commune in her newly empty nest. Liz, fifty-two, of Greensboro, North Carolina, had already sent both daughters off to college when her husband of twenty-eight years announced that because he needed some solitude, he was leaving her. So Liz adopted a fifteen-year-old foster child. Then she invited six other people to live in her home, to be part of what she called "an anarchist collective." With that many people, it costs each of them only about two hundred dollars a month to live in the home, including utilities, mortgage, and food and supplies. They shop for produce in grocery store Dumpsters. They get along really well, just like a normal family, she says, only better.[1]

If that's a bit extreme, or more precisely, insanely extreme, there is Leslie, from Chappaqua, New York, whose youngest daughter left for college on the same day that her husband announced he was leaving her. This was after she had quit her job and spent eight years caring for him while he battled non-Hodgkin's lymphoma. So she decided to start her own business, to try to sell the soup that she had been making at home for friends and relatives. She opened a tiny soup restaurant in a narrow storefront on a side street in a wildly diverse New York suburb. The place has become quite successful, and the store's Web site, which offers its products for purchase by mail, also tells the story of her ex-husband, the man who ditched her when she was at her weakest and most vulnerable.

This is just the tip of the freedom iceberg for hundreds of newly liberated mothers who have shared their plans with me, plans for today and plans for tomorrow. Plans they could never have imagined making before their children left.

Martha, a forty-nine-year-old divorced real-estate broker in Cleveland, puts it rather bluntly, if not exactly in proper English. "I can explore the freeness of being me again!" she says. "I adore my son and I will always be there for him, but I never want him to move back in with me. I spent twenty years working and living pretty much in his best interest," Martha continues. "I'm done with that now. This is his time to grow up, and my time to grow up and grow on, as well," she adds.

Deb, a fifty-four-year-old secretary and mother of two in St. Louis, puts it this way: "I suddenly realized that my desires, my wants, and my needs are just as important as everybody else's. But now I'm free to spend my time on myself and not feel guilty about it."

Guiltless freedom, that's what newly liberated mothers have found, and what could be more scrumptious? It's like double-chocolate brownies, macadamia-nut chocolate-chip cookies, and cherry cheesecake all rolled into one superdessert, but without the calories.

My own research confirms what these women say about the pleasure they feel in finally launching their children into the world. I conducted a Web-based survey of one thousand mothers. Most of the women are from the United States, as well as some from Canada, Great Britain, Australia, and Latin America. This is obviously not a randomly selected group of women, but I believe that they are fairly representative of middle-class women in the middle years. I recruited the women from several different sources: some were readers of the *More* magazine Web site, others were graduates of one of a dozen or so large universities, still others were regular users of Web forums such as about.com or collegeconfidential.com. (I have changed the names of all the women I quote.)

These mothers are, on average, fifty-two or fifty-three years old. They have two or three children. Three-quarters are married, for an average of twenty-four years. About three-quarters work for pay, an average of about thirty-five or thirty-six hours a week. They are librarians and special education teachers, registered nurses and receptionists, office cleaners and doctors, accountants and attorneys, administrative assistants and police officers, dairy farmers and secretaries, waitresses and ranchers.

In other words, they are EveryWoman and EveryMother.

They told me about themselves and their friends, their husbands and lovers, their children and their pets. They confided their secrets and their fears, like the woman who feels sexier "due to spending more time on the Internet, having phone sex, reading about erotic subjects, and writing my own erotic stories. Shhhh!!!" Or the one whose daughter is in the Peace Corps, so they see each other only three times a year. This mother's terrible fear is that she will see her daughter just sixty times more, and that's only if she lives another twenty years.

And when I ask about their feelings on the departure of their youngest child, they confess their secret pleasure: two-thirds say they are happy and joyful that the children are gone! Another 23 percent feel relieved to be on the leaving end of the offspring exodus. That's nearly 90 percent who feel fabulous about being on their own—child free and liberated from maternal responsibilities—despite the fact that they think about their children almost every day.

There are, however, a minority of moms—about 10 percent—who are truly saddened and in despair about having grown children, according to my research. They also say they feel a sense of despair about life in general. There may be a simple explanation for their distress, though. In any large group of women, a certain number are bound to be depressed or unhappy. Indeed, several major epidemiological studies show that, at any given time, between 10 and 15 percent of American women are suffering from depression.[2] So it's possible that any drastic life event—an empty nest, a death in the family, a divorce—will trigger an episode of depression among a small number of mothers. (For more about these mothers, see chapter 3.)

But let's get back to the not-so-silent majority of moms, those who are delighted with their newfound freedom.

My research shows that six in ten mothers whose children have left feel a strong desire to reinvent themselves. Half say they feel excited about their future, and nearly as many feel a sense of liberation.

There's Donna, fifty, from Urbana, Illinois, who has three children and has been married for twenty-nine years. She's an office worker for a math journal, but her heart is not in numbers. Here's what Donna says:

> Having no children at home is very liberating most of the time. I miss them, but my husband and I are having a lot of fun. We can eat what we want, listen to the kind of music we want, go where we want on vacations, watch what we want on television, have conversations that we want to have, have sex when we feel in the mood, and fix up the house the way we like it. The list is really endless. We have both been very devoted parents, but we feel like our dues have been paid. We've raised three decent human beings. But now we want our lives back, and we want to find each other again.

Donna's not being selfish; she's simply living her own life again. Other research offers similar conclusions.

A Texas sociologist analyzed six national surveys several decades ago, for example. While 46 percent of forty-something mothers whose children still lived at home called themselves "very happy," 61 percent of women that age did so if their children had left. Among moms in their fifties with kids at home, just 30 percent called themselves "very happy," but once the children were gone, 42 percent described themselves that way. This social scientist was surprised that no matter how much money families earned, parents in their forties and fifties were simply happier and enjoyed life more once their children were gone.[3]

Surprise, surprise!

It's our dirty little maternal secret: we love our children fiercely, but we breathe a sigh of relief when they're grown and gone.

A similar study in Australia reached the same conclusion. In the first year after the youngest child had left home, mothers' moods actually improved, as did their sense of well-being. In addition, mothers reported fewer daily hassles, a psychological measure of everyday problems that bothered or annoyed them, like finishing paperwork, dealing with bad weather, doing housework, and keeping the car maintained.[4] The hassles scale was developed in the 1960s, by the way, when the word "hassle" seemed like a hip way to describe minor personal irritations and turmoil. Now it just sounds quaint.

Finally, another study of New York–area women in their forties and fifties showed that 72 percent were happy, and nearly as many, 64 percent, were not at all confused about life. The secret to midlife happiness, the researcher said, is having good health, earning at least thirty thousand dollars a year (in 1998 dollars), and having a confidante or a group of close friends. To be happy, women didn't have to be wealthy, they just had to avoid poverty. The women were happiest, too, if the children were no longer at home, and it didn't matter if the women were married or divorced. The happiest women felt important in their own right, not marginal or useless. They had a vision of their own future, and they were able to fashion a life full of meaning, one that did not necessarily include their children.[5]

In other recent studies, social scientists also report that women's sense of vitality and confidence and strength actually blossoms as they grow older, although their looks fade.

The Fifties Are the Prime of Life

Some researchers insist that fifty-something is the prime of life for women. According to this view, women are at their physical peak when they are nineteen, and their marriages peak in happiness just before children are born, but they achieve a gold medal for all-around emotional security and comfort at the age of fifty or so. (Others say women peak at age sixty-three, as I report in chapter 9.)

Several psychologists who specialize in the study of personality focused their research on a group of seven hundred women whom they studied over several decades. They concluded that, among these baby-boom women, the prime of life occurs between the ages of fifty and fifty-six. It is during these years, they say, that women still have their health, they enjoy the highest household income, they feel happiest about their relationships with husband and friends, and they have launched their children.[6]

For such women, sending children out into the world provides a sense of accomplishment, of a job well done, a job that is finally over. In addition, life at home becomes pared down to a much simpler life, but one that is more rewarding, and they are able to refocus the enormous energy that they expended on children in places of their own choosing.

Take Cherie, forty-seven, who works for a government agency in Arizona and who lavished all of her love and attention and support on her two daughters for the past twenty years. She relies on them still, as shopping companions, as spa buddies, as manicure pals. Cherie and her husband, Ralph, fifty-three, always took several family vacations a year, and each daughter was allowed to pick one destination each year. The family has been to beaches in Spain, the Virgin Islands, and Jamaica; they've been to Paris and Turkey and Rome.

Cherie reminds me of Mrs. Bennet, the mother of five daughters in Jane Austen's classic *Pride and Prejudice* who missed her daughters terribly when they were away from home. Mrs. Bennet was especially bereft when her dopiest daughter, Lydia, ran off with the reprehensible Mr. Wickham before the two were even married—a terrible, horrific breach of social etiquette in the early 1800s.

Even so, Mrs. Bennet was distraught when the slutty Lydia left home. She refers to the loss of her daughters as an absence of friends, a rather modern view of one's offspring. " 'I often think,' said she, 'that there is nothing so bad as parting with one's friends. One seems so forlorn without them.' "

Like Mrs. Bennet, Cherie views her girls as the best of best friends. But unlike Mrs. Bennet, Cherie has the luxury of refocusing the energy and devotion she lavished on her daughters, turning to other causes now that her children are nearly independent.

A few years ago, Cherie took a job with a nonprofit branch of the local government, doling out money to nonprofit groups. She also started her own charity, which she called Cinderella Affair, to collect used-only-once prom dresses, evening bags, wraps, and shoes and then to distribute the party frocks to needy high-school seniors. It's a labor of love, one that makes Cherie feel as if she has five hundred new daughters every year.

"Some of these girls never had a dress, let alone a prom dress," she says. "My daughters helped me start the project," she adds, "but it's mine now."

Cherie has also gone back to college, to earn a BA for herself. It took her six years to get a two-year degree; she's working on completing the final two years in a lot less time. "I'll graduate between my two daughters," she brags. "That really helps the empty spot disappear."

Mothers of every age, in every era, surely feel that so-called empty spot, but how they react to the children's exodus depends very much on where they live and to what generation they belong. Social scientists refer to each generation as a cohort, meaning a group of people who were born at roughly the same time and who experienced the same things as they were growing up. Baby-boom women, for example, those born between 1946 and 1964, grew up during the Vietnam War and the sexual revolution.

There are about seventy-seven million women and men in the cohort known as the baby boom, and they comprise four in ten of all American households, according to the Census Bureau. Because the group is so huge, demographers refer to boomers as "the pig in the python," since they are a giant bulge, all moving through the life cycle at the same time and all riding the rising tide to later life together.

Baby-boom women and men are very different from their parents, the World War II generation, or their grandparents, children of the Great Depression.

Most boomer women think it's okay if a woman never marries, but their mothers disapproved. Many boomer women think that it's fine if a woman works while her children are young, but their mothers did not. Most boomer women believe that a husband should share household chores, but their mothers were likely to be shocked by such a suggestion. Women born during the baby boom have the gift of choice: they feel free to chose to work or to stay at home, to marry or to remain single, to divorce when they fall out of love.[7] All of this makes life more complicated and difficult, but also much more empowering and exhilarating.

The grandmothers of baby boomers, women born in the early 1900s, held much more rigid and sexist views about marriage and motherhood, including a strong and widespread belief that a woman's main purpose in life was to be a wife and mother. Thus, the loss of one of those jobs was often devastating to a woman's sense of who she was. But among baby-boom women, at least half of whom held a job while they were raising children, the children's departure may not have such a radical impact.

Indeed, psychologists compared a group of baby boomers who had lost their jobs to another whose youngest children had left home and found that getting fired was a lot more traumatic, painful, and difficult for boomers to deal with than was watching the youngest child leave.[8]

Age of Aquarius Meets the Age of Eternal Middle Age

Baby boomers tend to be loath to admit to having anything to do with "old age" because they are so consumed by the idea of youth, so get ready for brand-new expressions to be invented when boomers enter their seventies and eighties. In the near future, the elderly will no longer be called elderly. We'll be "late middle-agers," or even "late, late middle-agers," which may be especially appealing because it sounds so much like "teenagers."

When I was a college sophomore, nineteen years old and flippant about my youthfulness, my roommate, Susan, and I had a slogan that we repeated over and over, mostly to explain our view of the world. We said it with smug pride, never once believing that it would ever ring false. It was: "I've been young all my life!"

We couldn't imagine the day when that statement would no longer be true.

It might as well have been the motto of our entire generation, a group of die-hard Vietnam-era semi-hippies who, to this day, refuse to believe that the wrinkled, freckled, sagging face in the mirror is really our own. It's as if we believe that the great song lyric, from the Who's "My Generation," has come true somehow. It is "Hope I die before I get old," but what we really mean is that we want, always, to feel young and to think young and to be young in our hearts.

"We're in love with the idea that we're hardly ever old," agrees Abigail J. Stewart, a professor of psychology at the University of Michigan who is herself a baby boomer, and who has a special fondness for her own cohort. That's why, she adds, "we view middle age as very long in America."

Stewart has studied the course of women's lives for the past few decades, and she spoke to me at length by telephone about her research on the lives of boomer moms.

"To the extent that this baby-boom generation is going through these experiences collectively, that's what makes them different," she says. "It's not women alone at home feeling sad and blue, it's women talking with others about what middle age feels like."

In her extensive research, Stewart finds that **baby-boom women insist that their midlife is not the midlife of their grandmothers, or even their mothers**. They really believe, heart and soul, that fifty-five is the new forty.[9]

But just a generation or two ago, this was not true, and it would have been a laughable idea, in fact. In one 1965 study, for example, both women and men agreed that a woman was middle-aged by the age of forty or fifty.[10]

Now, don't even suggest that forty is the beginning of older age.

"For many women, middle age is experienced as a liberating period, a time when gender pressure, the pressure to live up to a feminine standard, drops away, and there's an opportunity to be more open, more direct, and more straightforward about what you think and feel," Stewart says. Mothers who have had a straight career path have always had such freedom, she notes, so it is women with what she calls "a more complicated trajectory through adulthood" who are most likely to experience midlife as liberating.

"And they're surprised by that," she adds. "They expected to find middle age depressing or discouraging, they expected to feel some kind of waning of femininity that was negative, and on the contrary, they experience middle age as very liberating. They have a sense of coming into their own, that's the language they use and that's the language that best captures how they feel," Stewart notes.

Coming into their own is a lovely way of putting into words the way midlife women feel about themselves.

Stewart sums up her life's work by concluding that women in midlife "feel at the top of their game."[11] And she doesn't mean at the top of their son's basketball game, or their daughter's soccer game, but the top of their own game, whatever that game may be.

In my own research, I find that age fifty represents a kind of mountaintop from which women can see the length and breadth of their life span. Looking back, they see themselves as young women who were full of energy but somewhat clueless about life. Looking forward, they envision a self with less energy but with a lot more awareness and confidence about how to live well.

Age fifty is when you know yourself best, you like who you are, and you enjoy how you feel. My own research supports this surprising conclusion: the fifty-something age group rocks.

Among fifty-somethings in my study, 70 percent are married, for an average of twenty-six years, and six in ten work full-time. Half have finished menopause and say they were, on average, about fifty years old when their last child left. Thus, they are living in their first decade of a mostly child-free life. They view this time period as a surprisingly productive interlude in which they are reveling in newfound freedom. For many women, it is the first time in their life that they feel a sense of safety and security, a kind of contentment with whatever hand in life they have been dealt.

I find that two out of three mothers in their fifties feel a desire to reinvent themselves, and almost half feel excited about their future. Half also feel a sense of liberation. Almost as many women in their fifties say that they expect to make new friends in the new phase they are entering, and also that they will fashion some kind of life that will be very different from the one they had before.

This is not to say that women in their fifties don't see any downside to having lived for five decades. Nearly half, about 45 percent, admit that they fear growing old. Even more, about six in ten, say they have trouble sleeping—but so do nearly as many women in their forties. Insomnia brought on by rampant, erratic hormones is an unavoidable biological fact of middle age. Having children at home, or not, will not make much difference in the snooze-ability factor.

Nevertheless, women's views of themselves in midlife are partly governed by the rules our culture offers for what it means to be a teenager, or a youngster, or an old lady. Age identity is based, in large part, on social expectations. Thus, **you are not just as old as you look or feel, but as old as everybody else tells you to feel**. In a study of twelve hundred upstate New Yorkers, a group of sociologists found that 80 percent of women in their fifties think of themselves as "middle-aged," and it isn't until women hit the age of eighty that a majority thinks of themselves as "old."

Here's a possible mathematical equation:

If 80 = Old, then 70 = Nearly Old, and 60 = Nearly Young!

The researchers conclude that, as long as women have their health, they view themselves as middle-aged, which is the time of life that offers them the greatest amount of respect and influence.[12]

Elaine just turned fifty, and she would certainly agree. She was surprised by how positive she felt about celebrating her half-century birthday.

"Fifty always looked and seemed so old," she says. "But I'm surprised at how young I still feel. I feel the world is there for me to do what I want with it. My life revolved around all the other people in my life, but now I can make my decisions based on me," she gloats.

At the age of fifty, she asserts, "I have a lot of life left to play with."

And she is absolutely right, for the simple reason that her life expectancy is so much longer than it has been for women at any other time in human history, a major benefit of being a boomer.

Up until the 1920s and 1930s, mothers did not have much time left to live after their children were gone, experts say. In 1900, for example, the average age of mothers when a last child married was fifty-five, but their life expectancy was barely fifty-five years.[13] So at the moment the last child left home, mom left the world of the living—no empty nest for her, mostly because she had left the nest herself.

Frances Goldscheider, an emerita professor of sociology at Brown University, has spent a lifetime studying social expectations about the ages at which children leave and return home. She, too, has written about the fact that few women lived very long after their children left home.[14]

"There has been a dramatic reshaping of the family life course," Goldscheider says, in part because women used to bear children until their mid- to late-forties, and those children tended not to leave home until they married. By that time, the mothers' lives were over, literally over. Women who were born in 1900 usually died by the age of fifty or sixty, just a few years, if that, after the last child had left. Right now, though, baby boomers will live longer than Americans ever have before: a man who reaches the age of sixty can expect to live another twenty years, and a woman who is sixty will live, on average, another twenty-four years.[15]

For this reason, Goldscheider notes, the postmotherhood phase of life, the one sometimes called "empty nest," lasts longer and carries greater meaning than ever before.

It's not just a brief chapter of adult life; it's a whole new book.

If we think of a woman's lifetime as a ring (see next page), then active motherhood is just part of the arc, perhaps a third of her life span. A woman becomes a mother in her second or third decade of life, at the top of the left ring. She and her children live together for about eighteen or twenty years, a time when both rings mesh and interconnect. When the child goes off on his or her own, the rings diverge. It is a natural process, dictated in part by nature, but mostly by our culture, which makes rules about when it is appropriate for children to leave home, and when, if at all, they are allowed to return.

Still, a mother and her child will know each other for forty or fifty or sixty years, barring disease or disaster. So they have a long time to figure out how to arrange their relationship when their life rings no longer overlap.

The Two Rings of Life

If we view this process objectively, the idea of a mother's life and her child's life as interlocking rings is intuitively correct. Mom lives life without children, then with them, then without them again. It's the natural circle of life, only with rings.

But, still, when a mother watches her child pack a suitcase, computer, video game system, and DVD collection and walk out of the house, she is bound to feel some kind of emotional wallop. Many mothers feel that punch as sharp pangs of loss and disorientation. How long those feelings last, however, varies dramatically from mother to mother. (For an explanation of the three stages of MotherLaunch, see chapter 3.)

Fighting the Best-Child Wars

Among a group of nine well-to-do suburban New York women I interviewed, for instance, just two had prolonged feelings of anguish and regret after their children left. I met these ladies in a group session held at Alison's house, a scarily neat suburban home tucked on a hilly, winding road in an exclusive village in a town just outside New York City.

These sleek, well-dressed, and well-groomed fifty-something ladies live in a place in which mothers are known for their tendency to fight the Best-Child Wars. The women wage a decades-long battle over who can send their children to the most elite Ivy League schools, preferably one of the holy trinity, Yale, Harvard, and Princeton. They have moved to this place specifically for its great-schools reputation, so that they can give their children the advantage of a supercompetitive education that only the highest New York taxes can buy. In 2007, an average home here, a smallish three-bedroom, sold for about one million dollars. Annual property taxes on those homes can easily reach twenty-five thousand dollars or more.

Because these mothers have engaged in relentless, though ostensibly friendly, child combat with their friends and neighbors for so long, it comes as something of a shock to them when their war is finally over. The endless child pushing and child prodding is done: Ivy League goal or not, the race is run, the battle ended.

Though most of these moms admit that they felt bereft and confused when the last child left, all but two said they were surprised at how wonderful they felt having no children at home. They argued less often with their husbands, they had sex more often, they had time for themselves, they settled into their partnerships and into their selves.

"It's our time to spread our wings," says Edie, a youthful, whippet-thin redhead who has been a real-estate broker here for twenty years. Her wide, open face is makeup free; her will-do attitude makes her radiate competence and self-assurance. She is thrilled that her children are gone, and she's not ashamed to admit it. "I don't worry very much about the children like I used to; the constant worries are gone," she says. "And now, there's so much time between three o'clock and seven-thirty, when my husband comes home, and I don't have the aggravation of the kids and their distractions." She can do her real-estate work or she can paint, and nobody is there to disturb her.

Edie and her friends know each other mostly through their children, so they haven't seen each other since last year's high-school graduation. They have genuine affection for each other, and for everybody's children, whom they have watched grow up over the past fifteen years. That's a powerful bond, one they are sad to have lost, as evident in their teary, bittersweet greetings as they catch up on whose child is doing what.

They are insulated by affluence, of course, these well-dressed women for whom working for money is just one option, like taking yoga or learning how to tango. It's almost as if they have too many options now that the children are gone, since getting a job to help pay college tuition is not essential for any of them. In fact, when I ask them if they've felt any family tension over the need to pay two or three college tuitions at once, they don't understand the question.

They literally do not understand why having to shell out an extra ninety thousand dollars a year for two tuitions could be a problem. Clearly, they are not on the same planet as the majority of mothers, and families, for whom college costs loom as a burden of monumental proportions.

We are talking in Alison's family room, a wood-paneled, A-frame space that is large enough to hold a sitcom cast, along with the entire crew and all of the heavy-duty camera equipment. It features a large pool table, polished oak floors, a giant stone fireplace, and a conversation pit with a wraparound leather couch and nubby Berber carpet. Alison has made coffee and serves homemade banana bread and biscotti, ornamented with a huge basket of tangerines. None of the elegantly slender women eats the sweets, but two of them daintily peel the tangerines, eating driplessly.

Very soon, they begin to confess how they really feel about this time of life.

Their feelings are intense, they say, almost as if they themselves are teenagers again. They have no children at home, but that doesn't matter, because they believe wholeheartedly in the aphorism that "a mother is only as happy as her least happy child." And they are aware, if not moment by moment, then day by day, exactly how happy each one of their children feels.

For these mothers, many of whom identify themselves as mothers first, the role of full-time mom is a difficult one to relinquish. It's like being a surgeon with no operating room, or a dancer without a stage.

Harriet is one of those who are having trouble viewing themselves as other than mother. She wears black-framed glasses and jeans, and looks as if she just stepped out of a class at Barnard College, in Manhattan. But she is fifty-two, mother of a twenty-two-year-old daughter and eighteen-year-old son, and is married to a bond trader. She is one of the few who admits that she needs to find a new purpose in life because her children have, so far, been her only purpose. She was a devoted sports mom, in part because both of her children were gifted athletes. Her son was a star forward on the high-school ice hockey team and an award-winning soccer player. Her daughter was a starting forward on the girl's basketball team. After her son left home, she missed watching high-school hockey games so much that she decided to attend them even in his absence.

But that plan backfired. When Harriet noticed that another player was wearing her son's jersey, number four, she burst into tears. She wept rinkside, in part because she was distraught to see that the team had moved on, though she had not.

"They didn't retire my son's number, or even wait to give it to someone else," she says, still hurt and indignant.

Bobby, fifty-four, tries to comfort Harriet, who is clearly bereft about the loss of her old life. "It's as if being a mother was your full-time job," Bobby points out. "We all really had that full-time job, but now we're involuntarily retired from it."

Their friends agree, but they also laugh at the pathetic nature of Harriet's hockey pilgrimage, where she had tried to worship at the shrine of her son's former glory.

Leslie laughs loudest at this behavior. She's fifty and works part-time tutoring math. She's openhearted and raunchy, with big curly hair and a bigger laugh. She was surprised at how happy she felt when her children left. "I miss them, but I'm okay," she confesses. "My mother-in-law was trying to rub it in, telling me, 'Oh, you're going to be so sad and empty,' " she goes on with a cackle. "But I'm not!"

Now that her children are gone, Leslie brags to her friends that her sex life is much improved. "The sex is exponentially better. Because we're relaxed, and nobody's coming in and nobody can hear us. And we're not tired," she adds.

Although confident about her sexuality, Leslie is not leaving the health of her marriage to chance. That's why she makes sure never to let her husband, an attorney with a large Manhattan firm, take business trips alone. "He goes on these boondoggles for work, and I won't let him go alone. The coworkers absolutely mess around with each other if the wife is not there. The single women hover," she says to the hoots of her friends, flabbergasted by this unsolicited confession.

But Leslie finishes by saying that she thought she'd be so sad when her two sons left, and she's not. Not at all.

Maria, forty-nine, agrees. She's thin and muscular, almost as if she's thirty-something, in part because she just took up long-distance running and started running half-marathons for women over forty in New York City's Central Park. She has no patience for complaints about yearning for gone children. "I'm surprised at how quickly I started to fantasize about selling the house and moving on somewhere else," she says. "I didn't expect that to happen so fast."

When Maria talks about missing the social ties her children gave her, though, that strikes a chord with the other women in the room. She misses the children less than she does the people she used to see all the time, because they all had children about the same age. Children are the glue that cements social ties in most communities, and when they go, those bonds often no longer hold. "I feel like I'm less connected to the community," Maria says. "I don't have the PTA connections anymore, and I don't recognize a lot of people."

Although she has been quiet for some time, Bobby speaks up to agree, and to add her own thoughts. A dark, sad-eyed woman with a large gap between her front teeth, she seems less self-assured than the others, and she's much more soft-spoken. But she is also more thoughtful than her self-effacing countenance would suggest.

Bobby has two sons and is married to a publisher. She, too, let go of her children rather quickly, she says. "I feel I'm more of a partner to my husband. The boys are independent, so I'm a participant, but I don't feel like a mother now, more like I'm sharing their experiences. I'm not managing their lives anymore," she remarks. "I'm enjoying their lives."

And she suddenly realizes, she adds, that "raising my kids, my life has been on hold," which she sees clearly only now, looking back on the past twenty years or so. "I need to make the most of the time I have left," she says, stating the somewhat obvious.

The truth and clarity of the point silence the room for a moment.

Then Edie admits that this is why she has just booked herself a month-long stay in Florida in March. "I realized that if I waited too long, I might never do it. If I wait, I might not be able to run anymore, or I'll have so many skin cancers that I won't be able to sit on the beach. So I thought, 'Come on, do it now!'" she says.

When Should Children Leave?

Bobby and her friends may think of the exodus of their grown children as an "involuntary retirement," but it actually represents a widely accepted social norm. In the United States, and in many other developed countries, there is a set of rules, or unspoken "shoulds," about which a majority of parents and their nearly grown children mostly agree.

Here are some of these shoulds:

❖ Children *should not* leave home before they graduate from high school.

❖ Children *should* leave home after high-school graduation, preferably to go to college or to join the military.

❖ Parents *should* help pay for their children's continuing education, if possible.

❖ Children *should* be allowed to return home after age eighteen, mainly for holidays and summers, until college graduation.

❖ Children *should* live on their own after college graduation and before marriage.

❖ Parents *should* assist children financially, if possible and if the children need help, after graduation, with a few exceptions.

- ❖ Children *should* be allowed to return home to live after college graduation, until they are able to afford to live on their own.
- ❖ Parents *should* allow grown children to return home at any age if it becomes necessary.

While most mothers believe that parents should pay living expenses for an unmarried child who is in college, only about one-third would feel equally obligated to pay for a married child's college expenses, according to one study. And if the child is single or married, but not in school, almost no mothers think the child should receive financial help. Their children, though, expect much more when it comes to being on the receiving end of parental charity: many more children believe that they should take parents' money, even if they're single and living away from home, or married.[16]

In his research on how age dictates these social rules, sociologist Richard Settersten says that a majority of Americans—about seven in ten women and men—believe that age is crucial for determining when children should leave home. Americans also believe that age matters for the timing of marriage, for the timing of first parenthood and its conclusion, and for the timing of grandparenthood.[17]

People hold strong beliefs about what is age appropriate, he says, and their views are supported by the agreement of nearly everybody they know. We have a mental map of our life cycle, and it is ruled by numbers that represent age. We think of this map as a kind of timetable, a guide for when we're supposed to make major life changes. Those numbers—eighteen years old, twenty-two years old, thirty years old— help us in the way we think about our lives and provide us with a way to measure and compare ourselves, and our children, to other people and to their children. That's why people believe that women shouldn't have babies after the age of forty, and women over forty-five, or maybe thirty-five, shouldn't wear bikinis. It's why people tell children that they should be married by the age of twenty-eight, and it's why people sense that by the age of sixty-five, women should become grandmothers.

We're supposed to act our age, and so are our children.

There are laws specifically tied to age as well. Teenagers can learn to drive in most states at the age of fifteen or sixteen, though they can't drive late at night until they turn seventeen or eighteen. They can join the armed forces at the age of eighteen, but they can't drink alcohol, at least legally, until the age of twenty-one. There are also biological functions tied to age—or at least there used to be. Most women can't get pregnant after the age of fifty or so, though medical advances have made that rule somewhat obsolete. And most men should not father a child after the age of fifty, either, if they want to live long enough to see the child grow to adulthood, although some do. These fathers, sometimes called Do-Over Dads, often include wealthy or famous men, such as real-estate mogul Donald Trump, former Beatle Paul McCartney, and comedian Robin Williams, all of whom sired children after the age of fifty or sixty. Apparently an exemption from age rules exists for the famous and wealthy.

But this insistence on living by numerical rules is not our fault: it's cultural rules that tell us what numbers dictate which behavior.

The vast majority of the Chicago residents in Settersten's study, for example, agreed that there is an age deadline for leaving home. People believe that both sons and daughters should leave home no later than age twenty-one or twenty-two. But they also agreed that there are no age limits for when grown children may return home, because home should always be a safety net, even for children who are adults. Thus, there are no age limitations on parental obligations—our children are always our children, regardless of whether they are precious five-year-olds or jobless thirty-five-year-olds.

The strong implication of Settersten's work is that parental obligations are forever. "Family support should not be limited by age," he writes.[18]

American women and men also adhere to a great many rules concerning social deadlines, according to another of Settersten's studies. The deadline for marriage, many people agree, is between the ages of twenty-six and twenty-eight; for parenthood, it's age twenty-nine or thirty. Women should be finished having children by the age of forty, but men are allowed to extend their child producing until the age of forty-four or so.[19]

We also have a deadline mentality when it comes to school and work, research shows. American women and men tend to agree that young adults should be finished with school by the age of twenty-five or twenty-six, and they should start working full-time by the age of twenty-two or twenty-three, settling on a lifelong career just a few years later, at twenty-nine or so.[20]

It's no wonder, then, that some mothers panic when their grown children don't seem to have met these unspoken deadlines. They wonder just how long they will have to support their children, financially and in every other way. (For more on grown children returning home, see chapter 4.)

Social rules also prohibit too-early behavior; a fourteen-year-old should not get married, for example, and a twelve-year-old should not go to college. Most people believe that children under the age of seventeen are too young to leave home. And although that situation is uncommon, it's more likely to occur in divorced or remarried families. The children of parents who divorce and remarry are more likely to leave home before the age of eighteen than are children of biological parents who remain married, researchers say.[21]

Likewise, adopted children, foster children, and those living with a stepparent leave home earlier, and daughters are more likely to do so than sons.[22] It may be that these children feel pressure to leave, or they may not receive the kind of financial and emotional support that children from intact families tend to have. In any case, leaving home too early breaks an age-related rule just as leaving too late does.

"Children of divorce leave earlier and are much less likely to return home," notes Goldscheider. "They have to make tough choices, and they don't have the ability to return home the way children of intact marriages do," she adds.

It seems clear that parents who have enough money—whatever amount that may be—use their financial resources to prevent their children from leaving home too early, but also to keep them from leaving too late, she adds. Parents with money pay children's expenses, either at home or when children have moved out.

Baby boomers were among the first generation of Americans to begin leaving home at the age of eighteen, which may be why we now expect our own children to leave at about the same age. And our children hold similar beliefs. Studies show that about two-thirds of parents, as well as high-school seniors, expect that grown children will live on their own before they marry. And that period of semi-independence begins almost precisely at the age of eighteen.

In fact, this home-leaving time has shrunk to a very specific age range—from eighteen to twenty-one—which is much narrower than ever before, experts say. In the United States, slightly more than half of children leave home at eighteen to live in "group quarters," the term social scientists use for dormitories. By the age of twenty-one, 70 percent of young American adults have lived away from home for at least four months at a time.[23]

But there is Leaving Home and there is merely Living Away from Home, two very different states of mind, not only for the children, but for their mothers as well. Children who are married, or who live in their own apartments or homes, have Left Home. But children who live in college dormitories, military barracks, or graduate-school housing paid for by parents are Living Away from Home.

The difference, essentially, is who is paying for what. If parents still pay for most of the child's living expenses, then their children are living away. If parents no longer pay, then their children have left.

In addition, most research shows that at least half of grown children who leave home come back at least once, or more often. Yes, that's right, **fully half of grown children return to the parental nest**, a somewhat shocking statistic. In her research papers, Goldscheider has taken to using the term "first exit" to describe that first departure, and to distinguish it from the many others that follow.[24]

It's enough to make a mother want to shriek with true horror!

Most parents and their nearly grown children seem to understand that those first few years, when students shuttle back and forth between college and home, are not really a time of complete independence. It's more like experimental independence, a limbo-like Pushme-Pullyou existence. Some researchers call it a period of "interdependence," because young adults can't really support themselves financially, although they seem to think of themselves as relatively independent. In a sink-or-swim world, it's often Mom and Dad who are throwing life vests to their grown children—to save them over and over again.[25]

Here are a few signs that children are merely living away from home, but have not truly left:

- They bring home dirty laundry to be washed.
- They accept money for living expenses, including rent, food, car payments.
- They are eager to snag home-cooked food of any type to take back to wherever they are living.
- Their cell phone is on the family plan, paid for by parents.
- They use an e-mail address from an Internet provider paid for by parents or a ".edu" address paid for by college tuition.
- They drive a car with insurance paid for by parents, in a car owned by parents.
- They never host holiday meals.
- They do not have their own medical insurance.
- They use a credit card with charges billed to parents.
- They don't buy their own underwear.
- They expect parents to buy prescription medications.

The time when children have moved out, but not officially left home, is an in-between time for mothers, too. It's a time of the not-quite-full but not-really-empty nest. A child's yo-yoing in and out of home can last between four to seven years, at least. And that's for each child. In fact, government agencies that give financial grants to students use age twenty-five as a cutoff point; that's the official age at which children become financially independent of their parents. Likewise, many health-insurance plans will insure children, at minimal extra cost, until they reach the age of twenty-five or so. But researchers agree that adulthood no longer begins at twenty-one, or even at twenty-five, for the vast majority of young adults.

Here are the five standard markers of adulthood, steps that young people must take in their voyage to being grown up, according to social scientists. To be an adult, a young person must:

1. Leave home
2. Finish school
3. Start work
4. Get married
5. Have children

By these standards, then, adulthood may not begin until age thirty or beyond.

That's a somewhat intimidating thought for mothers who may have hoped that their nest would be empty ten years sooner.

Take Janelle, whose oldest son is twenty-seven and still living at home. This makes her feel sad, she says, in part "because I feel that he's missing out on an important experience of living on his own and having responsibility." She admits that although he works full-time, it's easier and cheaper for him to live at home in Boston than to find an affordable apartment in an appealing part of this expensive city. And she is embarrassed to tell him, but she really thought he'd be long gone by his twenty-fifth birthday.

Part of Janelle's problem is financial; because she can afford to support her grown son, she does. It's an option that she and her family have chosen to exercise. In fact, the more money families have, the longer this period of dependence tends to last, because parents can afford to support children for as long as children are willing to be supported.

Baby-boom parents, especially, are wealthier than any previous generation, they have had fewer children, and they tend to use a more permissive method of raising children. Thus, they are likely to allow children to return home simply because they can.

It's this "why not?" logic that benefits children who are struggling for financial independence, although it is a deterrent to privacy and freedom for boomer mothers and fathers.

Obviously, families with money have bigger, less-crowded homes and can therefore accommodate grown children. They have more cars for children's use, and greater access to excess cash. They also take great vacations that entice adult children to come along. One friend of mine picks ever more exotic vacation destinations every year, ensuring that her grown children will be tempted to go: one year it was Spain and Morocco; the next, Moscow; then China; and finally, the Galápagos Islands. By that time, two of her children had graduated from college. But all of them still went on the fabulous family vacation.

Researchers disagree, however, about the ways in which wealth influences grown children's exodus from home. Wealthy parents support grown children who live at home, but they may also use their money to subsidize children who want to live away from home. That's the power of money: it offers the luxury of choice.

Whether sons or daughters stay at home or live away while being subsidized by parental funds depends on how well the family gets along, how much they value their privacy, and the type of solution that will make everyone happiest.

It's true, though, that children from wealthier families marry later in life and that wealthier parents tend to discourage early marriage. They do so because they usually offer children financial help. In one national study, it was clear that the more money parents had, the less likely the child was to leave home to get married, in part because they were more likely to be attending college for four years.[26]

In fact, parents often yearn for children's independence as much as the children do. That's why parents who are able to support their children tend to do so, according to sociologist Lynn White. "Better-off parents subsidize their children's departure in order to achieve greater privacy," she writes.[27]

This is sometimes called the disengagement stage of parenting, a tactful way of referring to the "Move Out of the House Already" phase.

Children's Exodus Around the World

While there is agreement among Caucasian parents about when children should leave home, there are distinct differences among parents of other ethnic backgrounds. Among African American families, for instance, children are less likely to leave home by the age of eighteen. The same is true in Mexican American and in some Asian families as well. In one study, for instance, 54 percent of Mexican American families included a child over the age of nineteen, as did 40 percent of African American families, but only 28 percent of white families did.[28]

Fewer black and Mexican American parents believe that it's important for children to live on their own before they marry. So in their eyes, the only legitimate reason for children to leave home is to get married.

In some industrialized countries, such as Britain, Australia, Canada, France, Germany, Japan, and the Netherlands, the "rules" are nearly identical to ours, so most mothers live for several decades without grown children at home. But in other countries, especially in Latin American countries, as well as in Spain, Greece, and Italy, grown children hang around the house for years. They are not expected to leave, so they don't.[29]

The situation is different in Japan, where longer life expectancy and a dramatic drop in fertility rates are giving Japanese mothers decades of life without children at home. Today, a Japanese woman's last child marries, on average, when she is fifty-one, giving her long years of a child-free life, according to Japanese demographers. Japanese women marry later than women in the United States or Canada, by almost three years, but they don't wait as long to have children, so they usually finish childbearing by their late twenties, just as American and Canadian mothers do. Japanese women's family life cycle, then, is becoming remarkably Americanized.[30]

This isn't to say, however, that there aren't a few bizarre exceptions to the Japanese children-leaving-home-by-twenty-one rule. A rare syndrome has arisen there recently, one in which children lock themselves in their room and don't come out for years. These victims are known as *hikikomori,* and 80 percent of them are boys who, by definition, stay in their room for at least six months. They watch television, go online, listen to music, and play video games, but only inside the house. Their mothers bring them food, a kind of at-home room service, and the boys rarely leave their room, let alone the house. Some of these young hermits imprison themselves for fifteen years or longer, and there is no known cure or treatment for the condition. If it lasts longer than a year, young men may never recover from this kind of paralyzing depression, which afflicts from 100,000 to 1 million young Japanese adults. This means, too, that between 100,000 and 1 million mothers become trapped at home with their immobilized grown children.[31]

The age at which children leave home is actually rising in some European countries, in part because of unfavorable economic conditions.[32] The situation is very similar in many Latin American countries, where grown children rarely leave home before they get married.[33]

"Here in Guatemala, because of our culture, our kids stay with us a long time," says Velky, a forty-year-old mother who answered my Web survey. She added that even after they marry, children sometimes still live at home.

"It's most common that parents build an apartment as a second floor in the house, so the children can stay," she comments. But this is mainly because children are expected to care for their aging parents. Still, Velky is teaching her daughter, now nineteen, to become more autonomous, and the girl has followed her advice by studying at an American school in Guatemala City. Velky has heard of the empty nest, but she doesn't quite understand what it means, she said, although she's hoping to find out someday.

In Buenos Aires, the largest city in Argentina, children rarely leave home before the age of twenty-four or twenty-five, according to Claudia Briones, an anthropologist who teaches at the University of Buenos Aires, also known as UBA.

"Social rules vary according to social class in our culture," Briones says, "but children live with their parents until they graduate from university, and then they still live with parents. Among educated people, children don't move out." Argentine children graduate from high school at age seventeen or eighteen, but their college education can last five or six years, because they earn a degree that is somewhere between an American bachelor's degree and a master's degree, Briones tells me in a lengthy telephone interview.[34]

I discussed this phenomenon with a lively group of Argentine working mothers whom I interviewed on a sunny afternoon in April, fall in the southern hemisphere, where drains swirl the other way and New Year's Day is a summer holiday. They told me their life stories, and about how their lives had been shaped by Argentine culture, at a time in which they could not leave home except to marry, and how that rule has changed for their own children.

Just a generation ago in Argentina, they agreed, only bad girls moved out of their parents' home before they married.

"In the days we grew up, in the nineteen sixties, it was unthinkable to leave home before marriage," Doria says. "I was twenty-two when I got married. But nowadays, the whole scenario has changed. Mostly, people have children first and very often they don't get married for a long time," she says.

Doria is a fifty-eight-year-old professor of American literature who also runs an English-language school. She is a dusky blonde, with dark-rimmed glasses and a highly competent, professorial air.

Married quite young, Doria had two sons, one of whom left home at the age of twenty to attend Bard College, in New York, and ended up staying in the United States to go to graduate school at Washington University in St. Louis. Doria says that she was the only mother she knew whose child had left home at such a young age, back then and even today.

"When my oldest left home for college, I thought I would die. I couldn't stop crying. It's very, very rare in Argentina to go to college and not live at home," she explains. "He was twenty, and I thought maybe I would never see him again. I was in a total state of despair," she says, now able to laugh about it.

In Argentina, mothers use the phrase "empty nest," or *"nido vacio,"* but there it carries a different meaning than in North America. Argentine mothers form empty-nest groups to commiserate when their children "undertake the flight," mostly because the children are emigrating far from home, says Silvia, fifty-nine.

A translator of Spanish, German, and English, Sylvia has three children, one of whom now lives in Toronto. All were in their mid-twenties before they left home, and her daughter lives nearby, having moved out at the age of twenty-seven. But Silvia and her husband still pay the girl's cell phone and car registration fees, as well as for her medical insurance.

These middle-class Argentine mothers have an additional five or ten years with their children before they finally move. But when their children leave, it is often to distant continents, not just to nearby cities or states.

The Emancipation of Mommy

For many years, and in many cultures, marriage has been children's best, and sometimes only, escape route from the parents' home, at least from the child's point of view. That primary reason for leaving home, however, has diminished in importance in recent years. Many more nearly grown children now leave home to live on their own long before they marry, and they delay marriage longer and longer.[35]

From the mother's point of view, the children's exodus, oddly enough, has the same purpose. She wants her independence as much as her children want theirs. For a mother who is ready and willing to launch her children and get on with her life, a child's marriage—or even college matriculation—is an emancipation proclamation.

This is a crucial turning point in mothers' lives. **It's a mother's entry into another level of adulthood, one that is more about her and less about the children.**

"It is taboo for mothers ever to openly articulate the ways in which the motherhood role is confining," says Abigail Stewart, a midlife researcher at the University of Michigan. "It's the last taboo, to ever talk about that. It's not a way of saying you don't love your children or you don't love being a mother. But it seems like it might be," she notes.[36]

To tell the bald truth, however, **motherhood can be extremely confining**, in ways that are both good and bad. It is a role that defines women from the moment they give birth, and one that remains central to their identity for years. In my Web survey, for instance, more than eight in ten women say they think of themselves as a mother first, even though many no longer have children at home. The role is immensely satisfying, but can also be draining and debilitating.

Once a mother, always a mother, for worse as well as for better.

The heroine in *The Mermaid Chair,* by Sue Monk Kidd, is a good example of this rule. She says that motherhood made her life feel stagnant and atrophied, a feeling she noticed only after her daughter left for college. "I felt there had to be some other life beneath the one I had, like an underground river or something, and that I would die if I didn't dig down to it," the woman confesses.[37]

Discovering that underground life is what many mothers hope to do when their children leave. And it is just as immense a transition for them as it is for their children, who must leap from adolescence to adulthood by leaving home. It's almost as if children and mothers are trading lives. The child becomes more like the parent, accepting responsibility for work and family and giving up a self-centered view of the world. And the mother becomes more like the child, shedding responsibility and living more for the moment—and for herself.

All of this happens when a woman's hormones start to go haywire, in the premenopausal years. It's somewhat like adolescence, only backward.

Midlife women are the new un-adolescents.

"As they've [her children] taken on more responsibilities, I've gladly let go," says Ann from Arizona. "Even when I didn't think they were ready for it, they've taken chances. It's a weight off my shoulders, when I no longer have to get them out of bed and make sure the homework is in the backpack," she notes. "I can celebrate their lives, and it's a pleasure watching them grow, but I don't have to be on top of them anymore," Ann continues, adding that she's become more like the carefree teenagers they used to be.

Another mother from Chicago points out that for the first time in ages, midlife mothers "are in a position to reinvent ourselves, which is a blessing and a curse. Our husbands don't have that choice, since they are pretty much always the same, but we have the chance to be different people whenever we want."

Believe it: this is the era of reinvention for mothers, and it is a beginning, not an end.

CHAPTER TWO

The Countdown Year

The year before the youngest child leaves home is the time to prepare for reinvention. Think of it as the Countdown Year.

After all, you know what is about to happen, so the transition does not come as a surprise. It's as if a big red bull's-eye is painted on the calendar, with a caption that reads: LAST ONE LEAVES. If you try to suppress this knowledge, or pretend that it's not going to happen, your child will probably remind you of it, over and over again. You'll hear her spout enthusiastic phrases like "I can't wait to leave" or "Only one hundred forty-seven days left." Or you'll hear him say, "You can't tell me what to do anymore," or maybe even "Get me out of here!"

These are symptoms of Countdown Year, a kind of Stage Zero for MotherLaunch, when it becomes crucial for mothers to organize themselves—emotionally, psychologically, and socially—for the imminent departure of their babies.

You know that the event is scheduled to happen, it is supposed to happen, it will happen. So how do you use this knowledge?

Some mothers are prepared for the event, because they've already experienced the departure of an older child. It's as if the leaving of the firstborn is a trial run for the departure of the last. In fact, some mothers actually say they had the most difficulty when the first child left.

Take Darla, fifty-five, who is one such mother. "When my oldest son left it was much more traumatic than when my second child left," she says. "It was a milestone, because the dynamics of the family changed forever when he was gone. It would never be the four of us again, back to the way it was," she continues, "even when he came back from school for vacation."

Because Darla was aware of the before-and-after drama of the firstborn's departure, she says, it wasn't nearly so traumatic when her daughter left two years later. Still, it was difficult, because she and her daughter are very close, "and she's more like my friend than he was."

As part of the mother-daughter ripping-apart ritual, she and her daughter enacted what seems to be a common rite of passage. It's one that includes an emotion-packed confrontation, full of tears and yelling, often set in the parking lot of Bed Bath & Beyond, a popular shopping site for future college freshmen. Mothers and daughters find themselves in terrible arguments while buying the sheets, towels, and shower caddies for the dorm room. They have these battles in the store aisles or outside, on the pavement. Darla had her two-generation fight after the purchase of an overpriced bed quilt, a fight that lasted from the cashier line until the duo hit the parking area.

"I walked out of Bed Bath with her, and we were barely speaking," Darla says, "and I remember crying into her new pillows when we got to the car."

It's the Bed Bath rite of passage, fighting and crying and making up, all in the context of shopping for school supplies. It's a multitasking event, trauma and heartbreak and consumerism all at once!

On the other hand, the leaving of the first child can be so much easier than the leaving of the last. Johanna's oldest child, a daughter, left home three years ago, and it was relief for the entire family. "Her high-school years were so stressful, with battles over everything, over curfews and classes and grades, you name it," says Johanna, forty-nine, who had her own Bed Bath scene.

"The summer before she left, she was picking fights about every-thing, and I know it was to ease our separation," Johanna says. "When we made the shopping trip to Bed Bath, we argued about which extra-long twin sheets to buy, because whenever I said one was nice, she'd make her signature noise, something between a snort and a Russian peasant woman, which was her way of showing disdain for any idea I had. No way was she buying any sheets that I liked. And here I thought the trip to Bed Bath was going to be a treasured moment, a beautiful rite of passage," Johanna says, finally able to laugh about the incident.

"During my daughter's senior year, we had so much conflict over the college application process that I couldn't wait for it to be over," Johanna confesses, slightly embarrassed by the eagerness with which she embraced her daughter's departure. "I told her that she needed to get teacher recommendations for her college applications," Johanna recalls. "But she said, 'Oh, that's totally unnecessary, they're really busy and I don't need to do that,'" Johanna says with disbelief.

Teacher recommendations are a required part of the student's application by just about every college and university, as Johanna knew, even if her daughter did not.

"Then, on the form where they asked about awards, I reminded her to write that she was a National Merit Scholar. But she said, 'I'm not putting that down, it's so braggy,'" Johanna says, still filled with horrified disbelief at her daughter's pointless stubbornness.

"The simplest things became the subject of fights. The most famous one is after we finished hammering out a list of colleges for her to look at; two nights before she was supposed to fly out to Oberlin College, in Ohio, she said, 'By the way, I'm not going to look at Oberlin, because there's no way I'm going to college in Idaho.'"

Johanna laughs again as she tells the story.

"And I said, 'Good, because it's not in Idaho, it's in Ohio.'"

"But my daughter just looked at me, and said, 'Whatever,' still refusing to go. She said, 'Give me one good reason I should look at a college there,'" Johanna exclaims.

"And my husband looked at her, and said, 'Two words: nonrefundable airfare.'

"The whole thing just reminded me how irritating her high-school years were, when everything was a confrontation," Johanna continues. "I knew she was trying to separate, but she made the whole thing pretty damn easy for me to separate from her. By the time my daughter left, I felt like she was too old to be living in the house anymore."

But the situation couldn't be more different with Johanna's second and last child, her son, Alec. "I'm heartbroken about his leaving, that's the only word to describe it," Johanna sighs. Alec is about to begin his senior year of high school, and Johanna has taken to staring at him while he sits at the computer, "mooning over him like a love-struck teenager," she adds. "I feel guilty because I'm so much more upset about the second leaving than the first. It's just that they are very different kids. He was always easier, and we were always closer. We're very simpatico, we have the same sense of humor, and we get along really well," Johanna says.

"So I'm dreading his departure. I've been worrying about it since he was about twelve," she adds. "He was very sickly as a baby, and he was hospitalized for asthma and he has terrible allergies, and he goes into anaphylactic shock if he eats shellfish, so I've always had a dread of losing him. And that's partly because he was so vulnerable when he was little, that's the underlying fear. I'm feeling anticipatory loss now in such a terrible way, and every moment is a bittersweet moment, because I am enjoying him but I know that he'll be leaving soon," she insists.

Johanna continues, "I've gotten really good about pretending to be enthusiastic about looking for colleges for him, but part of me thinks there's nothing wrong if he goes to the local community college. Still, I know that it doesn't matter if he's close by in New Jersey or in Maine or in California, the reality is that he'll come home only for Thanksgiving, Christmas, and spring break. After he leaves, he'll be gone, whether he is three hours away or across the country.

"I'm just hoping that because I'm dreading his departure so much, I won't feel so bad when it actually happens," Johanna concludes.

The Leaving-for-College Ritual

A majority of high-school graduates now leave home to go to college, which means that the going-to-college ritual is the rule rather than the exception. About 71 percent of graduating girls and 61 percent of graduating boys end up attending either a two- or four-year college, according to data compiled by the National Center for Education Statistics.[1] That's a significant increase from just twenty-five years ago, when barely half of graduating high-school seniors enrolled in college.

Thus, this life passage, the child's exodus from home, is determined by the timing of college entry, which in the United States usually occurs at the age of eighteen or nineteen. In Britain, many young adults take what is called a "gap year," in which the student either works or travels for a year or so before starting university. In Israel, most high-school graduates have to serve in the Israeli Defense Forces for two or three years before continuing their education. But elsewhere, and in the United States, a two- or four-year college or university is the socially accepted bridge to adulthood that begins a young adult's departure from the parental home. It's either that or joining the armed forces, an option that becomes less appealing as the risks of signing up become increasingly controversial, as well as life threatening.

The going-away-to-college rite of passage for American teenagers is as proscribed as a primitive initiation ritual, like the one for girls of the Kaguru tribe in Tanzania when they menstruate for the first time. Such girls are isolated in a special house and covered with ashes and herbs to cool them down from the heat involved in becoming a woman.[2] Or it's like the circumcising of teenage boys, to indicate that they have become men, as some tribes do.[3] The main difference is that going to college takes longer, is a lot less unpleasant, and is almost certainly a lot more enjoyable than having a painful medical procedure without anesthesia.

The American going-to-college rite begins in the senior year of high school, though in some communities it starts as early as ninth or tenth grade, or even earlier.

I know one father who enrolled his five-year-old daughter in an ice hockey program so that thirteen years down the road she'd have a better chance of being admitted to Princeton University. It's not clear yet if the tactic worked, since she's now a junior in high school. Meanwhile, she's been playing ice hockey, year-round, several times a week, for a decade. That's a really long Countdown Year.

In most families, the ritual begins later, whenever parents and children begin to think about where the children want to go to school, if they can get in, and how they will afford it. In some hypercompetitive communities, for instance, parents enroll children in SAT preparation classes in ninth or tenth grade. They hire tutors to help children write college essays, and they ship children off to college-visitation camp, a two-week program in which students are chaperoned on a college-visit blitz, seeing as many as twenty schools in thirteen days.

The application process begins in earnest in the junior or senior year of high school. Students take the SATs, they visit schools, they agonize about their decision, they consider the costs. Eventually, they apply to one college or five or forty. Next, they wait to hear. They get rejected or wait-listed or deferred by some schools, and accepted by others. They decide where they want to go, and where they can afford to go, and they send in a deposit. Some students, unable to make a decision, send in deposits to two schools, figuring they will decide which one to attend before September, when they have to show up somewhere.

Finally, they go to the senior prom, they attend graduation, they get a summer job, they take a vacation. In August, they shop for school and dorm supplies, they pack nearly everything they own, and they leave home.

Voilà, a rite of passage completed!

Looking back, some mothers insist that a child's senior year of high school—the year before leaving—was much more stressful than the year after. That's because this time is usually filled with an extraordinarily high level of family anxiety, most of it focused on the college admission process, as it was for Johanna. That stress is frequently a family affair, since many parents take on a large part of the burden of applying to college. More than eight in ten parents visit college campuses with their children, and just as many help the child decide where to apply. They also help with the applications, according to a recent study by College Parents of America.[4]

But college application stress is just one of many that mothers endure during eighteen years of child rearing. They have lived with all the direct stresses of working, raising children, being a wife, cooking, keeping a home organized, and living the complicated life that comes with being a mother in the twenty-first century. A majority of mothers feel stressed about finding time to relax, struggling to make ends meet and pay the bills, managing home responsibilities, and dealing with problems at work, according to one study. Half are also stressed about managing their children's schoolwork, sports, and social lives.[5]

In addition, a large number of mothers suffer from what some researchers call "vicarious stress," which means that they feel not only pressure from their own lives, but the pressure and problems of those they love. So a mother is stressed when her child fails a test, or isn't invited to the prom, or is rejected from a first-choice college. She's also stressed when her husband doesn't get a promotion or her nephew is arrested or a friend is hurt in a car accident.

Mothers feel the pain of others, **especially of those they love, and this can disturb their sense of inner balance** even when the pain is not, strictly speaking, their own.[6]

Watching a daughter get rejected from a school she wants to attend can be immensely stressful for a mother who has never before been unable to help the girl achieve her fondest wish. I remember sitting in the Admissions Office at the University of Pennsylvania, watching an Asian American mother beg the receptionist at the desk for an appointment with an admissions counselor. She kept insisting that it must have been a mistake that her son was denied admission, and if she could only talk to somebody about it, they would admit their error and rectify it. I cringed while I watched the woman's desperation and despair, mostly because I knew exactly how she felt. In fact, a few months later, my own daughter was wait-listed by the same school. If I thought that begging would have helped, I too would gladly have gotten down on my knees and pleaded.

Dozens of mothers tell me that they did an enormous amount of work on their child's college application, usually for what they considered good reasons. Their child was disorganized, they say, or the application involved a music audition they had to schedule, or they had twins, who needed their applications to be coordinated.

One mom admitted to me that she did so much work on the application, "I was like his secretary. He had to audition, and play his saxophone for a committee of teachers, but he also had to prepare applications and essays, and it was too much for him to handle on his own. So I helped," she says.

Another confesses that she worked so hard on her son's eleven college applications that she was relieved to be able to go to work during the week.

"I have to work to help support the family," she says, "so at least for ten hours a day, I was forced to think about something other than his college apps."

Confronters and Deniers

No matter who's doing most of the college-application work, a child's senior year of high school is fraught with anticipation and anxiety, both for children and for mothers. It's a time in which the child is yearning to leave, but afraid to leave. It's a time in which mothers can choose to prepare themselves for their child's departure, or they can pretend it isn't happening. Indeed, the way in which a woman reacts to her child's leaving home depends very much on the way she handles most stressful situations.

Some women are **Confronters**—they face problems and challenges head-on, willing to deal with any impending life-changing transitions. Others, though, are **Deniers**, who try very hard to act as if difficult or traumatic events are not happening and will never happen.

Jane and her family, for instance, are Confronters.

In the year before her eighteen-year-old son left home, Jane, fifty-five, girded her psychological loins for his departure in a way that helped her immensely when he finally left. "In the year or so before his leaving, we were participating less and less in his activities," says Jane. "I experienced a sense of loss and sadness about this, but by the end of his final year at home, I was used to it and rarely upset."

Jane's son helped her prepare by distancing himself from the family in the year before he left, by being there physically but not emotionally. His body was present, but his spirit was already on its way to college.

Jane adjusted to her son's virtual absence, in part because she and her husband have their own all-encompassing business. The couple owns a travel agency in Michigan, one that offers dozens of exotic treks: Botswana Bush Camping, Madagascar Nature Odyssey, Adventure Vietnam. In reality, she sells the kinds of trips that only women with no children at home would be able to take. At least women with, say, $2,695 to spare for a twelve-day voyage to vast tracts of far-flung wilderness, not including airfare.

At this point, Jane expects to feel happy when her son leaves, "because he's ready to go, and he's going where he wants to go." In addition, "I'm happy for me and my husband, for our freedom," Jane says. Because they live in a small house, "we'll definitely be less inhibited when we are alone. This will be one of the delights of an empty nest," she predicts.

With her son leaving in a few months, Jane already sees a change in herself, she says, and a positive one at that.

"I feel an increased excitement about my future, a shift from my preoccupation with my kids and their possibilities to preoccupation with myself and my own possibilities. I've discovered that I have much more self-confidence and much less anxiety than I had in the child-free stage of adulthood that preceded my kids. How nice!" she concludes.

Jane not only did her get-ready-for-empty-nest homework, she finished it long before it was due. Because Jane has done so much of the emotional preparation in anticipating her son's departure, she will probably zip right through the three stages of MotherLaunch like a power hitter sliding into third base at a World Series game. (I describe these stages—Stage One, Grief; Stage Two, Relief; and Stage Three, Joy—in the next chapter.)

Then there's forty-eight-year-old Holly, who is also a Confronter.

Youthful and perky, a special-education teacher who lives on Long Island, New York, Holly has long blond hair, and wears a chic gray pinstriped suit. She could be any New York power broker, trolling like a shark for new business ventures. But, in fact, she's a mother of three who has just finished with child rearing, and she's thrilled to be in this new phase of life.

Holly prepared herself in advance for the departure of her youngest son, now a freshman at Emory University, in Atlanta. "I took preventive action and went back to school, because my son was worried I wouldn't survive when he left," she says, giggling with surprise at what she's about to confess. "I overheard him and his friend talking about what would happen to their mothers when they left! They were actually worried about us," she gasps with disbelief.

"So my husband and I bought an apartment in the city, for when our son left home. I anticipated it and planned for it. Our place is on the West Side of Manhattan. It was something I always wanted to do, so I did it," Holly says. "I stayed there all summer before our son went to college, and now we're there every weekend, and if we have theater tickets, we sleep there," she says. "This year, I'm ready to give up teaching, and I'm going to school so that I can change careers, and learn to do counseling," Holly adds.

Holly used her family's considerable financial resources to make sure that she would have something to look forward to, for herself and her husband, when her children left. That's one of the advantages of having a lot of money—it offers the luxury of options and alternatives. Having financial means also means having freedom of choice.

Marjorie from Missouri didn't have that advantage, but she, too, threw herself into a new life just before her youngest son left for college. She got herself a job as a software manager for several Missouri school districts after spending twenty-four years doing school-related volunteer work, she says. She reinvented herself, at minimal cost, by losing fifty pounds (that's a whole second grader), winning a seat on the school board, redecorating her house, and discovering that "I'm pretty smart and capable and interesting on my own."

What surprised her most of all, says Marjorie, was the realization that she was a fascinating person, and a fairly decent mother. She was also surprised to discover that she could actually lose a whole second grader by exercising almost every day and not eating the junk food that her children insisted she keep in the house at all times. Also, because she was cooking less often, she spent much less time standing at the kitchen counter, nibbling her way through the food preparation.

While mothers like Jane, Holly, and Marjorie prepare themselves for a new life during this Countdown Year, others do their best to ignore it.

Susan, forty-seven, lives in Southern California, land of eternal youth and constant sunshine. She was desperate to make her youngest son's last year seem like it was also eternal. Susan says:

I wanted to appreciate every single moment of every day that he was still living at home, and I really didn't want to think about what my life would be like when he left, even though he really wanted to go away. When we visited schools on the East Coast with him, it was like my husband and I were just on vacation, sightseeing at places that happened to be universities. Instead of, say, spending the week in Rome or London or on a beach in Florida, we'd be touring Harvard and Tufts, Boston University, and the University of Rhode Island.

I wanted to pretend that this year would go on and on and on, that we'd always be thinking about and planning and imagining where Jason would go to college, but that he'd never actually have to leave to go anywhere.

Her dream life of denial lasted for a year, Susan says, but once it was over, and her son actually did leave, eventually—to Cornell University in Ithaca, New York—she was in shock. "I felt like I had been run over by a truck," she says, "although I knew it was headed right at me all along."

Denial is useful as a short-term solution to avoiding pain and loss, but it's one that tends not to work in the long run.

At least that's according to some studies of denial, which is also referred to among psychologists as "selective ignoring." It's ignoring what you need to ignore for as long as you need to ignore it. But in one study of 827 female twins, those who coped with problems using denial tended to be more anxious and were more likely to be depressed than the ones who faced their problems head-on. And if one twin was a Denier, the other was likely to be one as well.[7]

People who use denial tend not to want to discuss their problems with other people, and they also try hard to persuade themselves that everything is fine. They're the ones insisting that the tremors are not an earthquake, that those wisps of smoke are harmless, that the water seeping through the basement is a temporary trickle. Their denial calms them down in times of stress, but it can wreak havoc on their psychological well-being over the long haul.

Here's a simple test to determine if you are a Confronter or a Denier.

CONFRONTER/DENIER QUIZ

Read each statement and indicate how strongly you agree or disagree with each one.

1 = Strongly disagree   2 = Disagree   3 = Agree   4 = Strongly agree

1. I'm better off when I look only on the bright side of life.
    1   2   3   4
2. As long as I keep smiling, troubles don't get the best of me.
    1   2   3   4
3. Most problems are just a state of mind.
    1   2   3   4
4. For me, laughing is a good way to keep from feeling bad.
    1   2   3   4
5. I usually try to tell myself that everything is okay.
    1   2   3   4

Your score should range between 5, if you answered all 1s, to 20, if you answered all 4s. If your score is between 5 and 9, you are likely to be a Denier. If it's between 10 and 14, you are somewhere in between; if your score is 15 or above, you are probably a Confronter.[8]

What's most surprising about this trait, being a Confronter or a Denier, is that it may actually be genetic. The denial trait could be a personality quirk, like shyness or aggression, one that was always there, just waiting to blossom. Scientists figure out which traits are inherited by comparing both types of twins, identical and fraternal. Identical twins come from just one egg, are always the same gender, and inherit very similar physical traits, like eye color and build. They are also similar in psychological outlook, sharing tendencies to be extroverted and friendly, say. Thus, identical twins would be more likely to share the Denier trait than would fraternal twins, who come from two different eggs. Fraternal twins are siblings who were born at the same time, but are much less likely than identical twins to look alike or think alike. So if a personality trait is inherited, identical twins are likely to share it, fraternal twins are not.[9]

Your tendency to be a Confronter or a Denier may be inherited, then. If you are a Confronter, it's likely that you spent the year before your youngest child left home preparing yourself for the event. Likewise, if you are a Denier, you pretended that nothing was going to change, the way you usually do.

The difference between the two extremes is quite simple: **Confronters deal; Deniers don't**.

The process of letting go of nearly grown children is, of course, more complicated than just being able to deal with it, or not being able to do so. Most mothers have an emotional connection with their children and their image of themselves as mothers and wives. They have to untangle these issues before they can also untie their maternal bonds. There are probably hundreds, if not thousands, of ways to complete this highly complicated task. But here are four of the most basic ones.

Cutting the Motherhood Cord

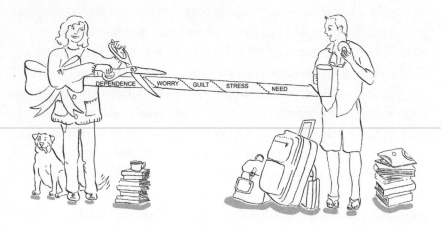

A group of sociologists at Boston College set out to examine the ways in which parents prepare to let go of their children by studying a group of thirty families with college-bound high-school seniors. They found that parents embark on four psychological tasks during the year to prepare themselves for the big event: they deal with conflicting emotions, they worry about readiness, they set limits, and they tackle identity issues.[10]

Untangling Your Emotions

Both mothers and fathers have to learn to manage their conflicting emotions about the child's departure, which is somewhat like the "sweet sorrow" experienced by Romeo when he parted from his Juliet. Parents tend to be sad about the temporary loss of their children, but they also feel happy that the child is ready and able to be launched into the world.

"Children have been at the center of mothers' lives in significant respects, even among women who have careers," says David A. Karp, one of the Boston researchers, in a telephone interview. "To the extent that women have so much invested in their children, and in the process of raising them, they spend a long time thinking about what their life is going to be like when their children go. And it's not just their relationship with their children," he adds. "It's their relationship with their work and with their husband, and they get to a point where they realize they may have to renegotiate everything pretty substantially."[11]

It's when children leave that mothers are forced to rethink their place in the family and in the world, and when they also have a chance to reinvent themselves as someone other than mother.

Mothers who realize this during the year before the last child leaves, says Karp, get a head start on moving on with their own lives. They are also likely to be Confronters.

Some mothers, though, seem to have an aversion to preparing for their children's departures. They are convinced that the children will almost certainly fail without their constant daily help, support, and guidance. They fear that the children will be unable to negotiate this incredibly important rite of passage, he adds, and that will reflect badly on them as mothers.

"Mothers look forward to this event with a measure of trepidation, and with the sense that if all goes well when the child leaves, it will reflect well on the job they've done," he concludes. But if it doesn't, then they believe that they're the ones who have screwed up somehow.

Thus, if a daughter becomes anorexic during freshman year or a son is caught buying alcohol with a fake ID, then a mother is likely to sense she is partly at fault, as if she has flunked her final exam in Advanced Mothering. Her child's crisis and troubles become her crisis and troubles, a reflection of something she did wrong. Mothers who buy into the **Child Fails = My Fault** equation tend to see affirmation of it all around them. Mother blame is a popular sport in American culture, one that never seems to go out of fashion. A few feminist scholars have agonized about how to conduct any research at all on what happens to children without, in essence, blaming moms for "child outcomes."

Several decades ago, for instance, well-respected researchers believed that mothers were directly responsible for their children's autism, schizophrenia, homosexuality, drug use, bed-wetting, poor school performance, and low self-esteem, to name just a few of the problems that they considered to be mother inspired. Even now, many social scientists who study children's troubles point the finger of blame at mothers, either because they work outside the home or because they are divorced or poor. Thus, there is a mountain of research comparing children who spend the day in child care with those who are at home. Another mountain of research is dedicated to examining the children of divorced mothers, both poor and middle class, and comparing them with children whose parents are together.

Because mothers tend to bear more of the daily share of child rearing than fathers do, they tend to shoulder a greater burden of blame. In addition, they have a stronger emotional involvement in the mothering role than most men have in the fathering role. As a result, mothers also tend to suffer from a greater sense of loss when children leave.

Among a few experts, there is even a thin thread of belief remaining in the power of "momism," a term coined in the 1940s to describe overprotective and domineering mothers, the ones who are easiest to blame for whatever ails their children. They are hyperactive, overbearing mothers, the stereotype of a Jewish mother or an Italian mama, and whether they even exist or not is almost beside the point. The belief in momism is the belief that what mothers do can irreparably harm their children. This view is, of course, a primary source of guilt and anxiety for women who buy into the notion that just about anything that happens to their children is their fault.[12]

Maybe that's why so many mothers are actually relieved when their children leave home: the Blame Game is finished!

In our telephone interview, Karp agrees that a majority of moms enjoy life when the children move out. "We wanted to take issue with the dour view of the empty nest for women, that their lives are over when the kids leave," he explains. "There is a measure of emotional turbulence that surrounds mothers when their children leave, but it's not that women feel bereft and uncertain about what to do with themselves once the children are gone. They do feel a vacuum in their lives with no children around, but they are also ready to go on to other things. They want to experience their marriage in ways that the child-rearing years didn't allow, in terms of intimacy and travel, for example," he says. "We wanted to clear up this stereotyped view of women being on the verge of a nervous breakdown when this thing happens," Karp adds.

He found no evidence for maternal breakdowns, impending or otherwise, when children leave; and neither do I.

Worrying about Readiness

During the year before a child leaves home, mothers spend a large portion of the transition period worrying about the child's readiness to leave, according to Karp's research. Although the list of potential worries is really endless, just one is most pervasive, and long lasting.

The Big Worry is: Can he/she live on his/her own?

All other worries are related to this central one: Will he make friends? Will she survive academically? Will he wake up in time to go to class? Will he survive basic training? Will she avoid getting so drunk that she passes out?

It's all about a child's ability to live without Mommy.

A mother is supposed to worry about her children; that's what she does; it's her job. Indeed, the mothering role is intensive and emotionally involving, which is one of the "shoulds" of modern motherhood in North America today, according to social scientists.[13]

So mothers worry when they are separated from their babies, and psychologists study their reactions. Mothers worry about the effects of working full-time on their young children, and sociologists study their reactions. Mothers worry about their teenagers using drugs, and educators study their reactions. There's an entire research industry dedicated to the examination of maternal worries, one that fuels endless research papers. Several psychologists have even developed a "maternal worry scale" to measure the degree of mothers' anxiety when their children get sick. They ask mothers of sick children how often they worry about their child looking different, or having trouble finding a boyfriend or girlfriend, or growing up too fast. They find that a mother's worry level is not related to how troubled the child seems to teachers, or even how seriously ill the child is.[14]

So the degree to which mothers worry has little to do with how much there really is to worry about.

It turns out, no great surprise, that worrying doesn't accomplish much. In fact, worrying has been compared to rocking in a rocking chair, because both give you something to do, but neither gets you anywhere.

Setting Limits

Aside from worrying about what will happen when a child leaves, mothers and fathers try to preempt their anxiety by setting limits on how far a child is allowed to stray from home, the Boston researchers say. Karp says that many parents, especially those on the East Coast, insist on a two-hour rule, meaning that the child has to choose a school within a two- or two-and-a-half-hour drive.

Indeed, one mother I know took out a large map—not of the whole country, but of the three states adjacent to Pennsylvania, where she and her family live. Then she set a small dessert plate on top of the map, drew around its circumference, and told her son that he had to go somewhere inside the plate. (It was about one hundred miles in each direction.) The boy chose to go to school in New York City, about as far as the plate allowed.

A few parents, though, have an even harder time letting go, so they don't.

Take the family whose teenage son left their home in Florida to become a center fielder for a New York Mets farm team. His parents bought a thirty-two-foot camper, equipped with microwave, air conditioner, and satellite television, so that they could follow their son from minor league game to minor league game. They have followed him, so far, for three seasons. The boy doesn't live in the camper, but he visits after every game, especially if he can snag a home-cooked meal.[15]

Their lives are like extreme Little League, with a paycheck, but they never have to supply the orange slices and Gatorade.

Tackling Identity Issues

Finally, the Boston sociologists say that a child's exodus represents a huge turning point in a mother's identity, since she tends to be the one responsible for the day-to-day care of children. The year-long countdown to launch is a perfect time to assess what this turning point will be, although it's not clear how many mothers are willing to take this step before the child's actual departure. That will certainly be a monumental event for mothers, who must rethink their own careers, their own marriages, and their own lives. It's the start of seeing themselves in whole new ways, whether they want to or not.

Here's an example of how one New York City mother, Rory, refused to change her view of her role in her daughter's life. And, by the way, neither could her daughter, Lisa.

The year before Lisa left for college, Rory cried a lot. This was her way of trying to let go, especially when her daughter would go on and on about how eager she was to leave her home in the city and move to a college dormitory. A few years before Lisa was due to leave, Rory had toyed with the idea of getting pregnant again, so that her soon-to-be-empty nest would be full of baby again. As far as Rory was concerned, having another baby was the perfect solution to facing a life without a child at home: just make another one!

I was surprised by Rory's revelation, in part because she seems so together and professional, and so much more than just a mother. At forty-eight, Rory is a tall, slim lawyer who specializes in bankruptcy cases. She's had an engaging and demanding career as a partner in a prestigious law firm since before her daughter was born. But none of that seemed to matter when Lisa finally left home. Rory was devastated, she says, and is on the verge of tears when she talks about it now, a year after the event.

The month after Lisa left "was terrible," Rory says,

> because I miss her, and I feel as though my best friend has moved away. She came back home a couple of times, because she was really sick and I had to take care of her. I still speak to her on the phone five or six times a day, about everything. She'll call to ask, "Mom, how do I buy a heating pad?" or "Mom, should I go to the dorm first and then the library or the library first and then the dorm?" She also calls my husband every day. She's very happy in college, but she's very dependent on us in many ways. I'm trying to force her to make her own decisions. She gets out of class, and immediately she's on the cell phone to me.

Rory is half thrilled and half embarrassed by her confession. Rory and Lisa were so close, in part, because Rory's husband goes to sleep at nine o'clock every night, while she and her night-owl daughter used to stay awake for hours. "We had four hours together every night, so we were together, in the same room. When we're home together, we're this close," she explains, as she points to a spot three inches from her side. "It's a little bit abnormal, actually. I'm not proud of it," she adds.

Rory still longs for that late-in-life baby, so that she can postpone altering her identity as a mother, but it's not in the realm of the possible. Her husband has had his fill of diapers and sleepless nights and nursery-school applications and teacher conferences, even if she hasn't. He refused to consider having another child so late in life.

I interviewed several mothers whose husbands were much more open to the idea of adding a midlife baby to the family. That's why they had an eighteen-year-old college freshman as well as a newborn or a toddler. These couples won't have an empty nest until thirty-five years after they had their first child!

A much simpler, and more biologically feasible, way to prepare for the last child's departure is to surround yourself with beloved pets. Many women admit that they don't feel all that alone because they still have a dog or two around the house to keep them company. I'll confess right here that I'm among the dog-as-pal group, since my Jack Russell terrier, Kippy, is my constant companion. She greets me at the front door, she follows me around the house, and she sleeps at my feet, in the nearest patch of sunshine, day after day, week after week. I'm not sure I could ever send her off to college, in fact.

As long as my husband and I have Kippy, our nest is definitely not empty.

The Nest Isn't Empty Until the Dog Is Dead

Some women, like me, feel so strongly about their relationship with their dogs that they agree their nest won't be empty until the dog is dead. Those who have a beloved pet will know that I am not making this up; everyone else will have to take my word for it. In some ways, a dog can be more loyal and faithful than any human companion, since a dog will not talk back or be ungrateful. And a dog is always, always happy to see you come home, whether you've been gone for two hours or for two weeks.

Stacey's youngest son left her New Jersey home this year to go to college, but she says that her two bearded collies, Riley and Daisy, "are a big comfort. They are really like my children, and I never feel totally alone, because I always have my friends." She means the dogs here, in case there's any confusion about the identity of those "friends."

"They listen to me, and they're always happy to see me," Stacey adds, unlike her two sons, who sometimes seem to have no interest in her presence.

There is actually some evidence that more American households contain a pet than contain children, although that may be hard to believe. Still, as baby boomer's children age out of the house, more and more older adults are living with their dogs and cats and parakeets, instead of with their kids. It turns out that caring for the pets is mostly the woman's job, too, according to one study of pet owners.[16]

While that may be obvious, what's most striking is that almost nine in ten pet owners view their dog or cat as a family member. If you doubt this, think about all of those Christmas cards you received in years past, featuring photographs of the family or just the children. How many of them included a shot of the dog or cat, along with the kids? Probably most of them—precisely because so many families feel that Rover and Kitty are like small, furry offspring.

This particular study of pet owners divided families into seven life stages: newlyweds, parents of infants, parents of preschoolers, parents of school-age children, parents of teenagers, parents of young adults, and postparentals. It was the postparental pet owners, as well as the newlyweds, by the way, who were most attached to their dogs, according to this research.

Whether you own a dog or a cat, a horse or a ferret, here's a quick test to find out how close you feel to your pet.

THE PET TEST

Indicate how much you agree or disagree with each of these statements.

I = Strongly disagree   2 = Disagree   3 = Agree   4 = Strongly agree

1. No family is complete until there is a pet in the home.
   1   2   3   4
2. I feel closer to my pet than to some of my friends.
   1   2   3   4
3. My pet accepts me no matter what I do.
   1   2   3   4
4. My pet keeps me from being lonely.
   1   2   3   4
5. My pet is more loyal than a lot of people I know.
   1   2   3   4
6. My pet gives me someone to take care of.
   1   2   3   4
7. I sometimes judge people by how they react to my pet.
   1   2   3   4
8. My pet makes me feel loved.
   1   2   3   4

Your score on this admittedly odd test should range from 8, if you answered all 1s, to 32, if you answered all 4s. Any score over 25 means that you are deeply, madly, truly a pet lover. And if so, you might not feel as sad when your youngest child leaves home, at least for as long as your pet is alive.

Preparing for the Big Day

There are two aspects to preparing for the departure of the last child. First, the child has to be ready. And, second, you have to be ready.

I'm not so sure that at this late date you can do much more to prepare your child to leave home. You've had seventeen or eighteen years to train the kid in ethics and values and what matters most in life. You can, however, give booster lessons in basic, semi-independent living. First, **you can teach children to do laundry,** if they don't already know how. Write out a list of laundering instructions, hand over a jug of detergent and a roll of quarters, and you've got that covered.

Second, **children should know how to cook at least one basic meal,** something that they can prepare in a tiny kitchenette or in a microwave. Maybe it's just packaged macaroni and cheese, or a pot of pasta, or scrambled eggs, but they should know how to prepare their own sustenance.

Finally, **children should know how to fend for themselves,** which may be the trickiest and most difficult skill to teach in a short period of time. They should be able to visit doctors on their own, fill their own prescriptions, and recognize when they are truly sick or troubled. They should know when they've had enough to drink, and when they've had so much to drink that they shouldn't drive and that they shouldn't get into a car with someone who's had too much to drink. This kind of what-you-should-know list is almost endless, and doesn't bear thinking about too closely if you don't want to induce a panic attack.

You'll just have to trust that you've done your job, and that your children are capable and aware and have basic street smarts and skills. Still, your nearly grown children will probably surprise you every so often with questions that reveal how much they don't know. Some real-life examples of questions asked by twenty-somethings, according to their mothers, include: How do I make a self-addressed envelope? If I buy a bed, don't I get a mattress, too? Why can't I put lemon and cream in my tea? If there's no microwave, how do I heat up the soup?

As for mothers, there are several steps you can take in the Countdown Year to help prepare for the day your youngest waves good-bye.

Savor the remaining moments. Appreciate the time you have left with your youngest, even the bad parts, when he's cranky and nasty, when she's rude and uncommunicative. Remember that your children's job is to separate from you emotionally—that's why they are so awful to you, to wrench themselves out of your orbit. Think of it as being similar to the ninth month of pregnancy, when you became so physically uncomfortable that you began to look forward to the agonizing pain of childbirth, just so you would no longer be pregnant. The last few months of living with an outbound eighteen-year-old may be nearly as unsettling, all so that you won't be as heartbroken when the day of departure finally arrives.

Many mothers seem to relish the savoring. One mother lovingly transcribed her son's soccer schedule in the fall before he left, anticipating that these would be the last games she would ever see him play. Another attended every performance of the high-school musical, knowing that she'd probably never see her daughter in a starring role again. One mother I spoke to even had her son's final high-school report card framed, although he was far from being a straight-A student. "I just wanted a memory of his school years," she says.

Worry in advance. Try to do some anticipatory mourning and worrying the year before the last leaves, to try to get some of it out of your system. That's what Joan says always works for her. "I worry about things ahead of time, so it's not so bad when it happens," she says, comparing her sorrow about her son leaving to her fear of flying. "I get really anxious about the flight two days before I have to go, and then when I actually get to the airport, I'm mostly finished with all the worrying," she says, admitting that she also takes a tranquilizer or two.

Joan didn't expect to have to worry in advance about her son's departure, since she works full-time as a hospital lab technician and is busy all day long. "When I thought about the empty nest before, I thought it only applied to women who were not working, because they had nothing else going on in their lives," Joan explains. "But that's not true. I have a job I love, and work that interests me, so I'm not wondering how I'll fill up the days when he's gone. Still, even though he still has a year before he leaves, I literally get an aching in my chest when I think about him going away."

For this reason, Joan plans to start mourning her son's departure in the first week of September—when her son begins his senior year of high school!

Make a wish list. Write down all the things you've postponed doing because you were too wrapped up with your children. Then do one of them, right now.

In the year before her youngest child left home, Nadine, a divorced mother in Maryland, told me that it helped her to make a wish list "of all the things I had chosen to put off in favor of devoting time/energy/resources to my children and family." At about the same time, she was laid off from her job. With the help of savings and severance pay, she decided that it was her turn to do what she wanted right now, and sooner rather than later.

"A few months before my son left home, I joined a gym, lost a ton of weight, and I began to go out with similarly childless friends. I also started to take classes, began making jewelry, started to read again, and much more," Nadine reports. "Though I know I will miss him when he leaves, this is My Time, and I have never felt younger, happier, or more carefree, and I intend to enjoy it."

According to Nadine, she's glad she began her transformation while her son was still at home. "I wanted my son to see how much I could change my life, and how well I was doing on my own, rather than doing all this stuff in private, as if I was hiding some dirty secret," Nadine says. "I think he was actually proud of me, too."

Practice on the firstborn. When your first child leaves, pretend he or she's your last. Focus on your feelings and how you are coping, as if it's a rehearsal for the last one leaving. Some mothers find that they have the most difficulty when the first leaves, because that departure signals the beginning of a new stage of life. Still, after you've experienced one child's departure, you get to know what it feels like and how well you cope. If you have enough children to practice on, by the time you hit the lastborn, you'll have the process down cold. Of course, if you have only one child, then this is not an option.

Start a group. Several moms tell me that in the year before their youngest left home, they joined a group of other women in the same situation, or they actually formed one themselves.

Toni from Santa Cruz says that she started meeting every month with other mothers of high-school seniors, to talk about themselves, for a change, and not the children. Quite soon, she says, "we realized that it is wonderful to have the support of great women, and that we can all help each other prepare for when our daughters leave home."

Many nearly empty-nested moms belong to similar groups, which can center around anything, as long as it's not mainly about the kids. Midlife moms form book clubs, they band together to walk on Saturday mornings, they agree to go out for a drink on a weeknight. The point is to do something you like to do, with other women who have no children at home, or who are about to have none at home. They don't even have to be your age, or in your stage of life, as long as all of them are relatively empty nested, not including dogs or cats, of course.

Send them to sleepaway camp. You may have to turn back the clock for this one, but mothers who seem to be the most well prepared for children leaving home tend to be those who sent their children away to summer camp. Many moms tell me that the first time they waved good-bye to their children for a few weeks in the summer, they were weeping. But by summer number two, they cheered as the camp bus left the parking lot. The college departure, they say, follows the same trajectory, only it happens a lot faster. First, there's the leaving, then there's the weeping, and a few days or weeks later, there's the cheering.

Get busy, now. Start expanding your life before the last one leaves, not after. Show your lastborn that you have your own life, one that does not require his or her presence to be fulfilling, exciting, and entertaining. Join a group, take a class, go back to school, get in shape.

Sean was so nervous about being without her twin sons that she spent the year before they left figuring out what she would do with her-self when being a mother no longer filled the part of her day when she was not at work. "I was very nervous. I thought I would have tremen-dous emptiness in my life," Sean says. "So I started painting, I learned to play bridge and tennis, and I even tried to play golf. I take an art class in Chicago and I learned how to paint furniture." Sean did all this after work and on weekends, which gave her more energy than when she just worked and went home to cook and do her mothering chores. Her twin sons were so amazed by her transformation that they actually became more considerate and started to do more around the house, including laundry and some cooking.

"Now that my kids are in college," Sean reports, "my husband and I have a whole new life for ourselves."

Treat your depression. For mothers who have suffered from serious depression in the past, the year before the last child leaves home is a good time to seek professional help. For women who are prone to depression, experiencing the departure of the last child may trigger another episode. It did for Sandy, a sixty-year-old Connecticut Realtor who had suffered from depression when she was in her forties.

Sandy's first bout with depression came after she had her first and only child, Brian, at the age of forty. She was treated, and recovered, but eight years later she was widowed when her husband died of a brain tumor. Rather quickly, she became overly doting and quite de-pendent on her son, as he was on her. When the boy was little, he told her that he'd never, ever want to go away to what he called "sleepaway college."

When Brian started his senior year of high school, Sandy realized that she had to unwind the seriously long apron strings that she had wrapped around her son. They saw a therapist together, who helped them see just how strong their attachment was and how helpful it would be if both eased off a bit. Brian attends the University of Michigan now, a plane ride away from home, so he's fine with their separation. Sandy, though, started taking Zoloft, an antidepressant, the year before Brian left, "just to help me out," she says. "That played a big part in making the transition seem really, really easy. My friends were worried about me that first year, because they thought I'd have a nervous breakdown. But every year it gets easier, and I have the Zoloft to thank for that," she notes as she laughs.

Move. Another single mom, Kay, decided to sell her home before her only child, a daughter, left for college. She did so, she says, "only because I didn't want to have to move by myself." When her daughter was a senior in high school, Kay sold her suburban home and bought a small condominium in a neighboring town. As a result, her daughter had to drive to school for a year, a prospect that didn't please the girl. Still, Kay says that having her daughter help her move, and live in the new place with her for a while, helped ease Kay's transition to the solitary living that she faced after her daughter left.

"I know she wasn't happy about it," Kay says now, "but moving while she was still living with me was the best thing for me."

Prepare to let go. You are going to have to let go, sooner or later, so try to loosen the reins of control over your child before he or she leaves. Give her wiggle room in her curfew if she's trustworthy. Let him drive himself to soccer practice if you don't need the car. Next year, you won't know where she is at midnight or when he goes out to a party, so give yourself some practice in letting go right now.

Whatever you do or don't do during the Countdown Year won't change the final outcome: your youngest child will leave. Although it's possible, even probable, that one or more of your almost-grown children will come back home to live for a while, you are about to face a home and a life that is child free. What will happen to your sense of inner balance when that day comes? Will it vanish, receding slowly, like the tide? Or will it come rushing back in, as an unexpected benefit of all those years of intense mothering?

The answer depends on how quickly you progress through the three stages of MotherLaunch. So read on.

CHAPTER THREE

Three Stages of MotherLaunch

It doesn't matter how you approach the departure of your lastborn. You may have been counting the days to freedom ever since your youngest child became an obnoxious adolescent. Or you may have been dreading this moment for years. Either way, it's pretty much guaranteed that on the day that your last child leaves, your nerves will feel raw and exposed. Nothing will feel quite real. The world will seem off kilter. You will be "in a funk," as several mothers describe their initial state of mind. You will feel very much the way you felt when you brought your firstborn infant home from the hospital, as if you are not yourself and nothing will ever be the same again.

That was certainly true back then, and it is true once again now. Your life is about to change, almost as drastically as it did when your first child came into the world.

You are about to become a new you. You are still a mother, but you are on your way to becoming someone else as well. You are becoming someone who is other than mother, someone who is moving on, moving beyond the mommy years.

You are entering MotherLaunch, the stage of life in which you become a mother to children who no longer live at home. **As you launch your children into the world, you also launch yourself into a different phase of adulthood,** one in which you are no longer responsible for the day-to-day and hour-to-hour job of mothering. You send them out into the world, and you send yourself out into the world, too. In doing so, you will begin to see your life with new eyes; everything old will seem new again.

You will see your husband and your friends, your work and your television set, your dog and your cat, your yard and your kitchen, and your face in the mirror. All of them are old, but all will begin to seem new and altered in some way, not younger or better, but certainly different.

In a bizarre way, you are living a life that mirrors your children's. As they adjust to becoming independent adults, daughters and sons who are separate from their mothers, you adjust to becoming newly independent, a woman who is more than just a mother of sons and daughters.

It's an Alice in Wonderland, through-the-looking-glass time, both wonderful and frightening all at once. Maybe that's why closing the door on that last child is a gesture ripe with amazing ambivalence for mothers.

We have a natural urge to hold on to and protect our children, but also a normal need to let them go. We may yearn for freedom, but we also long for the days when our little children needed us for everything. That's why this time of life is one of sadness tinged with elation, one of happiness spiced with melancholy. It's a smorgasbord of feelings, all of the ones you've ever felt and more, and they all bleed and converge and blend until you're not sure what you're really feeling or even which end is up.

You may feel a sense of regret about a job mostly done, but with no chance for do-overs or rewinds. You may have lingering fears about a child who might not be ready to leave, as well as a slice of anxiety about whether you did a good enough job. And there is exquisite sadness when you truly understand that your little children are now gone children. The little boy with no front teeth, the baby girl clutching her bear by the ear, they have vanished. Instead, in their place are these large almost-adults who no longer worship and adore you. These former children insist that they are all grown up, that they don't need you to tell them what to do or how to do it. Still, they're overgrown teenagers who need financial support, home-cooked meals, from-a-distance encouragement, and a tacit assurance that they can come back home to live whenever necessary, as a measure of last resort. (For what happens when they do, see chapter 4.)

They are more like "in-betweeners" than adults, not teenagers but not yet mature grown-ups, either.

So it is that mothers don't lose their mothering job when children leave home; it's just that their job description becomes radically altered. With children at home, motherhood requires daily chores and worries and problems. But after the children's exodus, when that parental Red Sea parts, the chores are nearly gone, the worries are muted, and the problems become long-distance ones. Most of the heavy-lifting duties of motherhood are gone.

Poof! Welcome to MotherLaunch.

By this, **I am not saying that mothers whose children leave are no longer mothers. A mother is always a mother to her children, whether that child is six or sixty**. Nearly every one of the hundreds and hundreds of mothers I interviewed agrees on this central point. It is a kind of mantra of all other-than-mother mothers: "I think about my children every day, even though they are not here." They repeat this, over and over again, almost as if to reassure and comfort themselves. Whatever the reason, the sentiment resonates with truth.

Not at Home, but in Our Hearts

The children are no longer at home, but they are still in our hearts. That's part of the empty-nest mother mantra.

Children who live away are still an integral part of a mother's life, especially now that there are so many electronic options for staying in touch. You can call a child's landline or cellular phone, you can send an e-mail, you can instant-message, you can text-message, you can video-conference, you can speak over the Internet, on Skype. You can stay in touch every which way, except maybe by telegraph or carrier pigeon (unless, of course, you are a pigeon person).

And most mothers are in frequent contact with their children who no longer live at home. In an eight-year-long national research project completed in 1990, for instance, sociologists found that 80 percent of parents of grown children had either seen or talked to their child the previous day.[1] The researchers concluded that out of house does not mean out of sight, or out of mind.

And that study was conducted eons ago, technologically speaking. In 1990, no one had cell phones or the ability to send instant messages, text messages, or e-mails. Now, with the pace of communications technology racing ahead of itself, there are more ways for parents to stay in touch with grown children than ever before. This doesn't mean, of course, that your son will call or e-mail you every day. And it doesn't mean that your daughter will text you or put you on her instant message Buddy List. It's just that he could if he wanted to, and so could she.

In a 2006 study of freshmen at Middlebury College, in Vermont, parents made an average of slightly more than ten communications a week with their children, including cell-phone calls, e-mails, instant messages, text messages, old-fashioned phone calls, and even snail mail.[2]

One of my neighbors, Jennie, was prepared to be devastated when her youngest son left for college. But she found that she couldn't feel sad "because he's so excited about everything." When he first left, "he was e-mailing us at three a.m. with updates about his lectures and his professors and the things he was doing. He didn't close me off. I could e-mail him whatever I wanted, and I could ask him anything, even 'Do you have a girlfriend yet?'" she says. (She did ask the girlfriend question, and no, he didn't have one yet.)

Part of her secret may have been that most of her contact with her son was by e-mail, a less invasive way of getting in touch than by telephone. E-mail messages don't insist that you answer right away, right now. Thus, mothers who make e-mail inquiries generally seem much less pushy than those who do so by telephone. That's probably why so many mothers tell me that they prefer to stay in touch with absent children by e-mail or instant message.

"When I call him on the phone, I feel as if he's not really listening to anything I say," Jennie says. "It's like we need to speak on his timetable, when he's ready to talk. That's why I gave up calling him, and I just wait for him to call me. And if I really need to know something, or feel like I want to make contact, I just e-mail him and he usually answers within a few hours," she adds.

Even months after her son had left, Jennie tells me that "I still feel very much a part of his life." And that was all she wanted, really. That almost daily connection was like an emotional dam keeping at bay the floodwaters of sadness and grief that she expected his departure to bring.

Maura, a mom in Chicago who answered my online survey, also adjusted rather quickly to her newly empty home. A fifty-two year old single mother of two, she says that she likes the fact that her days belong to her now. "I like to have my kids come home on college breaks, but I like the convenience of doing whatever I want when I'm home alone, not having to think about what's for dinner, not having to share the television, knowing that the condition I leave a room when I depart for work is going to be the condition it's in when I come home."

Both of Maura's children call often, from their cell phones, she says, "and my nineteen-year-old daughter called in between this question and the one I just answered!" And she loves the fact that she gets these unsolicited calls at odd hours of the day and night.

Still, the way that mothers adjust to this remarkable change in their lives varies dramatically.

For some moms, like Jennie and Maura, a few days or weeks is all it takes to become adjusted to life as other than mother. Meredith was the same way. "I got over being sad about my son leaving within about two weeks, much faster than I thought," she tells me. "And I think that's partly because I know that whenever I need to talk to him or contact him, I can, depending on whether I want to use my cell or my computer," Meredith says.

Heather, forty-nine, also recovered quickly, though she says that the first two weeks were terrible. "I was very, very melancholy. I was wandering around the house, not catatonic, but in a funk. I was calling friends and reaching out and looking for reasons why I wasn't the world's worst mom. I was going over everything I'd done, and wanting to do it all over again," she says.

Yet, after that initial period of shock and despair, Heather says that she perked right up. "Watching my daughter adapt and begin to love om hating it to loving it, I started enjoying my freedom t was kind of nice," she admits.

ers, though, struggle for months to rid themselves of loss and worry about their newly gone children. They're the ones driving loops around the child's former high school, serving on the school board for years after the children leave, attending fund-raising committees for the child's former athletic teams, and driving for hours to attend the child's college rugby or college lacrosse or college tennis matches. For these mothers, it's a matter of not being able to let go, or of letting go, but just one bare millimeter at a time.

Ashley, forty-one, is a copy editor in Seattle, and she has a supreme inability to let go of her son, Adam, to an almost pathological degree. If you think I'm exaggerating, listen to this.

Ashley goes online nearly every day, checking the Webcam at the University of Chicago, hoping to get a glimpse of Adam walking along the path. She haunts the online blogs of his friends, too, hoping for a mention of him so she can feel part of his life. He doesn't have his own blog, she admits, or she'd be visiting adam.com all the time.

And there's more.

"He'll send me a quick little text message, and I'll save it so it can't be erased, and I'll look at the message—"Hail and sleet"—when I'm feeling lonely. I'll click around at his university's Web site, looking at pictures of his dorm, or what's on the lunch menu, anything to catch a glimpse of his life. It's almost like a junior-high crush, where everything about the person just seems incredibly fascinating," Ashley says.

The woman has become a son stalker, with equal measures of creepiness and sadness and an inability to get on with her own life.

Here's how she explains it: "At first, I was just at loose ends. So much of my life had revolved around meeting Adam's needs and, as I realized more and more, chatting with him. We find similar things funny, and it's relaxing to talk to someone to whom you don't have to explain anything. I became more and more gloomy after he left, and felt as if I were sort of exposed on one side—like I was wearing a shirt with one sleeve torn off."

The Three Stages

Ashley is an extreme example of a mother stuck in the first stage of the adjustment process when children leave, the one I call the Grief stage. All newly empty-nested moms experience a similar process of adjustment when their last child leaves home. This progression includes three stages: **Stage One, Grief; Stage Two, Relief; and Stage Three, Joy.**

This is a three-stage psychological journey, one that requires a different amount of time for every mother. If you could see the progression with time-lapse photographs, the pictures might not vary much from day to day, or even week to week. Eventually, though, over time, each mother's stage of adjustment would become obvious. Women progress through the stages at their own rhythm and pace, depending on several factors.

The speed with which mothers traverse these stages has to do with their relationship with the child, their personality type, the reason the child left home, if the child is happy, and how well the child copes. I've spoken to a mother whose son enrolled at a school three thousand miles away and was pleased to discover that the boy was fine living on his own. I've interviewed mothers whose children left home to join the army, or to travel for a year, and after an initial period in the Grief stage, they, too, have entered Relief. As long as children are happy about their destination, the process tends to go smoothly, and it becomes all that much easier for mothers to move on.

It's when children struggle with unhappiness that mothers find themselves having difficulty adjusting. If a child has been rejected by several colleges and is attending a fourth- or fifth-choice school, one at which she is miserable, that makes for potential maternal distress. If a child suffers from anorexia or severe depression, then mothers may not exit the Grief stage for a while. And if a child calls home to say it was all a big mistake and can somebody pick her up, then mothers struggle to feel guilt-free relief at being on their own.

Andrea, forty-nine, a woman I interviewed from Morristown, New Jersey, sent her second son off to school at New York University, not far from home. But he had trouble adjusting there, his roommate would not speak to him, and he didn't like any of his classes. A month after he left home, he called to say that he hated school and could he come back home.

After that phone call, Andrea suffered almost as much as her son did those first few months. She and her husband argued about whether they should just drive up to New York City, pack everything, and bring the boy home. But they couldn't afford to lose the money they'd already paid for tuition, so they decided to let him tough it out. Andrea resisted the impulse to be her son's savior. Instead, she talked to him every day, trying to assuage his anxiety and depression. Eventually, the boy learned to cope on his own.

Edith, forty-four, another New Jersey mother, had a daughter who joined the air force and was sent to Afghanistan. She admits, quite understandably, that "it was truly hard for me to let her go under those circumstances." There were times, she says, "when I just did not want to get out of bed in the morning." But finally she saw that "either you live the remaining years to the fullest, or you see yourself in a life that makes you miserable and sad. Life is a gift to be appreciated and lived," she concludes, in a heartfelt way. She left Grief, stayed for a while in Relief, and now she's feeling Joy.

Another mother, Mandy, who lives in Amherst, New Hampshire, had to send her daughter off at the too-young age of fifteen, to a rehabilitation facility for drug addicts, by court order. After the girl had been weaned from her addiction, Mandy had to send her daughter to boarding school so she wouldn't relapse.

"I am still working on letting go of my guilt feelings about this," Mandy says. "My husband and I sat down and cried together when we came home. It was the hardest thing we ever had to do." It was understandably difficult for Mandy to let go of her daughter, in part because the girl was so young, but mostly because she left for such an unfortunate reason.

A mother's progress through these stages will also vary according to how well she has organized her life to reflect her own needs and interests. If she already has a steady focus on what matters in her own life, she will be that much more ready to live life on her terms. One woman who answered my Web survey offered one simple reason for her relatively easy adjustment to letting her children go: "I've worked all along, and that made a difference," she says, "because my children don't define me, and never did."

What Stage Are You In?

Most mothers should be able to figure out which stage they are in simply by reflecting on their own feelings.

Are you sad, feeling a little blue or unhappy? Is your sense of loss still keen, cutting through your heart like a knife? If so, then you are most likely in Stage One, Grief.

Have those feelings been replaced by a sense of relief and freedom? Do you marvel at how much of your time is now your own? Then you have probably progressed to Stage Two, Relief.

Finally, are you giddy with a sense of possibility and promise? Do you look at your partner, and the world, with new eyes, as if you have been reborn? Don't look now, but you're in Stage Three, Joy.

If, however, your feelings are muddied, and examining them feels like peering into the depths of a bottomless well without your reading glasses, then you might need help deciphering which stage you are in. It's possible to be in two stages at once, both sad and relieved, say, or both relieved and full of joy. If you are confused about which stage you are in, answer these ten "what if" questions and add up your score. Your score should range between a 10—if you answered all 1s—and a 30—if you answered all 3s.

THE "WHAT IF" QUIZ

1. Imagine that you are in the grocery store, and you pause in front of the refrigerated dairy section. What do you do?
    1. Look with longing at the gallon jugs of milk, and wish that you still needed to buy that much.
    2. Reach for the gallon, but remember with gratitude that you probably need only a quart.

3. Happily buy the smallest container of milk possible or, maybe, none at all.

2. Imagine that you are walking past your child's empty bedroom. Do you:
   1. Walk in, sit on the neatly made bed, and cry?
   2. Peek in and marvel at how orderly it is?
   3. Decide to move some of your own stuff in there?

3. Imagine that you are driving near your child's former high school at dismissal time. Would you perhaps:
   1. Detour around front to see if you know any of the children leaving or entering?
   2. Smile at the parents forming a conga line to pick up spoiled offspring who refuse to take the bus?
   3. Make sure to avoid the neighborhood so you don't get stuck in the daily traffic jam?

4. Imagine that it's spring break, and your children are due home any day. Do you:
   1. Make some calls to see which of their friends will be home, too?
   2. Try to remember to pick up some of their favorite foods before they get home?
   3. Remember only at the last minute that they will be home?

5. Imagine that one of your children calls you while you are working on a complicated project. Would you:
   1. Drop everything to talk, no matter what?
   2. Say hello and chat briefly?
   3. Answer the phone, but ask if you can call back later?

6. Imagine that you are watching a television show featuring a teenage boy with cancer, or a mother throwing a birthday party for a

three-year-old, or a young girl visiting her mother in the hospital. How does this televised heart-wrenching make you feel?

1. Like bursting into tears.
2. Nostalgic and wistful.
3. Engaged, but not personally involved.

7. Where are your children's LEGO bricks or books, especially the classics like *Goodnight Moon* or *Love You Forever* or whatever you used to read aloud over and over again?

1. They're still in the children's rooms, on shelves, or in closets.
2. I've packed them away, to save for grandchildren.
3. I tossed most of them, or gave them all away.

8. Imagine that you are dining out at a fairly expensive restaurant and a family with three young children takes the table next to yours. How do you react?

1. I'm jealous of the mother, because she still has her children with her.
2. I'm pleased to see an apparently happy family.
3. I'm annoyed, because they'll probably get noisy and ruin my meal.

9. Imagine that you are walking through the mall and you spy a new store that features cool clothing for young people. What do you do?

1. Walk in and decide to buy a little something for one of your children.
2. Look at the window display with fond nostalgia.
3. Walk right on by.

10. Imagine that you are about to have grandchildren. Which is closest to the way you will react, or have reacted?

1. I would seriously consider moving so that I could live near my grandchildren and help take care of them.

2. I would renovate my home, to make guest rooms for prolonged visits.

3. I would make sure I could chat often, on the telephone or online, with my grandchildren.

The first answers, the 1s, represent the Grief stage. The second answers, number 2s, are Relief; and the third, the 3s, are Joy. Add up your answers. If you score between 10 and 14, you are still grieving the loss of your babies. If you score between 15 and 22, you are probably closer to feeling Relief that they're gone. And if you score between 23 and 30, you are almost certainly full of Joy about your child-free state.

The stages are not definitive, though. They are not black and white, like being pregnant or turning fifty, both of which you either are or aren't. Instead, these stages are suggestive and ambiguous, they blend and merge into each other, and as one begins, a prior stage may still be lingering. If we illustrated the stages, they'd look something like the art opposite.

Stage One: Grief

The Grief stage is the most devastating, but it also tends to pass quickly.

In my research, I asked mothers how they felt in the week or two just after their youngest child left home. Recalling that time, nearly 50 percent say they felt shocked and upset or sad and depressed in those first few days or weeks. It's the same feeling you might have when recovering from surgery, or breaking up with a boyfriend, or losing a job. Everything feels slightly unreal, as if you are not yourself, in part because you are living a life different from what you're used to. It's a feeling of disorientation, one that can take days, weeks, or even months to wear off. But this stage rarely lasts longer than six months or so. If the Grief stage lasts longer than a year, it means that a mother probably has additional, and more serious, problems to resolve. (See "Stuck in Stage One," on page 78.)

In the first week after my youngest child left for college, I was extremely upset and sad. And I remembered a fantasy I'd had when both

The Three Stages of MotherLaunch

Grief

Relief

Joy

of my children were preschoolers, a time when I couldn't leave them home alone. It was a Sunday morning, and I had to wait for my husband to return before I could go out for a run. I was itchy to escape, and annoyed that I couldn't leave as soon as I was ready. My daughter was four, my son was two, and both were cranky and upset that I was leaving.

As soon as my husband walked in the door, though, I was out of there, yelling, "I'm leaving; bye!"

I shut the door and ran away, as if escaping from prison.

As I ran, I began to have a kind of *Twilight Zone* fantasy. What if, I fantasized, when I returned from my run, both children had magically grown up? What if I came back and, instead of my two little munchkins, I returned to find two twenty-somethings, adults who barely noticed that I'd been gone?

The idea, while crazy, seemed somewhat possible, and it both horrified and thrilled me. While I didn't want to miss my children's babyhoods, the prospect of all that freedom was enticing, alarmingly appealing. I shuddered as I tried to block the notion from my mind. When I got back, forty minutes later, I was relieved to see that my little ones were still little.

Now, all these years later, I feel as if I've entered that *Twilight Zone* episode after all. These days, when I return from my Sunday-morning run—more like a Sunday-morning walk—my children are, in fact, grown and flown. I can go whenever I want, for as long as I want. My husband and I are alone, and there is no prison from which I need to escape.

I thought about that fantasy a lot during my Grief stage, because it seemed so bittersweet that I'd finally gotten what I wanted, but no longer felt as if I did. Luckily, though, this feeling didn't last that long, and neither did my Grief stage.

Miranda's first stage didn't last long either, but she felt her Grief most keenly the second day after her youngest daughter left home. "I didn't realize my kids were really gone until I went grocery shopping for the first time," says Miranda, fifty-one, who lives in Rochester, New York. "Then, it was as if everything was symbolic. It was a shock, too.

It's like, 'What do I buy? Like, two potatoes, four bananas, what?'" She felt her sadness in the symbols of what she no longer had to provide for her children, the food that she bought and cooked for them every day for years and years.

This food shock is among the most common Grief reactions among mothers whose children have just left. They feel it when they no longer have to buy so much milk, or a daughter's favorite sugary cereal, or the special Doritos that a son ate every afternoon. Mothers' distress is not so much about the food itself, it's about what that food represents: decades of loving and caring and nurturing.

In that first month or so after the last child leaves, mothers become upset about a number of painful issues, in addition to the grocery blues.

Four in ten mothers say that they are sad about no longer being involved in their child's life, according to my Web survey. Quite simply, the children are not at the dinner table, they are no longer in the car, they're not in front of the television or the computer screen.

Here's what a fifty-year-old mother of three from Phoenix misses: "I miss the loss of some traditions that I valued, like the give-and-take of ideas at the dinner table." She used to keep up with her children's political views on a daily basis, she says, and argue about those positions almost every night, but now she's completely out of their loop.

That's why she is still in Stage One, she says.

Marie, a forty-seven-year-old mother and stepmother from Sheboygan, Wisconsin, says that when her youngest daughter left for school, "I felt like I had been hit by a train, and I cried on and off every time I thought about her, for three days." It was especially painful, she says, when she realized that her daughter's days were a complete mystery to her, that they would no longer chat at the end of every day to catch up on what had happened, where it had happened, and why.

A smaller group of mothers, about one in four, says they are upset when they see the child's empty bedroom, according to my Web survey. That unusually pristine space is a visual reminder of what is gone—a beloved child. The cleanliness is nearly as shocking, because it, too, is irrefutable evidence that a messy, busy teenager is no longer at home.

Vicki missed her daughter so much when she left their home in Philadelphia for the University of Wisconsin that she turned the girl's room into a kind of memorial shrine. She left the room as it had been on the date in late August when the girl left for school. The high-school awards stayed on the wall, the old stuffed panda bear was on the bed, the unwanted shoes still spilled out of the closet.

Vicki is a shy, somewhat insecure woman of fifty-four, and her puffy face makes her seem as if she has just finished weeping. When Vicki's daughter left, she says, "I was devastated. I really missed her. We were very attached. I'd go into her room, lie on her bed, and cry. I'd think the same wrenching thought, over and over and over again. It was like a prayer. I'd think, 'Oh, God, she's gone.'"

One in five mothers feels bereft because she is not cooking or shopping for the child anymore. These are central chores for the motherhood role, and although they can be onerous—dinner tonight, and again tomorrow, and again the next day—meal preparation is a way in which many mothers express their love and affection for their children. In fact, sociologists who study family activities sometimes ask parents to keep a time diary, listing every single thing they did in the previous twenty-four hours. (There's even a category called "none of your business.") Meal preparation, meal cleanup, and food shopping are usually included as a subcategory of housework, which also includes housecleaning and repairs.

In a recent comprehensive national study that used such a time diary, researchers found that American mothers spend about 107 minutes every day caring for children.[3] And in another study, one of the largest ever, a government-sponsored questionnaire polled twenty-one thousand people to discover exactly what they'd done the day before. By their estimates, women say they spend, on average, 47 minutes a day cooking meals and cleaning up afterward.[4]

So let's do the math, using 47 minutes as a guideline. If a mother cooks for a child for, say, sixteen years (we'll subtract two years for nursing and baby food), just six days a week (to be conservative), she will have spent 234,624 minutes cooking meals and cleaning up. That's about 3,910 hours, or 163 days, around the clock, of preparing meals and washing dishes. Add extra hours for each additional child. Subtract extra hours for a husband who loves cooking or cleaning up. (And count yourself extraordinarily lucky if you've got one of them!)

Mathematically speaking, then, we miss that chore because it took up almost an hour, every day of every week of every month of every one of at least sixteen years.

In addition, one in five mothers is upset when the last child leaves because she can no longer participate in the child's school activities.

Two of the Philadelphia moms I interviewed confessed that they started to take night classes at their children's former high school. They had always envied their children being able to take fascinating classes with great teachers, and they saw this time as a chance to finally get in on the act, especially since their easily embarrassed teenagers were no longer around to protest. One of them took a class in which she had to read a new Jane Austen novel every week. The other signed up for what she considered an intriguing offering, called "The Poetry of Yoga."

Finally, one in ten mothers says that she is upset about paying the tuition bills, no small matter when one year of private higher education costs about forty-five thousand dollars, in 2007 dollars. "Okay, I really miss him sometimes," says Phoebe, fifty-two, about her son, who attends Stanford University. "But then I remember that we're shelling out over forty thousand dollars for the privilege of letting him leave home, and that disturbs me so much that I can't even see straight!"

This litany of sorrows can't possibly cover every little event or each special moment that mothers cherish. We all have our own special something that we miss most of all.

One mom tells me she misses hugging her son, the daily physical contact. Another says she misses a daughter's smile, seeing it whenever she wanted. A third confesses that she misses all of her daughter's friends who used to drop by, and even the horrible, loud music that she always thought she hated so much. Another mother even admits that she misses receiving all the telephone calls that weren't for her.

Despite their wrenching sense of heartache when the last child leaves, many mothers are shocked to find that their Grief lifts much more quickly than they expected. Indeed, for the vast majority of moms, the disorientation and sadness fade as soon as mothers accept the idea that their new, mostly child-free way of life is enormously liberating.

With the passing of time, my research shows, only a small group of mothers—around one in ten—feels a persistent, lingering sense of Grief, one that they cannot seem to shake for months, or years, after their last child leaves.

Why can't these women recover from the loss of their full-time-mom jobs, when so many others can and do?

Stuck in Stage One

The women who seem stuck in Stage One are likely to be clinically depressed.

Women who suffer from depression tend to have trouble laughing or singing, enjoying movies or music, and they often lose the ability to fantasize, not just about sex, but about anything positive, like winning the lottery or telling off the boss. There are about a dozen common signs of depression, and the more often you have them, the more likely you are to be seriously depressed.

Ask yourself how many days each week you have felt each of these symptoms; then add up the number of days. The higher the number, the more likely it is that you are depressed.

During the past month or so, how many days did you feel:

- ❖ Bothered by things that don't usually bother you?
- ❖ Lonely?
- ❖ Like you can't shake the blues, even when your family and friends try to help you out?
- ❖ Unable to sleep well?
- ❖ Sad?
- ❖ Like everything is an effort?
- ❖ That you were having trouble keeping your mind on what you were doing?

- ❖ Afraid or nervous?
- ❖ That it was difficult to speak?
- ❖ Not very hungry?
- ❖ That you couldn't get going, first thing in the morning or at any time during the day?
- ❖ Depressed?

Women who are stuck in Stage One, usually with some form of depression, may have at least one other source of sadness or despair in their lives. It can be a troubled marriage, a health problem, a sick or dying parent, a lack of friends, a terrible or humiliating job—any of which can act as a trigger for a bout of depression. It's as if having a child leave home becomes final straw, the catalyst that brings on a flood of pain and depression.

Petra is a good example of how a child's exodus can become the tipping point for an avalanche of despair. She's fifty-five and lives in Evanston, Illinois, and couldn't escape from the Grief stage after her son left home. Her first problem was that the boy left home too young, at the age of fourteen, long before the socially mandated age of eighteen, viewed by most Americans as the proper home-leaving time. But Petra allowed her son to move out, she says, "to follow his career path in the pre-professional performing arts, so he could be surrounded by intelligent and like-minded gifted students."

She let him go for his own good, although she says that both she and her husband grieved for his loss for four solid years, the entire time that he still "should" have been home. Now that he's a sophomore in college, "his father and I are finally accepting that he will never again come home to live," she says.

For seven long years, though, she did not accept that he'd never return. Those years, she says, "have been grueling, and full of grief and worry and guilt and loss over my child's intimate life during his teens."

Although Petra knows that her son and her older daughter have lives "that are blossoming into their own," she admits that "I will never get over letting him go too soon."

But Petra has other, bigger problems, troubles that compound her sense of loss over her son's early departure. She has had a stroke and heart surgery due to thyroid disease. She is responsible for taking care of her mother and her mother-in-law, both of whom are in poor health. She works almost eighty hours a week as a database developer and has no close friends, no one to turn to for comfort and companionship. Finally, she is stuck in a marriage that she regrets deeply, and admits that if she could rewind the last fifteen years of her life, the one thing she'd do differently is that, this time, she'd get a divorce.

Her sex life didn't change much after her children left, she says, because she doesn't have one.

It's no wonder, then, that Petra's children's departure sent her over the brink, into depression and self-pity and gloom. Her sole advantage is that she understands what has happened to her, and knows what she has to do to make it right. "It is a matter of finding my soul and the me I lost a long time ago," Petra confesses.

Petra is clearly vulnerable to depression, though the fact that she is aware of her condition means that she may be capable of doing something about it. Many experts believe that more women than men suffer from depression, in part because it's their job to feel everybody's pain. In fact, one major national study found that 16 percent of American women will suffer from depression at some point in their lives. The same researchers also demonstrated that women are more likely to suffer from anxiety disorders, including panic attacks; agoraphobia, or the fear of going out in public; social anxiety; obsessive-compulsive disorder; and post-traumatic stress disorder.[5]

As part of my research, I examined women like Petra closely, under a statistical microscope, to try to discover what it is about them that makes them so supremely susceptible to despair. I wanted to find out why it is that some mothers are stuck in Stage One.

I discovered that these women tend to see life through gloom-colored glasses: for them, the grass is greener elsewhere, they're never on the sunny side of the street, the glass is always half empty. About half of them realize that they have become depressed, according to my research. Not only that, a majority say they feel empty, afraid of growing old, and anxious. They are significantly more likely to have had such negative feelings than women who are in Stage Two or Stage Three. Four in ten women stuck in the Grief stage feel irritated with their husbands, and only 15 percent are excited about their future, compared to 60 percent of mothers in Stage Three.

But these unhappy moms are not without self-awareness. Indeed, six in ten feel a need to move on, it's just that they can't see a way in which it's possible for them to do so. It's almost as if they have been blinded to what's positive and hopeful and uplifting about this stage of life—yet another symptom of depression. And they also suffer from several other signs of that disease. Two out of three mothers who are stuck in Stage One say they have trouble sleeping, and four in ten have felt a serious loss of sexual desire, although they are not more likely to be suffering from the hot flashes or mood swings associated with menopause.

It's almost as if whatever happens in their lives has the potential for creating sadness, and watching children leave home is up there in the top three reasons for feeling anguish, self-pity, and despair.

But why does one woman get stuck in Stage One, and her friend, in the same situation, thrive on the newfound freedom?

The answer may lie in genetics, since vulnerability to depression tends to be hereditary. It's an enormous oversimplification, but if you have a parent or sibling who suffers from depression, you are between two and eight times as likely to get hit with it yourself as someone whose close relatives were never depressed.[6]

Happy gene pool to you.

Some researchers even believe that women who readily fall into depression have what they call "hostility syndrome," meaning that they tend to be cynical and paranoid, believing that the world is threatening and everyone in it untrustworthy. This kind of nastiness can also prevent hostile women from making friends and finding people who care about them, which is in itself, of course, also depressing.[7]

Welcome to one of the more vicious cycles of life.

In addition to genetics, some mothers may become stuck in Stage One due to a personality trait, one as simple as a tendency to view oneself as unlucky. People who view themselves as unlucky are not extroverted, open, or agreeable. When they meet someone new, they do not engage in conversation; they rarely keep track of friends; they are often afraid to take the first step in any social situation. It's as if, one author says, they repel other people, unlike those who view themselves as lucky. Lucky people are like "social magnets," with a natural ability to draw other people to them. They trust people they have just met, and they expect to be liked; not coincidentally, that's what usually happens, since most of us tend to get what we expect.

In observing self-described lucky people, British psychologist Richard Wiseman finds that people who think of themselves as lucky smile twice as often as others and make eye contact more often. This habit not only makes lucky people seem friendlier, but actually results in the fact that they have more friends. They're also more open to new people, new experiences in life, and various quirks of fate, he says. Ironically, lucky people expect to be luckier, so they are. It turns out that the way they view the world influences how the world acts on them.[8]

Mothers who get stuck in Stage One clearly do not view themselves as lucky.

Paula has never viewed herself as lucky. She raised three children in California, partly on her own, but now, at the age of fifty-eight, she still can't get over how empty her house feels. "I need to find more friends my age," she says.

After moving two years ago, for her second husband's job, she is completely cut off from everyone she used to know. "I find the isolation and loneliness to be difficult. I have to go back to work, or else give up and go live under a bridge," Paula says, with a rising note of pessimism.

"Still, I believe that raising a child is much more important than pleasing clients or running a factory," Paula explains. She did, in fact, run a plastics factory, but sold it so that she could be at home to raise her youngest son, now eighteen. With the idea that she has at least twenty years left to live in good health, Paula has decided that her new motto should be "Have more fun."

It's just that she doesn't quite remember how to do that.

Stage Two: Relief

One in five mothers are lucky enough to slide quickly through Grief and land on Relief when their children leave home. Perhaps they have engaging work to distract them, or a vibrant marriage, or a gang of friends to amuse them.

Or maybe they have all three.

For whatever reason, these moms do not spend much, if any, time sitting around weeping and bemoaning the flight of their babies.

"I have always felt that a child's leaving at a certain point is life's natural progression," Eloise says rather bluntly. Eloise is from Stamford, Connecticut, and has a twenty-one-year-old son; she notes that "we teach them to fly so we can set them free," which she admits is a Hallmark-card-type sentiment, but one that gets at the heart of the matter.

Then there's Patty, fifty-seven, who felt the loss of her oldest child, a daughter, as sharp pangs when the girl first left their home in Pasadena, California, to begin school at George Washington University, in Washington, D.C. "In general, I was surrounded by kids my whole adult life, organizing them and keeping their lives running. I was really afraid I wouldn't be exciting after they left, and I didn't want to be a burden to my husband. So I have a support group of women I can turn to for sympathy," she says.

Indeed, that group became Patty's secret weapon, a source of emotional support that helped her through the pain, and made her realize that what she felt was less sadness and more like simple relief at the lifting of so much responsibility.

Patty and her friends gather once or twice a month, she says, and "we're all really aware of the need to move on with our lives, physically and mentally. But we have to move on in a positive way, and not say, 'Oh, God, life is over!' "

Most important, she says, is that "I don't want to live in the past. I want to continue having a great life."

Patty's friends also made her realize that "if I fail to accomplish something, it is my own fault. I can't think of my children as an obstacle to my success."

If any mother could rightfully claim her children as an obstacle, it is surely Patty. Her oldest child, a twenty-one-year-old son, was diagnosed with a brain tumor when he was four years old, and she gave up her career to care for him, through years of slow and painful recovery. "My son was considered a miracle child," she says, "and he changed our lives."

Now that the boy lives in a residential school on the East Coast and her daughter also lives on the other side of the country, Patty is left on the Left Coast with her husband, an investment banker who spends all his free time training for long-distance bicycle races. The man spends thirty or forty hours a week riding his bike; it's his second career.

This leaves Patty with way too much time by herself, so she decided to find herself a new career, using her own rule of three: she had to be her own boss, she had to have flexible hours, and she had to make a lot of money.

She found work that satisfied all three of her goals. Patty now operates her own clothing business, selling high-end women's business clothing out of her home. She works sixty hours a week, but she makes a healthy income, all on commission.

The stage in which Patty finds herself, Relief, is quite often a transitional phase, one that becomes a station stop on the continuum to Joy. For her, and for many women like her, it's just a matter of time before Stage Two, Relief, becomes Stage Three, Joy.

In my interviews with a group of fifty-something mothers on Long Island, New York, it is clear that several are now in the Relief stage, but most seem destined to find their way to Stage Joy.

Cassie is a fifty-six-year-old kindergarten teacher with three children, the youngest of whom is a freshman at Duke University. She explains her position quite simply: "I felt really happy when the kids moved on. They were ready to go somewhere else. I felt good about them leaving, mostly because my kids were immediately happy when they left, and that made it easier for me."

Cassie has understood a basic maternal equation, one that is echoed by many mothers in the same position:

Children Gone + Children Happy = Mother Relieved

Simple, sweet, and nearly universal.

Cassie is one of six women, all of whom have gathered in their friend Marilyn's elaborate and expansive dining room to discuss their absent children. They live in a community where looks really matter, where what you earn is written all over your car and your clothing and your house and the huge rings on your well-manicured fingers. It's a place with supercompetitive schools, and the parents that fund them. It's a place where average home prices can exceed one million dollars and annual taxes can easily reach forty thousand dollars or more. It's a place where bigger is always better.

There are big homes on big lots on fancy streets, and smaller homes on smaller lots on not-fancy streets, and everybody knows which is which.

We are sitting in one of the big homes right now—a huge white monstrosity, with an iron-gated entry, surrounded by a fake stone wall, and fronted by a large circular driveway, paved with huge stones. The rooms are gargantuan and coffee-table-magazine perfect, with half a dozen elaborate seating areas arranged around a fireplace or a coffee table or in a great room.

The brand-new kitchen is mammoth, and everything but the sink and the refrigerator seems to be made of granite. Everything in the house matches everything else; the place is decorated to perfection, and it is spotless: there is not a rug askew, not a frame off balance. There is not a speck of dirt, not a bit of clutter, nothing out of place. It's as if everything has been glued into position, and dust has been prohibited from gathering. If there were such a thing as designer air, the oxygen in this house would be Air by Prada.

The insidious perfection makes it seem as if no one lives here. Actually, that's nearly true: only two people live in this twelve-thousand-square-foot home.

The hostess, Marilyn, confesses that she and her lawyer husband bought this house not before their children left home, but after. "We think of it as a place for them to come home to," she says, adding that "we're house people."

This group of women, many of whom envy Marilyn for the vastness and flawlessness of her place, reflect their look-good culture. They come to our four o'clock brainstorm interview session dressed to kill, in skintight jeans and sweaters and boots, with large diamond rings and perfect hair and makeup. Most of them are thin, but the kind of thin that takes a lot of work, thin-with-effort thin. A few have personal trainers; most have gym equipment at home. They are afraid to look old, and they are fighting it. For the most part, they are winning the fight. They're on the cusp of looking-not-so-young and looking old, but none has yet had cosmetic surgery.

Or that's what they say.

All of them, too, seem to be haunted, in varying degrees, by the somewhat realistic fear that their husbands will be tempted to leave them for someone who is younger and prettier. Someone who, as Marilyn puts it, has "bigger boobs and is more attentive to a man's needs."

Cassie expresses her relief about her children's departure over and over again, perhaps to convince herself that it's true. At fifty-six, she is a thoughtful woman who dresses like a teenager, in jeans, Ugg boots, and a flashy scarf, perhaps to hide a sagging jawline. Still, she worries that her personal style is no longer appropriate for her age, adding that "I need to find my niche."

But she finds that being without children gives her a new ability to relax with her husband. "We can just sit over a bottle of wine and spend time together. In the morning, before we both go to work, I make the coffee, and he'll come down early and sit with me in the kitchen while I putter. I do the dishes and feed the dog, and he comes down to be with me. We enjoy our time together, without being interrupted," Cassie says.

The fact that her children need her less comes in handy now, she notes, because her mother needs her so much more. "She's not well, and she lives just fifteen minutes away. I was never able to go there after work when the kids were here. So now I can give her more time, and I feel better about that. I knew she was resentful when I didn't visit. My father died thirteen years ago, and it's very hard for her, so I go on the weekend and spend two or three hours with her. Now I have time for my sandwich-generation work." She sighs.

She's not alone in that labor, since caring for an elderly and infirm parent tends to be midlife women's new work shift, one that replaces caring for children.

Experts estimate that between 6 and 40 percent of middle-aged women between the ages of forty and sixty-five will end up helping both their parents and their children at the same time, thus earning the name "sandwich generation." A majority of baby-boom women under the age of sixty, about seven in ten, have at least one living parent, according to recent research. But by the age of sixty, only two in ten women still have a living mother or father.[9] How's that for horrifying?

In fact, at least one-third of women over the age of eighteen will end up caring for two generations at some point during their lifetime. Perhaps most surprising, though: women will spend the same amount of time caring for parents with health problems as they do raising children, an average of eighteen years.[10]

This is not to say that mothers and fathers stop caring for children so that they can take care of their own aging parents. Part of being the filling in the sandwich means that they do both, mostly at the same time.

In one study of more than thirteen thousand Americans, for example, large numbers of parents said that they routinely help their grown children. Forty-four percent of parents in their forties help grown children, as do 67 percent of those in their fifties and 58 percent in their sixties. Slightly fewer help their own parents; 38 percent of those in their forties, and just 20 percent in their fifties, probably because fewer have two living parents.[11]

What kind of help does the sandwich generation give? It's not always monetary help; in fact, it's mostly physical labor. Middle-agers help their grown children by babysitting or doing child care, by offering transportation, by doing home or car repairs, by working around the house, and by offering advice or emotional support. When it comes to giving money, though, midlife parents are much more likely to provide financial aid to their children than to their parents. As the researchers put it, money flows down, from parents to children, more often than it flows up, from children to parents.

Stage Three: Joy

Finally, believe it or not, there is Joy.

Even in the first few weeks after a last child leaves, about one in four mothers zips through Stages One and Two and lands in Stage Three. These women feel happy and joyful about the situation right from the start. One such woman, a psychotherapist in Philadelphia, misses her daughter, but crows that now "I don't have to cook vegetables anymore!"

For her, that's a joyful life: no string beans, no broccoli, no peas!

One mom admits that she's thrilled not to "have to deal with parents of kids I don't like, but didn't want to offend." Another is sheepish about her secret pleasure in "not having to see school performances anymore!"

Few mothers will say the unsayable, that their lives are infinitely improved after the kids leave. But as their life stories unfold, that seems to be the unspoken message.

Take Connie, who at fifty-four and with no children at home is happier than she has ever been. Remarried, with two grown children, she suffers from fibromyalgia, a disease like rheumatism, which is accompanied by chronic muscle and tendon pain. You'd think she'd be miserable. She was at first, but no longer.

Connie started MotherLaunch in what she calls "a major, horrible funk. I had zilch self-esteem when my children left." She explains that "when my kids were at home, it was like I was paralyzed and I couldn't make anything happen. At the time, my psychiatrist told me I had an 'executive functioning disorder,'" a problem with a fancy name that may not actually exist.

To top off the family's run of bad luck, Connie's daughter was diagnosed with multiple sclerosis at the age of nineteen, the same week Connie's father became terminally ill, and her son was thrown out of high school and "we were forced to send him to a boot camp in Arizona. And my husband is a manic-depressive."

Connie would seem to be a modern-day female Job, a woman whose life is filled with disaster, as if under some kind of biblical cloud. If anyone has a right to feel unlucky, she does.

But, like Job, she prevailed, and without divine intervention. It seems that luck really is in the eye of the beholder. "If someone had told me ten years ago that I'd be doing as well as I am, and living where I am, I'd never have believed it," Connie says. "I'm incredibly thankful, to myself, I guess, for the second chance."

Here's what she did, and most of it was for herself. First, she lost forty-five pounds—always a sign of female rebirth, as well as great determination and willpower. Then she began to sell her own handmade jewelry and paintings to stores and spas in Charleston, South Carolina, where she moved, so that she could live near the ocean, a lifelong dream. Then she got a job as a Realtor, selling vacation homes at a beachfront resort. She divorced the manic-depressive second husband and found herself a new boyfriend, a lost love from junior high school, whom she rediscovered on classmates.com. "We are like kids now, the way we were in seventh grade," Connie says, with some disbelief. Like seventh grade, only with real sex.

Connie felt joyful quite soon after her last child left. But many mothers need to work their way into bliss. In my research, I find that six in ten mothers eventually say they feel happy and joyful that their children have left home.

For the majority of mothers, then, Stage Three becomes not the exception, but the rule.

Six in ten of the joyful moms are married, about the same number as those in the other two stages. So it's not having a hubby that thrills them. They are, however, slightly older than mothers in the other stages, and they also work more hours a week, so they tend to have work that gives them pleasure. They also have more close friends, women to whom they could tell a terribly embarrassing secret, like, say, "My husband is having an affair" or "I pluck the hairs on my chin" or "I can't bear to spend time with my own mother." Women in the Grief stage have two of these dear friends, but women in the Joy stage have at least four.

Mothers who end up in Stage Joy tend to be cockeyed optimists, as the song from *South Pacific* goes. They're "stuck like a dope with a thing called hope," and they can't get it out of their heart.

And here's how I know that: in my Web survey, more of these moms than any others describe themselves as "excited about the future." Six in ten do, as compared to half as many moms in the Relief stage, and only 15 percent of those in Grief. Half feel a sense of liberation, and they are incredibly hopeful about their future. Although these mothers are in the fifth or sixth decade of life, half of them expect to make new friends anyway. Nearly as many, slightly more than four in ten, expect to fashion new lives for themselves.

The Joy-stage women are full of zest for life, raring to go, eager to dive into whatever postmotherhood phase life has to offer. Dozens of moms in this stage have the same epiphany as Talia, the mother of four boys, who realized one day, like a bolt from the blue: "I am somebody without my kids."

That's not as obvious as it seems.

Several of the Long Island moms in my brainstorm group have achieved the joy of Stage Three, and the insight of child-free self-fulfillment. Stacey, for example, is fifty-three and does full-time volunteer work. Her husband is a stockbroker, so they don't need extra income. She has three children, the youngest of whom, a daughter, is a freshman at Tufts University, in Medford, Massachusetts. Stacey wears her curly hair long and looks like a hippie who came into money late in life.

She lives a looser life now that her kids are gone, Stacey says, one that she didn't expect would be so, well, wonderful. "People say you have a midlife crisis when the children leave, that there's a void," she says. "But there's a whole great psychological thing going on with me now. It's like I'm entering a new phase." She pauses, looking for the right way to describe the feeling. Then it hits her. "I'm balanced," says Stacey, with enormous calm.

If nothing else, mothers who enter Stage Three have received a gift, a sense of balance and inner harmony that is sometimes so unexpected that the shock takes time to wear off.

Stacey's life is more relaxed now, she says, because "when my daughter was home, I always felt anticipation, waiting for a major blowup between my husband and my daughter. It was like walking on eggshells. Now I feel the level of stress has diminished."

Stacey's point is a good one, since mothers of daughters often find that their relationship is so fraught with intense emotion that they are either stuck in the grief of Stage One or transported right into the glee of Stage Three.

The Daughter Dance

Psychologists who study mother-daughter relationships agree that they are among the most complex and emotionally charged bonds in any family. Even more astonishing, though, is the fact that adolescent daughters, age thirteen to twenty-three, are confronting the same developmental issues as their mothers, who are between the ages of thirty-five and fifty-five. Both daughters and mothers are trying to separate from each other, to gain a sense of autonomy, and to seek a new definition of self. The daughters are trying to find themselves for the first time, the mothers for the second or third time.

Daughters cling to the simpler life of childhood, while also longing to become more adult. So they hang on to mom for dear life, but they also push her away as hard as they can. Mothers, too, cling to the mother role, while also longing to become a separate adult, one whose first thought is not always "my child, my child." Both must try to enlarge their own boundaries, as the shrinks say, or to move beyond the safety of family and explore the uncertainty of independence.[12]

It's a scary world out there, for daughters without their mommies and for mothers without their little girls.

In the best of all possible worlds, mothers and daughters will help each other move and grow beyond the status quo. To do so, a mother must learn to treat her daughter as an adult, not as a child. She must let go of her little girl, while holding on to the almost-woman. A daughter must also begin to view her mom as other than mother, as a woman with dreams and desires that have little to do with the fact of motherhood. It's not a simple transition to master for either one, and both mother and daughter must be prepared to invent a new relationship for themselves.

That's what happens ideally, or in the movies, perhaps. In real life, though, daughters tend to become divas who detach dramatically.

Diva Daughters Who Detach Dramatically sounds like a newfangled tongue twister, but it's actually what happens. Daughters separate themselves from mothers in several ways, most of which involve quite a bit of drama, emotional upheaval, and torrents of tears and yelling.

In the daughter-mother struggle for independence, girls use at least five tactics for tearing themselves away from Mom's center of gravity. That is to say, five at a minimum; there are surely an infinite number of others. Here are the top five:

1. **Daughters know it all.** They refuse to listen to whatever Mom advises, no matter how obvious or sensible or correct. The more Mom tries to convince her daughter that something is true, the more her daughter is convinced that it never was, is, or will be true, in the history of the universe.

2. **Daughters argue.** They disagree with Mother about anything—the time of day, the weather, the number of children Madonna has, it doesn't really matter. Here's the rule: if Mom says it, then it is wrong. That's adolescent-daughter logic, impossible to breach.

3. **Daughters withdraw.** They build walls around themselves, pretending to shyness and sensitivity, all to prevent Mom from entering the daughter castle. They censor their true feelings and thoughts, sharing with friends, but almost never with Mom.

4. **Daughters rebel.** They try to become whatever Mom is not. If Mom is careful about what she wears, Daughter is a mess. If Mom is an intellectual, Daughter is an artist. If Mom is religious, Daughter is an atheist. The possibilities are endless.

5. **Daughters get mean.** They say whatever hurts most. Then they say it again.

These tricks of the daughter trade may last only through the teen years, or perhaps into the twenties, but they are a trial and tribulation for loving mothers everywhere. Some mothers accept these daughter tricks as expected forms of psychological separation: they are the saints among us. Other mothers deny that the daughter separation is happening, pretending that everything is fine (the Deniers, again). Still others are deeply hurt by what feels like permanent rejection from a beloved little girl. A few mothers even retaliate with envy, looking on their daughter's youth and potential and yearning to have all those lost looks and lost years back for themselves. Who hasn't felt even a twinge of such an embarrassing sentiment? If nothing else, when a middle-aged mother walks in public with her young daughter, and Mom gets noticed instead of ignored, that's a heady sensation for sure.

Chloe, an African American single mother from Arkansas, describes her daughter's technique quite simply. "She has to do it her way, no matter what I say or how right I am. So if it's raining tomatoes, and I say, 'It's raining tomatoes,' and you can see the red tomatoes smashed right there on the ground, she'll say, 'It's not raining tomatoes, those are eggplants.'"

Whatever happens to the mother-daughter relationship, it must by definition change as the girl becomes a woman. Mothers and daughters will know each other as adults far longer than they did as moms and little girls. And if a mother wants a loving and respectful relationship with her grown daughter, she will have to re-create their bond as one of adult to adult, and not as mother to child. But as far as mothers and daughters go—and we've all been at least one of those—intimacy and irritation are intertwined. You can't have one without the other.

It's part of the Daughter Dance for mothers and daughters to drive each other crazy.

Dee's nineteen-year-old daughter has been dancing that dance for years, to the point that Dee finds herself unable to read any books about mother-daughter relationships "because I find it too aggravating." Dee is a soft-spoken artist, and at fifty-one she is lovely, with long, ashy blond hair and a come-what-may attitude that any daughter might find difficult to resist. Dee's daughter has had to find a truly creative route to provoke her laid-back mom, but she arrived at one of the few guaranteed to drive her mother around the bend.

"My daughter wears all her clothes inside-out," Dee says, the dismay painted across her exasperated face. "It makes me insane, and she's been doing it since she was five years old." The girl refrains from indulging her inside-out fetish while working at a stuffy New York office for her summer job, but otherwise, she's inside out 24/7. Oh, and there's one other thing. "My daughter has very long hair, but she refuses to comb it, so it's a nightmare," she sighs. "This is all about our separation," Dee says, adding that she prays the daughterly rebellion stage will end someday.

Mothers engage in this Daughter Dance for years, but there are enormous benefits to maintaining strong ties to those former little girls. Mothers and daughters tend to find the same things funny, but they also find the same things sad, so they laugh and cry together. They become boon companions, shopping, going to spas, going to the gym, getting a manicure, going for coffee, driving around. Mothers and daughters who get along love to hang out, an aerobic female activity that involves lots of talk, laughter, gossip, and unbridled affection.

Who wouldn't want all that?

Serena certainly does. Now fifty-one, Serena moved from suburban New York to Chicago when her only child, a daughter, graduated from a fancy day school in Connecticut. Serena owned a teacher-placement service in New York and had to sell the business before she moved to the Midwest, where her husband had been made chief counsel for a large corporation based there. Serena is neat and simple, and laughs as she calls herself "an L. L. Bean kind of gal." She wears no makeup and is athletic and sporty. "I'm a very plain Jane," as she describes herself.

But Serena's twenty-year-old daughter, Jeannie, a freshman at Trinity College in Hartford, Connecticut, is a slim and gorgeous knockout, a girl who dresses in ultrachic clothing-of-the-moment with perfect nails and flawless skin and stylish hair.

She's the anti-Mom, the un-Mom.

But as unalike as they are, the two love being together.

"We're pretty close," Serena says of her daughter. "She tells me and we talk every day, and that's because she calls me. She likes do the girlie stuff and I don't, so much that my friends laugh at me. But I go shopping with her, even though I hate it, because that's maternal love."

Unfortunately, many mothers of daughters may not achieve a truly adult relationship until the daughters marry or have their own children, which tends to shuffle the bonds so well that they are newly renewed, according to one study. While young adult daughters push Mom away, once they have their own children, they often try to revitalize and restore their mommy ties. In fact, both suddenly desire to see each other more often than before, usually because both are focused on the next generation, of grandbabies.[13]

When Maryann's daughter had her first baby, she was devastated because the girl was in West Virginia, about two thousand miles away, she says. "I got a Webcam so I can see them on the computer," Maryann notes. A full-time nurse in Caldwell, Idaho, Maryann is thrilled that her youngest daughter will be moving back home, along with husband and new baby, while the couple start medical school. Both generations are excited for the chance to live together again—at least for a little while, Maryann says.

Perhaps the best thing a daughter can do for a mother, though, is not to hand-deliver grandchildren to the doorstep, but to help Mom see herself in a new way.

When Nora's daughter left for college in Los Angeles, it made the forty-nine-year-old woman examine herself more closely. Though she lives just a short distance away from her daughter, in Santa Monica, their separation was eye-opening for both.

"Watching her experience new things and watching her blossom and go through the idealistic stage when she wants to change the world made me take another look at myself," Nora says. "I realized that this stage should never end, that I should never stop growing. That's why I started my own business, because I felt that I had sold out by working for a big corporation just because it was easier. My daughter got me

...thing with myself. I am more open to try new
...he concludes.

...n daily money-management company and is in
... Rob, a computer-company executive. Inspired
...ted taking classes to learn sign language and is
...oo.

... learning to play golf, which was a big deal for our marriage," Nora says, laughing. "That was a gift to Rob; it was an expression of my love that I learned to play golf, and he gets that. Now I'm a sponge again. Observing my daughter grow has gotten me excited about my life again. I'm jumping back into the pool, from the sidelines, where I've been for ten years," Nora crows. "It's scary, but exciting."

Launching Yourself

Like Nora, some mothers just need to watch their daughters flourish after a launch so they can become inspired to do the same. For others, the transition from Grief to Relief, and from Relief to Joy, will happen naturally. A few, though, may need extra help to find a catalyst that will propel them through the three stages of adjustment.

For those who need prodding in the right direction, and for those who didn't prepare themselves during the Countdown Year, here are a few suggestions.

Make a list. In one column, list all the bonuses of having no children at home. Include things that you didn't really like to do, such as cooking or laundry, chauffeuring, or watching the annual musical at the high school. Be realistic, too, about how much surly, sullen teenage behavior you had to put up with during the past year or two. Think about your newfound privacy and the extra time you have to spend with your husband and friends. Making such a list doesn't mean you don't love your children, it just means that you can look on the bright side about their absence.

In another column, list all the negatives of having no children at home. Include everything you miss about not sharing their lives, not cooking for them, not doing their laundry (really?), not chatting with them in the car. When you look at the pluses and the minuses, you might be surprised to find that both lists are similar. But which one is longer?

Find work that matters. If you need to earn some, or most, of the household income, you may not have much choice about where you work. Still, if you have any flexibility at all, try to find a job that makes a difference in the world. If doing this for pay is not possible, then volunteer, even for just a few hours a week, for an organization or a cause that matters to you. Otherwise, seek paid work that offers moral and ethical rewards. Become a teacher or a counselor, find a job with a nonprofit organization, or start your own company and hire unpaid interns. The point is to raise your level of generativity—that is, to do good for the next generation, above and beyond what you do for your own children.

Go back to school. If your ideal work involves getting credentials, go out and earn them. If money is tight, take one or two courses at a time, preferably at a low-priced community college or a state-funded university. Study for credit, or study for fun, but enlarge your intellectual horizons and show your children that school is not just for children. This is a good way to prove to yourself that you are never too old to learn, and that it's possible to expand something other than your waistline and your dress size.

Start a blog. If you are feeling frustrated about moving past the Grief stage, go online and start a blog about how you feel and what you plan to do about it. A few of the mothers who have done this rave about how great it makes them feel, even if almost nobody else reads what they write. Confession can be enormously liberating and therapeutic, as priests and shrinks can testify.

Make a no-matter-what date. Pick a friend, or two, and agree to go out every week or every month, no matter what, to see a movie, have lunch, walk, whatever all of you agree will be fun and give you something to look forward to. Then just do it.

Look to your partner. Your husband or your mate is also going through a dramatic transformation right now, so try to work your way through it together. Make an effort to spend time as a couple, doing new things. Take a ballroom-dance class, join a gym, learn pottery, take yoga. Launch yourselves into something totally different from your old life, and then do it as a team.

Fix up your house or your garden or your car. Dive into some do-it-yourselfism and work on things that are important in your new life. You might need to take a course in woodworking or mulching or car mechanics, but so what? Wouldn't it be great if you could finally retile that cruddy second bathroom or you could grow a butterfly garden or you could learn how to replace a spark plug? Well, maybe you don't want to go that far, but you get the idea.

Find surrogate children. If you are consumed by the thought of children, and by your need to be near them, volunteer at a local day-care center, tutor middle-school students, or babysit for grandchildren. If you are desperate to redo motherhood, you can take in children for the summer through a Fresh Air Fund, or even become a foster parent.

Get TiVo. I'm not suggesting that you lock yourself in your house so you can watch television while you mourn the absence of your children. Still, for a really busy woman who likes to be entertained at home, there's nothing better than TiVo. Unlike your children, your TiVo always wants to please you, and it will try and try to become adept at figuring out what you like to watch. Then your TiVo will become relentless in its pursuit of finding and recording only those shows you love. As far as I'm concerned, there's no other electronic device as easy to operate, as friendly, or as helpful. And with no children at home, your machine will be devoted only to your needs and your taste. It's a way of making your television your own digital slave.

Pray. Look into your heart, whether it's by praying or meditating, doing yoga or exercising. Do whatever you need to find a calm, still place to think and reflect on your life before, your life now, and where you want your life to go next year and in the years to come. With the children gone, you've got a head start on the silence and solitude you will need to take this step, so capitalize on the situation and use it for your own benefit.

Don't get sidetracked. If, or more likely when, your children

return home, don't regress to an earlier stage. Make sure that you remain true to the new you, the mother who is other than mother. Don't
be tempted to jump backward, becoming the mother who always put
her children first. Your returning children are adults, so you should treat
them as such. Whether or not you expect them to help pay household
expenses is up to you, but they should certainly share in household
chores, like grocery shopping and laundry. You might also instruct
them to be considerate of your needs, so that they inform you when
they won't be home or when they'll be late for dinner.

MotherLaunch begins when the youngest child leaves, and it is an
evolutionary process with three stages. Think of yourself as a train on
the MotherLaunch track, and don't let yourself be derailed, even by
circumstances beyond your control.

CHAPTER FOUR

Back to Stage Zero

Once your children have been gone for a year, and you've progressed through the three MotherLaunch stages, you'll be ready to revel in Joy. You'll realize that it's finally time for you to live your own life again, and you'll feel pretty good about yourself, your life, and the world as you know it.

The moment that this insight creeps up on you is a crucial psychological turning point. When it happens, your view of the world flips upside down, like the first time you realize that your child is no longer a boy, but a man. Or when you suddenly understand that your parents need your help more than you need theirs. It happens when you realize that you no longer wish that all of your children lived at home again. Instead, you come to relish the idea that they are gone. You are relieved to know that your job is done, that you no longer control their daily sense of well-being, that they are living their own lives.

Insert big sigh of relief here.

But guess what? Just as you've tipped yourself over this psychological edge, they're back!

Insert horror-movie music here.

The odds are 50 percent—or one in two—that at least one of your children will come back to live with you after leaving home for the first time, and the chances increase the more children you have, according to national statistics. Social scientists refer to this increasingly common event as "coresidence," which is what happens when grown children live with their parents. The children are not home just for the summer or just for vacation, but for a "perma-stay," a prolonged dual residence.

Researchers have even coined an awkward acronym, ILYA, to describe the phenomenon. ILYA is not a Russian spy sent by Moscow to steal top-secret nuclear warheads. Instead, ILYA refers to an "Incompletely Launched Young Adult," which describes the grown boy in your house who shaves twice a day, works full-time, and expects a hot meal at dinnertime, and the young woman who uses up the toilet paper without replacing it and lives rent free while she finishes getting her master's degree.

ILYA refers to the children who were gone but have now returned, those not-so-prodigal sons and daughters who are sleeping in their old beds in their old rooms. There are hundreds of thousands of them, and their numbers increase every day. Social scientists in most of the industrialized countries of the world state emphatically that parents should not expect their empty nest to stay empty for long.

It's as if an entire generation of youngsters have clicked their heels three times and chanted in unison, "There's no place like home!"

Onward to Oz, or to your house, whichever comes first.

Remember that it's not just your children who are returning to the family homestead; **more than half of grown children leave home more than once**.

This is a cultural trend, one that affects a large proportion of mothers who believe they have finally launched their twenty-something children, only to find them back home. And it happens in the United States as well as in other first-world countries, including Great Britain, Australia, and Canada.[1]

"My children come back every now and then, when things aren't going well for them," says Barbara, forty-nine, a carpenter who has two children of her own, two stepchildren, and a brother she raised from the age of eight. She accepts this bing-boinging back home and out again as part of what it means to be a mother. "They always know they have a place to go if they need help in starting over," she says, "if they need to regroup or to refocus or just to have plain old sanctuary. They've stayed two to six months, and then moved on, refreshed and empowered to see what their future has in store for them."

This is not to say that Barbara doesn't make sacrifices when those newly returned children invade her space. She and her second husband live in a small three-bedroom house in Jacksonville, Florida. Her husband is a construction worker, though he's been without work for about six months, and she's had to pick up the slack by working overtime and on weekends. They can't always afford extra mouths to feed, Barbara says.

But that's not the worst part. Sexually speaking, she says, having the grown children at home cramps her style. "When they're gone, you don't have to control your volume levels," she points out. "The fact that you can go for it at the drop of the hat without wondering if you're gonna get walked in on makes for some hot times, sexually and mentally."

It's safe to assume that her children may never have considered that possibility.

Still, many mothers and fathers come to realize what Barbara already knows—that the exodus of almost-adult children is a very gradual process, one that requires years and years, and several departures and returns, before the final kickoff farewell. Youngsters use their parents' homes in two ways: first, as a safety net in times of trouble, and second, as a home base, a place from which to relaunch. Home becomes a safety net when a child loses a job, breaks up with a partner or spouse, or flunks out of school. Home becomes a home base when a child needs to save money for a car or a down payment on a condominium or is in between jobs or schools.

As the grown-child-returning phenomenon has become more common in industrialized countries around the world, it has acquired all sorts of nicknames. America has "boomerang kids," according to American social scientists. Australians use goofy names like "adultescents" and "kidults." Germans call these young adults "nesthockers"; in Italy they are "mammone"; and in the United Kingdom, they are KIPPERS, short for Kids In Parents' Pockets Eroding Retirement Savings.[2]

The number of youngsters making a second return home has indeed exploded during the past few decades, according to Frances Goldscheider, the Brown University sociologist I quoted earlier who has spent her entire career studying the timing of and reasons for home leaving. The whole process, she tells me, has become less of a one-way street, and "more like a circular migration."[3]

The Boomerang Cycle

All of the international catchphrases describe the same thing—nearly grown children who live at home. In the United States, some experts call it "the refeathered nest," as if parents have to redecorate when the children move back in, spiffing up the family domicile for the return of their overgrown sons and daughters.

But if we pursue the avian metaphor for a moment, comparing nearly adult children to nearly adult birds, there is some consolation to be had from bird research. Some kinds of baby birds don't leave the nest, either. Among Siberian jays and some woodpeckers, for instance, one fledgling may refuse to leave home, horning in on mom and dad bird long after most other siblings have flown the coop.

Avian experts call this reluctance to leave the nest—an actual bird's nest, in this case, not a metaphorical one—"delayed dispersal," which apparently occurs rather often. After jays and woodpeckers hatch, at least one dominant baby bird tends to stay behind, basically kicking out weaker bird siblings, thus leaving himself more room to hang around the house and fatten up.[4]

Apparently, parent birds are helpless in the face of their bossy offspring's desire to stay in the home nest. This is quite unlike a cartoon that appeared in the *New Yorker,* one that depicted a mom and dad bird standing on their nest, looking down from a treetop, while one says to the other, "I'm all for pushing them out of the nest, but maybe next time we could wait till they hatch."[5]

It doesn't really matter whether you push them out of the home nest, or pull them back into it for as long as you can. The reasons that nearly grown children return home may not have much to do with how you raised them or how well-adjusted they are. It doesn't matter how well they did on their SATs, what their GPA was in college, or whether they are warm and caring human beings. Instead, many of the reasons that children return home have to do with conditions not under your control.

Some researchers suspect, for instance, that previously launched children return home for purely demographic reasons, reasons related to the time and place and economic conditions in which they grew up. For instance, social scientists say that the more babies born at around the same time, the more difficult it will be for them to find jobs as near-adults, due to supply and demand, since they will all be job hunting in the same period. Thus, they will be more likely to live at home or to return there while they spend longer looking for work. Those born into smaller families, too, will be more likely to receive financial help from their parents, including offers to move back home, since the family resources are divided into fewer portions. And finally, young men are slightly more likely than young women to return home.[6]

When young adults leave home to marry, though, they are much less likely to return, according to Goldscheider's huge study of 12,205 Americans. In addition, she finds that those who leave to go to school or to join the military are actually more likely to return later on, as are those who leave young, before the age of eighteen. And finally, those who were born outside the United States tend to leave for the first time much later, but are less likely to return once they are gone.[7]

Why Children Return

The reasons for leaving home the first time, returning, and then leaving again are extremely complicated, and tend to be difficult to study and to explain. Still, here are six of the key social and economic reasons that nearly grown children leave home at eighteen but move back into their parents' home a few years later:

- ❖ They postpone marriage into their late twenties.
- ❖ They postpone childbearing even longer.
- ❖ They spend more time completing their education.
- ❖ They rely on parents for financial help, even after graduating from college.
- ❖ They are unable to afford to live on their own, even when employed.
- ❖ They belong to a new stage of life, one that did not exist just a generation ago, called "emerging adulthood."

American men marry for the first time, on average, at the age of twenty-seven; American women marry at age twenty-six, according to the most recent census data.[8] If that seems about right, and not so out of whack, consider the ages at which men and women married just fifty years ago. Census figures show that in the early 1950s, men married at the age of twenty-three, and women married at age twenty. That is a four- to six-year difference in age, or about half of the twenty-something decade. This is not solely an American phenomenon, either. In Sweden, women now typically marry for the first time at the age of thirty, in Spain and France and Finland it's twenty-eight, and in the United Kingdom and Germany and Austria it's twenty-seven, about the same as in the rest of the European Union countries.[9]

It's not so surprising, then, that American women are also delaying childbearing, which is not just a national trend, but something that is happening in most of the world's industrialized nations as well. Right now, American women have their first baby at about age twenty-seven, an increase of three or four years over the past three decades.[10] In the European Union nations—including Sweden, the United Kingdom, Spain, Ireland, Denmark, France, and Germany—the average age at which women have their first baby is twenty-eight or twenty-nine or even thirty.[11] (If it seems as if the age of first marriage and the age of first childbirth are remarkably similar, that's because they are. The world is hosting an increasing number of weddings for pregnant brides, apparently.)

What are these youngsters doing while they postpone getting married and having children, the major markers of adulthood? They are not all having one long high-school romp, partying and staying out late and drinking way too much, although some of them do just that. But many young adults do stay in school for many years after they graduate from high school. At least six in ten high-school seniors go to college right after they graduate, and nearly half of those between the ages of eighteen and twenty-four are either still in college or have already graduated.[12] Even more astonishing is that one-third of college graduates continue their education even further, going to graduate school for an advanced degree.[13]

This prolonged passage to adulthood is one that is receiving more and more attention from social scientists, who admit to being shocked at how dramatic the difference is between this generation of young adults and those in the not-so-distant past. In 1960, for instance, about 70 percent of women had left home, finished school, become financially independent, and were married with children, all by the age of twenty-five. In 2000, though, just 25 percent of twenty-five-year-old women had achieved all these markers of adulthood. Among twenty-five-year-old men in 1960, 44 percent were adults by this definition, compared to just 13 percent of men in 2000.[14]

Because young adults take so much longer to mature and to become ready to start a career, they also tend to need financial support from parents for much longer, borrowing early and often from the Bank of Mom and Dad, an unusually forgiving financial institution that rarely requires repayment, let alone interest. Parents bankroll adult children in a multitude of ways—from doling out cash to paying credit-card bills, or by simply not charging for room and board while the almost-grown children live at home.

Baby-boom parents tend to believe that their financial obligations to their children don't end with any single event. They don't cut off support after high-school graduation, or even after college graduation, according to research conducted by William Aquilino, a professor at the University of Wisconsin. Most parents, for instance, agree that they should help pay for children's college education. But at least half go on to say that they should also help grown children who are having financial troubles, at least in some situations. One exception to this rule, he says, is parents who are in second and third marriages. They are much less willing to help out their stepchildren.[15]

Bev, fifty-four, runs a day-care center at a community college in Philadelphia, and has two children, twenty-three and twenty, whom she raised as a single mom for fifteen years. She remarried nine years ago and lives in a five-bedroom house that she and her second husband bought. Although they have plenty of room at this time, Bev's husband is adamant that the children will not be allowed to move back in, for any reason. "He insists that they have to sink or swim in this world and that we shouldn't help them any more than we already have," says Bev. She seems resigned to this point of view, but confesses that "I think of myself more as a teacher than a mother now."

Bev and her husband are a typical stepparent family, one that draws a strict, do-not-enter line over the home threshold after their children leave for the first time. But parents who are still in a first marriage tend to be a lot more tolerant.

"There is some consensus among American parents in general that it's quite okay to have adult children at home, as long as they aren't completely supported financially," Aquilino tells me in a telephone interview.[16]

Parents want to make sure their children "don't flounder" and are willing to give them money and help, as long as they seem to be trying, he believes. But, he notes, "It gets testy when parents don't see kids making progress and not getting their act together, when they're completely relying on parents' financial resources and not going to school."

Aquilino goes on to say, "The children who have a good relationship with their parents are most likely to move back home. Parents know that the kids are there for the long haul, until they can get their lives together and move on. But even so, most spells of returning coresidences are fairly short, just a year or two. As long as the parents see that the children are making progress and moving forward in their lives, they don't mind it. 'This is a type of support we can provide,' is their thinking."

Parents who think this way tend to put their money on the line. Mothers tell me that they pay for their grown children's cell phones, credit-card bills, health insurance, rent, vacations, gym memberships, and car payments, depending on the child and the circumstances. One mother even confesses that "both of my boys are going bald, and I feel guilty about that, so we pay for their Propecia, the hair-loss treatment."

A large number of Americans between the ages of eighteen and thirty-four receive cash from parents, according to one large national study. In fact, parents report giving each child in that age range about twenty-two hundred dollars a year, for seventeen years in a row! That's why **one-quarter of the cost of raising children is spent after the child reaches the age of seventeen,** and not before. Indeed, about two in three children in their early twenties say that they take money from their parents, as do 40 percent of those in their late twenties.[17]

Kris, fifty, subsidizes her twenty-five-year-old son's living expenses, although he hasn't lived at home since he graduated from high school. The boy dropped out of college after sophomore year and has had a series of jobs in Nevada, as a ski instructor, brewery worker, nursery-school teacher, and organic gardener. Still, Kris gave him a car, pays his credit-card bills as well as for gas and food and clothes, and sends him a check for a few hundred dollars every so often. She estimates that he costs her at least six hundred dollars a month, with no end in sight. "I really need to put him on a budget," she says, "but I can't seem to bring myself to do it."

It's not that young adults are terrible slackers, trying to take advantage of their trusting and gullible parents, despite what Kris may fear about her freeloading son. More often than not, they simply can't afford to live independently on what they are able to earn. In a complex analysis of the earnings of young adults worldwide, economists used recent data to show that a majority of young men and women in the United States do not earn enough to support themselves until after the age of twenty-five. The same is true of young adults in Germany, France, the United Kingdom, Italy, the Netherlands, and Sweden.[18]

Take Alice, who learned about the inability of near-adults to earn a living wage firsthand, since all three of her children ended up living at home after graduating from college.

Now fifty, Alice sells advertising for a medical trade publication and lives with her accountant husband in northern New Jersey. Her children range in age from twenty-three to twenty-eight, but she and her husband have not yet lived in a child-free home. She and her husband, Lou, say they don't mind helping their nearly grown children, to a point. "I enjoy them being around, as long as I'm not their maid," she says. "And I don't mind cooking, since I'm cooking anyway and I love to cook. Also, they've been doing their own laundry since high school, when I told them, 'If you are old enough to drive a car, you are old enough to operate a washing machine.'"

Yet none of Alice's children has ever helped out with grocery shopping, doing dishes or housework, gardening chores, or car repairs, so in many ways, she has been a kind of long-term, unpaid maid. She just doesn't think of herself that way. She insists, too, that she enjoys having the children home, and that they are not really a burden.

"It's nice on the weekends," Alice explains. "I'm Italian, so I make fresh sauce every Sunday, and we all get together for dinner." As an Italian American, she says, she expects to host Sunday dinners with the whole family, no matter where the children are living, so if they're already at home, the arrangements are that much simpler.

Alice's twenty-three-year-old son has lived at home for the past two years, ever since he graduated from Providence College, in Rhode Island. He has had a series of part-time jobs, but no real career, and she's worried that he is "a lost soul who is not sure what road to take."

Alice and her husband pay only for this son's car insurance, and they don't give him any allowance. But the boy doesn't contribute any money to household expenses, nor does he help out around the house. He does his own laundry, though, and Alice says he keeps his bathroom clean. But that's about it. "If I ask him, he'll empty the dishwasher," she says, "but I have to ask."

Sabrina, Alice's oldest child, was still living at home at the age of twenty-five when Alice decided that she needed to take a firm stand. "I told her, 'I love having you here, but I really think it's important that you have your own place before you are in a committed relationship.' "

Alice felt strongly that she didn't want her daughter taking the same path that she did, at twenty-two, going directly from her parents' home to her husband's home. Alice feels that she never learned to be independent, and she wants her daughter to get a taste of that heady freedom before she is tied to a husband and family of her own. "Sabrina was getting a little too comfortable here," Alice admits, "so I had to give her a little push."

All three of Alice's children lived at home in their early twenties while they saved enough money to launch themselves into the world. They were waiting to be able to afford to live on their own, to travel, and to find themselves, but in style and comfort rather than in wretched semipoverty.

Today, many young adults also move back home because they were raised to believe that their parents would always shelter them from setbacks and disappointments. They were raised with the belief that they were entitled to live a middle-class life, regardless of how much money they actually earned. And they were raised with the belief that their parents were the ultimate financial safety net, ready to provide monetary aid upon request.

Children as Fallers or Rebounders

Children's sense of entitlement, as well as their feelings of independence, self-confidence, and willingness to ask for help, are personality traits that result from genetic disposition, but also from the ways in which children were raised. Were their mothers indulgent and giving, always there to perform a rescue? Or were they strict and authoritarian, forcing children to be self-reliant? Are both parents in agreement about how much help they owe to almost-grown offspring?

While parents and children may not discuss how much aid and comfort and help emerging adults should get, families usually have unspoken rules about who owes what to whom. In Alice's family, for instance, the children knew they could live at home rent-free, all meals included, but they wouldn't get any cash subsidies. In other families, the returned children have nearly unlimited use of the parental credit cards for most of their expenses, and they live without paying rent. And in some single-parent households, children help out by chipping in for mortgage payments and groceries. The type of household financial arrangements for still-emerging adults is almost as unlimited as the number of families that host them.

When it comes to almost-grown children returning home, most families make up the rules as they go. Thus, some adult children use their home as a safety net, a place in which to fall when life gets tough. They have learned that their parents will always be standing underneath, like a spotter for a gymnast, watching and waiting in case the child stumbles or tumbles or crashes to earth. Others are careful to use the family domicile only as a home base, a place that becomes a temporary retreat, a kind of springboard to the future.

The first group, the **Fallers**, know that if they are ever in an economic pinch or have any small failure, they will always be welcome at home for as long as necessary. The Fallers are the ones most likely to return home, due to their family's somewhat indulgent parenting style.

The second group, the **Rebounders**, use their parents' house as a trampoline from which to spring off for a second or third try. Their stays tend to be brief, and they don't require as much monetary aid or emotional support. Still, these kangaroos may bounce back home more than once or twice.

Although social forces steer large numbers of nearly grown children back home, Fallers may have an extra push built in, simply because they are less able than others to cope on their own. It's possible that some

dren of helicopter parents. These parents hover for years,
children to the point of suffocation and, perhaps, at the
children's independence and maturity.

Are You a Helicopter Parent?

"Helicopter parent" is a newly coined term that has been the focus of recent stories in both *Time* and *Newsweek* magazines, and has its own entry, dated May 2006, in Wikipedia, the free online encyclopedia.[19] Helicopter parents are defined in Wikipedia as people who pay "extremely close attention to their child or children, particularly at educational institutions. They rush to prevent any harm from befalling them or letting them learn from their own mistakes, sometimes even contrary to the children's wishes." The online resource goes even further, and defines "Black Hawks," as in the combat helicopter, as parents who "cross the line from a mere excess of zeal to unethical behavior such as writing their children's college admissions essays."

Think of it this way: riding in a Black Hawk is good; being one is not.

Even the College Board deals with helicoptering. The New York–based company, which has a stranglehold monopoly on college admissions tests, as well as college handbooks and scholarship and loan applications, posted an essay on its Web site titled "Are You a Helicopter Parent?" The article attempts to help parents recognize when they are "overmanaging" their children's lives. The site scolds that if you call your college-age children too often, if you contact the school's administration about the children's problems, and if you feel bad when your children don't do well, "you are hovering."

The College Board also warns that helicoptering can stunt children's maturation and lead to unnecessary parental anxiety.[20]

Many baby-boom parents have, in fact, been pioneers in the overprotective-parent movement, which has rewarded the urge to put children first, regardless of the consequences, for several decades now.

It is this generation of parents, for example, that first placed "Baby on Board" stickers on car windows, in the naive hope that other drivers would be more careful around their precious cargo. They lobbied for mandatory child-safety seats, and some even promoted the family bed, in which parents happily slept in the same bed with their infants and toddlers. A few years later, these were the parents who were yelling at referees and umpires they considered unfair when their nine-year olds played soccer and baseball. They were the ones who complained to middle-school teachers and principals about their children's less-than-perfect grades in social studies or science. And these parents were the ones who made sure that their children received trophies and prizes and awards for the smallest of achievements, in order to inflate children's self-esteem. (Thus, "Most Improved First Baseman" and "Best Level Three Saxophone Player.") Finally, these parents badgered high-school guidance counselors about writing glowing recommendations for their children or having them certified with a learning disorder so they could take college admissions tests with no time limits.

Now these parents are oversupervising their college-age children and are welcoming them home when the children decide to boomerang back.

Although Rita has never heard the expression "helicopter parent," she embodies the concept.

Rita, now fifty-three, says that she always helped her son with his schoolwork, because "I thought I was making his life easy." A skinny redhead with long hair and the special flamboyance that comes with living on the wealthy Gold Coast of Long Island, Rita is proud that her life was centered around her two children, neither of whom had ever left home before going to college.

"My son got into American University, and I helped him find his roommates and I set up his dormitory room," Rita recalls. "I bought matching carpeting and lamps and pillows, everything. I'm really into design, so everything matched. He was away from home for just one night, then he called and said, 'I can't stay here.'"

"So we said, 'Okay,'" she recalls.

Within twenty-four hours, Rita and her husband had packed up the carefully selected furnishings and driven their son back home to Long Island.

"The next morning," she says, "we were at Hofstra University, registering him for classes." They put all of his new things in the basement, and he lived at home for the next four years. After graduation, the boy got into law school, and they moved him out all over again. This time, though, it was after a few weeks that "he wasn't sounding so good," Rita says. They figured they'd rent an apartment in Philadelphia, near the boy's law school, so they could be close by. Rita's husband drove down at two o'clock in the morning to be with him, but their son called middrive, to say, "Never mind."

But Rita's hovering wasn't over yet, since her daughter was about to leave for college. The girl had been admitted to Columbia University, just an hour's drive from Rita's suburban home.

"We got her set up great, and I went into the city every other day to see if she was okay," Rita says. "We'd have lunch and spend time together."

After a few weeks, though, Rita's daughter was back home. Again, Rita welcomed the girl and immediately registered her at Hofstra. She lived at home for four years, until she graduated.

"I used to meet my daughter on campus, and we'd go shopping," Rita says, although the girl was living at home. "We looked like the Bobbsey twins, and we did everything together," she adds.

Rita earned her Black Hawk stripes in helicopter parenting, for sure, and her children responded by embracing that hovering. It's only now that both children are in their late twenties, Rita says, that they are truly independent adults living on their own.

Helicopter moms and dads suffer from the three "overs": they are overprotective, overinvolved, and overamped about their children's progress and success and happiness. It's as if they believe that their children are incapable of fending for themselves and that parents must be children's champions, a bizarre modern-day version of medieval knights facing down the impossible and frightening challenge of adult life.

All of this sincere and loving effort to prevent children from potential failure and pain may backfire, because such children often have difficulty learning to cope on their own. And the kids may also be more likely to end up living at home, for longer periods of time, than other near-adult children.

Of course, there is no evidence for this theory, except that it makes sense, common sense. So here's a way to figure out, fairly easily, if you are a helicopter parent or not.

HELICOPTER PARENT QUIZ

Have you:

1. Called, e-mailed, texted, or instant-messaged your college-age child at least five times a week, all semester long?
2. Called or e-mailed a child's professor or administrator about a poor grade?
3. Had your child e-mail you a copy of a paper or report so that you could edit or proofread it?
4. Contacted a resident adviser about your child's living situation?
5. Attended all or most of the college intramural or varsity athletic events in which your child was playing?
6. Made all of the arrangements for a summer job or internship for your child?
7. Called your child in the morning to wake him or her up for an important test or class?
8. Driven more than two hours to pick up your college-age child for every holiday or school break, and then back again?
9. Balanced your child's checkbook every month?
10. Considered yourself your child's best friend?[21]

If you've done three or four of these, you are a borderline helicopter mom, but if you've done five or six or seven, you are in the serious helicopter zone. Nine or ten, and you've earned Black Hawk status.

A mother who checked many of these items is someone who is unable to cut the motherhood cord. Taken one at a time, however, these habits seem fairly harmless. Indeed, if you checked one or two of them, you may have an explanation, or at least an excuse. Think of it as a kind of asterisk: helicopter symptom, but*. And the * means "Wait, I had a good reason for that!"

Take symptom number four, for example. A woman I know quite well—me, actually—would like to offer an asterisk on number four. I almost interfered on behalf of my son during his freshman year of college. I didn't want to think of myself as a mother who would do such a thing, but there I was, doing it anyway. My son had been assigned a roommate who drank heavily and often. One night in October, when my son had been a college freshman for barely a month, the roommate came in at two o'clock in the morning and fell into bed in an alcoholic stupor. A few hours later, he woke up, staggered to my son's side of the room, and urinated in the corner of the room. Three pairs of my son's shoes were in that corner, on the floor.

In the morning, the roommate claimed not to remember having used the room as a urinal, and insisted that he'd been sleepwalking.

It happened again ten days later.

Granted, I was worried about my son's ability to adjust at school, and granted I was somewhat neurotic about his departure, but this was beyond even the realm of imagined troubles. So I felt compelled to do something. Especially since my son called, asking me what he should do.

I advised my son to rat out the roommate and try to get another one. Wisely, he refrained from such a drastic course of action. Instead, he moved his desk chair every night to barricade his side of the room, thus preventing the drunken roommate from trespassing with intent to pee.

Not only did the solution work, but by the end of the year, my son and his roommate had achieved a kind of détente, living together in silent cooperation.

While most colleges and universities do not have policies for dealing with in-room urination problems, many are tackling the helicopter-parent issue head-on. They focus on pushy parents who meddle in student-orientation and student-registration periods. They try to deal with parents who make it their business to oversee their children's progress in the classroom and in the dormitory. The situation has escalated to the point at which college deans, university administrators, and embattled professors need to find their own version of garlic and crosses to ward off these parental vampires.

Many schools organize special programs and activities for parents during freshman orientation, for instance, to inform them about the school and to ease the separation process. But they also print a formal schedule, one in which there is a line, usually around four p.m. on the last day of orientation, that reads: "Parents leave." In case the moms and dads don't get the message, the next activity listed says: "Students only."

The University of Vermont has gone so far as to train workers to be "parent bouncers," whose job it is to distract potential mom and dad helicopters while their children are trying to register for classes. Their express purpose is to "keep parents involved in other activities while their children make key decisions independently," according to a university publication. "Some parents can't stand to not help their children pick courses, and some even get a little mad," when they are foiled in their helping attempts, according to the director of orientation and parent relations at the University of Vermont.[22]

Their response to such intrusive parents: tough luck.

Many colleges and universities also publish guides for parents of freshman, to teach them proper, nonhelicoptering behavior. Dickinson College, in Carlisle, Pennsylvania, for instance, offers a Web guide called "Being the Parent of a College Student." It offers tactful hints, like sections titled "Time of Transition for Parents Too" and frequently asked questions, such as "How often should I call, visit or e-mail my son or daughter?" (Helpful hint from Dickinson administrators: "Most students need some 'space' to effectively create their routines at college.") Even if the child calls "in a panic and sounds really upset," here's what the ideal, nonhelicopter parent should do: "Resist the impulse to intervene."[23]

Maybe American universities and colleges should just relent and hire a full-time, year-long parent wrangler, somebody whose job it is to fight off interfering and pushy parents and keep them away from their overly vulnerable children.

Youngsters who are stuck in a groove between adolescence and adulthood, one from which they can't quite escape, are sometimes called "start-up adults." A pediatrician writing about the trend says that these young adults are not really ready for the real world, especially when it comes to holding down a job. They are confused, naive, and unprepared for the frustration and effort involved in establishing themselves in a career and a mature life.

In addition, as children of helicopter moms, they were overprogrammed as teenagers, forced to engage in too many activities that left them incapable of working on their own, thinking originally, or taking any action on their own initiative. Mom and Dad supervised their homework, and their sports, and their volunteer work, and their college applications, so they've never had to be motivated and organized on their own, with incentive to finish work on a strict timetable.[24]

In other words, he says, a lifetime of being helicoptered can disable grown children.

When a start-up adult finds a first job, for instance, he is often unable to delay gratification and think long-term. "They have trouble starting at the bottom of a career ladder and handling the unexciting detail, the grunt work, and the political setbacks they will have to bear," one expert says.[25]

Basically, these children are little more than grown-up toddlers.

Living with Your Emerging Adult

Most of us don't have helicopter tendencies, fortunately. Still, as baby boomers, many of us are parents of children in a newly invented stage of life, one that didn't exist when we were young and newly sprung from home. Social scientists call this stage of life, which lasts from the ages of eighteen to twenty-five, "emerging adulthood." This is a time when not-adolescents but not-quite-adults learn to find their way in the world.

For emerging adults, finding the way to adulthood can take a long, long time. They emerge a little bit, and then some more, and later on they are still emerging. They're like caterpillars who need several seasons, instead of several weeks, to become butterflies.

Other researchers call these the "volitional years," a time in which youngsters are supposed to explore their identity and to experiment with life. It's a time when the lives of young adults should be dynamic and changeable and fluid. They live their lives without roles; they are sons and daughters, but not husbands and wives or fathers and mothers, and they don't really see themselves as adults until their late twenties or even their thirties. They move more often than people in any other age group. The only thing guaranteed about this time of life is its lack of guarantees and its high level of instability. It's a time in which young women and men tend to engage in risky behavior, in part because they have so few responsibilities. So they are likely to do lots of binge drinking, they have unprotected sex, and they drive too fast.[26]

Young adults consider these risks fun, which proves how not-quite-adult they really are. Think of this time as an extended teenage life, only with paid employment. Or, rather, we hope paid employment is involved.

But this kind of slack-headedness is not really their fault, because social definitions of what it means to be an adult have vanished. You are no longer a grown-up simply because you turned twenty-one or graduated from college or started a career. Indeed, twenty-one is the new sixteen, a kind of backward equation for the later years, when fifty-five is the new forty.

Lilian, a New York City mother, says that her children's thirty is our twenty-one. "When we were twenty-one, we were already financially independent and on our own. We wouldn't have dreamt of asking our parents for money or calling them about what to wear or insisting that we use their credit cards," she says. The fact that Lilian's daughters feel they can live at home whenever they want makes her feel a bit like a failure, as if she hasn't prepared her girls to live like adults.

But what does it really mean to live like an adult or, more to the point, to feel like an adult?

The vast majority of Americans say that **being an adult means reaching a certain psychological state,** one in which you accept responsibility for your actions, agree on your own beliefs and values, and establish a relationship with your parents on equal terms.[27] So adulthood is a state of mind, not a state of timing or social roles. This definition is so fuzzy that it's no wonder that twenty-somethings take forever to reach adulthood.

It's also no wonder that mothers and their almost-grown children have such complex and shifting relationships, like two small boats on rough seas trying to move through the water together. They crash into each other, and they move at cross-purposes, but eventually they steer parallel courses.

Many mothers also harbor unspoken fears about their returned child's future. Will he ever live on his own? Will she ever be able to move out? Many mothers are pleased to be able to help their struggling adult children, but their concerns are never far from the surface, although they may remain undiscussed and unspoken.

Are such children failures in the eyes of the community, or in their parents' eyes? And if so, does that mean that mothers have also failed?

Melanie, a fifty-one-year-old social studies teacher, lives on Long Island in a modest home, along with her husband, one cat, and one of her three daughters. The girl is twenty-four, and working full-time, but can't afford to live in Manhattan, so she lives at home. She is saving her money so she can afford to rent an apartment on the Upper East Side. Melanie never expresses her fears about her daughter's ability to succeed in life, but she voices her concern in other ways. "I worry that she won't be able to meet young men her age, and that her social life will get more and more difficult as her friends begin to pair off to live together or get married," Melanie says. "I'm happy that we can afford to let her stay with us, but I'm beginning to think we might all be better off if we kicked her out."

This kind of ambivalence is common among parents, especially when their children seem unable to achieve financial independence, according to some research. In one study of mothers over the age of sixty, for example, the women report having mixed feelings about grown children whom they still support. Mothers say that they are sometimes "torn in two directions or conflicted" in their feelings toward grown daughters and sons, and that they get on each other's nerves. This is especially true, the researchers say, if the mothers believe that the child's problems are voluntary. Thus, if a son falls ill, his financial dependence is not his fault. But if he has problems with drug abuse, then he is responsible for his situation, and his mother is more likely to resent his presence at home.[28]

Of course, the nature of a mother's relationship with her children changes drastically when they return home after living away, in part because she has gotten used to their absence. The first time that children leave home, their relationship with their mother shifts. By definition, they are out of sight, so much of the bad stuff is suddenly out of mind. Mothers tend to remember the chubby baby elbows and the sweet Mother's Day cards of the seven-year-old, not the grumpy, truculent sixteen-year-old or the willful high-school senior. Indeed, when children first leave home, their ties to mothers and fathers are instantly reduced in intensity, and there is much less conflict and struggle for power, according to William Aquilino's research. He studied parents and children at two points in time: first, when the children were teenagers, and then again when they were in their early twenties. He found that mothers who live with children in college get along better than those who live with children who aren't in school. Also, mothers whose children work get along better than those whose kids are unemployed.

Generally speaking, when nearly grown children are back home, mothers prefer them to be doing something productive, rather than simply hanging around the house. I'm not sure you needed a scientific study to figure that out, but there it is.

Finally, when adult children move back home after living away, they tend to have more arguments with parents, although they also feel closer and share more activities, according to Aquilino. Mothers yell more often at a returned child, shouting and arguing, and they disagree with their children more often, he finds.[29]

Take Jane, a forty-one-year-old African American nurse in Oklahoma City, who has been a single mother for twelve years. Her twenty-three-year-old daughter, Keisha, has come back home three times, the first when she was nineteen, in college and newly pregnant. Now Keisha brings her own daughter every time she returns home. So Jane has to deal with her not-quite-adult, unmarried daughter, who has returned as a mother herself, as well as a young granddaughter.

Jane is thrilled to see them, but with reservations. "One night, Keisha and her friends came into the kitchen and went into the pot of pasta I had made from a Martha Stewart recipe, and they wiped out the whole thing. They left everything on the table, with the pot on the stove, and they were picking their teeth when I came back in," Jane says with indignation.

"Then she said, 'Mama, what did you make?' as if she thought it was disgusting, but they ate it all up anyway," Jane says. "That really got my goat."

Even worse, Keisha was "all the time grooming herself in the living room, leaving her brushes and combs and bottles of soap there. And when I say to her, 'You have to clean up the kitchen' or 'Change the toilet paper' or 'Don't eat in your room,' she'd look at me, all confused, and say 'Why should I listen to you? I'm a grown-up now!'"

That really, really peeved Jane.

"I didn't feel I was getting any respect from her," Jane says. So she developed her own way of coping with Keisha.

"When eagles build their nest, they put brambles on the bottom, and cover them up with soft feathers," Jane says. "After the eggs hatch and the birds get heavier, they touch the brambles, and they get uncomfortable. So eventually they leave."

Inspired by this example, Jane turned her daughter's bedroom into a den, which she uses for herself, to exercise and watch television. When Keisha comes home, she has to share a room with her younger sister, a prospect that does not please her.

That's fine by Jane, who loves her daughter and hopes that she becomes fully independent real soon, with the help of a few homemade brambles.

Leaving home shakes up the ways in which mothers and children relate to each other, but returning does the same thing, in the opposite direction. Mothers of gone children don't feel as close to them, but they also don't argue as often. Mothers of returned children feel closer but fight a lot more, just as Jane and Keisha do.

Boomeranged children may not like having to return home, but they often enjoy the benefits of free room and board, and the comforts of a home in which they first felt at home. From their point of view, frequent disagreements may just be the cost of living chez Mom and Dad.

Some mothers feel that allowing a grown child to live at home, rent and chores free, is a way to be supportive, but that it's wrong to hand out cash so the children can move out. Sandra, fifty-four, a travel agent in Houston, is one such mom. "I have an issue with parents who are supporting their kids for years and years," she says. "When do you say 'enough' and stop paying? At what age or at what salary? What's your exit strategy?" she asks.

But Sandra doesn't really have any easy answers to her own questions. In fact, she herself supports her twenty-four-year-old daughter, who has been living at home, rent free, since she graduated from Emory University two years ago. The girl contributes no money to household expenses, although she does pay her own bills, except for her cell phone and her car insurance. Somehow those costs have become the family's responsibility.

This month, Sandra's second daughter, who just graduated from Emory also, moved back home as well, to look for a job. But Sandra feels that it's her children's right to have a safe place to return while facing the brutal world of work. "I want to see them get on their feet in a good place," she says. "I want them to feel safe, that they have a bed and food on the table and that they're not thrown out on the street." Still, she worries that they will begin to take the luxury of living free for granted.

"I don't want them to feel entitled, I want them to feel motivated," she explains.

The best thing about having her girls home, Sandra says, is although they argue a lot about doing dishes and taking out the garbage, they talk to each other now more as peers than as parents and children. Their conversations are much more open and honest than before, when the girls were teenagers and Sandra's role was mostly to tell them what to do.

"I like having time to influence them," she says. "I like to talk to them about making smart choices, financially and relationship-wise, in a way that I couldn't talk to them when they were living far away from home."

Sandra doesn't resent having a refilled nest, at least not yet, because she feels "it's an extra last chance to teach them about making smart choices in life."

Sandra and her daughters, who feel close but who also argue, are somewhat typical, according to research.

After interviewing 609 parents who had at least one child at home between the ages of nineteen and thirty-four, Aquilino found that, for the most part, parents and children get along with each other, at least some of the time. This is despite the fact that only about one in four emerging adults makes any financial contribution to the family's expenses. Still, about seven in ten parents say they argue at least occasionally with their boomerang kid. They have disagreements about the following: how the child dresses, about his or her boy- or girlfriends, about other friends, about staying out late, about getting a job, about doing housework, about sexual behavior, about drinking or using drugs, about money, and about making an effort to get along with people in the family.

In other words, they argue about everything possible.

In addition, Aquilino finds that older parents, those who gave birth later in life, get along better than other parents when their nearly grown child is back at home. But there is much more conflict, he says, if the mother has remarried and is living with a second husband who is not the child's father. Finally, parents get along slightly better with returned daughters than with returned sons. Everybody fights more, though, if the children have returned home with their own children in tow. Mothers who live with their children and grandchildren tend to be stressed out—very stressed out.

Finally, he says that mothers and their returned children have to figure out a way to live together in harmony, or else tension and hostility blossom.

No kidding.

The best solution, Aquilino submits, is "when parents are involved with adult children in pleasurable activities and when adult children are more self-sufficient."[30]

Other researchers agree that mothers' relationships with their boomeranged children are enhanced in some ways and harmed in others. Although grown children are grateful for the support and understanding they receive from parents who allow them to live at home, the children say they feel they get less respect and fairness from Mom, and trust her slightly less, according to a study of 435 young adults and their parents.[31]

Is Moving Back Good for the Kids?

Overall, it's probably helpful for young adults to know that they will always have a place to come home to, no matter what. And many actually benefit by returning home, experts find.

Parents feel a strong obligation to provide shelter for children, no matter how old they are, and children take advantage of that sentiment. In most studies, the vast majority of mothers and fathers agree that parents ought to provide housing to children having problems.[32]

When children move back in, the experience can be positive in several ways. Just about all the research confirms what most of us probably suspect: that these emerging adults don't help very much around the house, nor do they contribute to the family coffers. In essence, they behave as if they were teenagers, but with jobs and cars and the legal right to play drinking games.

In one large national study of parents and their children over the age of twenty-one, sociologists discovered that about one-third of mothers of all ages—those in their forties, fifties and sixties—lived with at least one returned child.

Even with an almost-adult at home, guess who does most of the chores around the house, including grocery shopping, cooking, laundry, driving, home repairs, yard work, and cleaning?

If you didn't say "Mom," you must be joking. Mothers do all of that, with returned daughters chipping in only slightly more often than returned sons. Daughters do about 18 percent of domestic tasks, and sons do about 10 percent, these researchers say. And the amount of help children offer is not related to how much money the children pitch in, so they aren't trading off work for cash, the researchers add.

In households where grown children live with single mothers, though, children tend to help out a bit more. Sons tend to contribute some financial help when they live with just Mom, and daughters tend to do slightly more housework when living with a single mother.[33]

Clearly, adult children live high on the hog, with few, if any, household responsibilities. Indeed, sociologists conclude that in these situations, families live together for the children's benefit, and not for the parents'. Overall, the boomerang kids say that their relationship with their mother is more important than their relationship with their father, and that they get along better with her than with him.[34]

There is even some evidence that the longer children stay dependent on parents, the more education they will attain. This makes sense, of course, since it is difficult to earn a bachelor's degree, or an advanced degree, while also having to earn a living.

Sociologists at the University of Nebraska interviewed about thirteen thousand Americans and concluded that "children benefit from continued parental sponsorship into their early and mid-20s." This was true for those who left home for the first time to go to school, as well as for those who left for another reason, at least the first time. The new reality, they conclude, is that children benefit socially and emotionally from having between twenty-two and twenty-four years of financial dependence on parents, as well as from living at home during most of that time.[35]

Many young adults live at home because they can simply live better than they would if they had to support themselves. So they forfeit some degree of independence for the luxuries of home. Why drive a falling-apart old car, live with three roommates in a dump, and scramble for change to pay for beer on weekends when you can live at home rent free, buy a new car, and have enough left over to take a beach vacation in the winter?

"Why suffer if you don't have to?" may well be the motto of emerging adults who choose to live at home.

Life is certainly easier for grown children who move back home. But does depending on parents for so long help them mature and grow at the same pace they would if they were on their own?

That's difficult to know, of course, but researchers who studied a large group of young men and women over a fifteen-year period believe they have the answer. For young women, living an independent life turns out to be much more beneficial than staying at home, they say. Young women who don't live with their parents are more likely to make work plans, to expect fewer children, and to become more open-minded and less rigid about family roles. Independent young women come to believe that it's acceptable for women to work and to have children, and for fathers to work and also do the cooking and cleaning. The researchers speculate that young women who live on their own develop more self-confidence, as well as crucial social and domestic skills, like maintaining a home and a car, paying bills, having friends over for dinner. These advantages do not show up, however, for young men.[36]

Perhaps that's why young men are more likely than women to return home: in the long run, it's easier for them and does little harm.

Is a Refilled Nest Good for Moms?

Emerging adults take their time entering adulthood while being subsidized and supported by parents, most of them quite happily. But how do mothers feel about their formerly empty nest being refilled?

Michigan psychologist Abigail Stewart says that most mothers feel a unique ambivalence about the return of their formerly gone children. "When the children are gone, it's a deprivation, but when they come back, it's an intrusion," she tells me.[37] "This captures the very ambivalent experience that it is. You enjoy having this independent adult life when your children leave home, but of course you miss them. Still, when they return, it isn't on the same basis," she says. In part, that's because everything seems different and not quite as wonderful.

Just about all of the mothers I interviewed who have college-age children expressed this sentiment, though in slightly different ways.

"You can't wait for them to come home, and when they do, you can't wait for them to leave again," is the mother's-eye view of college children who come home for summer or winter break. Moms don't like living without the children, but they can no longer live with them, either.

Mothers often love to have the company of their nearly grown children at home, while at the same time regretting the loss of their former freedom. That reentry can alter the nature of their marriage and their sex life, for the worse, as well as slow down the process of their own self-discovery. It's as if you took a cocoon and stored it in the freezer for a while. The caterpillar would be really cold, frozen in a pre-butterfly stage, until you finally liberated it from cold storage.

Some mothers sense that cocoon freeze when their children move back home, as if the next part of their life has been put on hold. Of course, grown children tend to move back only when they get along fairly well with their mothers and fathers, so the situation is usually bearable.

In fact, a large portion of young adults who return home describe their relationship with their parents as "excellent," according to a recent Canadian study. That study also shows that at least three in ten young adults return home after leaving for a first time.[38]

Which mothers are most likely to have children who bounce back, boomerang, or yo-yo back home? They are:

1. The ones with fewer children
2. The ones with more sons, who are more likely to return than daughters
3. Those with unmarried children
4. Those with higher-than-average income
5. Those who are African American or Hispanic
6. Those still married to their children's father[39]

Some researchers also find that the children's return has an adverse effect on marriage, especially after couples have settled into their routine of being alone again. It's especially stressful for marriage when the child returns home for a second and third time, according to a study of 420 Canadian families.[40]

Having a grown child at home can subtly alter a marriage in many, many ways: it can create pressure on wage earners to bring in more income, it can limit parents' alone time together, and it can place more of a burden on mothers, who tend to be responsible for all the extra household chores. The situation disrupts marital routines, and it makes midlife sexual activities more complicated.[41]

Looking at parents over a five-year period, sociologists compared how well couples got along after their children left home, and then again after one child had returned. They found that wives' happiness with marriage decreased in the latter situation, and that the women said they argued more with their husbands. The husbands, though, didn't seem to notice any difference. Still, both wives and husbands observed that they spent less time together once a grown child had moved back in.[42]

In my Web survey, I examined mothers who had at least one child return home, after leaving at least once before. About one in three of the mothers was in this situation, and I compared them to mothers whose children were all out of the house, at least for the time being.

Though about two-thirds in each group are married, more of those with a nearly grown child at home say they often feel irritated with their husband. More of them say they feel a loss of sexual desire, too. And more say they feel "a need to move on." There's a sense of frustration among these mothers, as if they are itchy to get past a stage of life they thought they had completed. In fact, about four in ten say they often feel anxious; but only one in four moms with no kids at home does. More of them also say they have become depressed lately.

The bottom line is that many mothers blame themselves when their children struggle, or seem to be failing to achieve an independent life. This is especially true if the evidence of that struggle lives in the house, day after day.

Gillian, twenty-two, flunked out of college two years ago and had been struggling with addiction problems for a while. Her mother, Caroline, blames herself for her daughter's failures:

> I didn't have her until I was thirty-nine, and I worry that maybe I pampered her too much and she'll never be able to establish her own home. I have to set limits, but I haven't thought of them yet.
>
> My daughter has lived at home for nearly two years, but she doesn't contribute any money, really, or help out around the house. We gave her a curfew, and we say, "If you have to come home later, we'd appreciate a phone call." At times, she goes along with it, but other times she disappears for two weeks, and we don't know where she is. And she doesn't answer her cell phone, the one that we pay for.
>
> I feel I have failed. My daughter is not self-sufficient, she's not ready to fly, and she's already twenty-two. I'm her mother, so . . .

Caroline's voice wavers, and the rest of the sentence, the "it's my fault" part, remains unspoken.

Dealing with Stage Zero

While most mothers expect to have to cope with an empty nest when all of their children are gone, few are prepared for a time when the whole process goes in the other direction. It's as if you played a family videotape forward, and then back, in slow motion. The children gather their grown-up selves together, they pack everything they own, and then it all goes in reverse, zip, zoom: they move back home, as if time itself has been put on rewind.

It's no wonder that so many midlife mothers are befuddled when the kids come back—it's real-life time travel!

Still, although the odds are even that this will happen to you, the good news is that it probably won't last that long, and it will give you a chance to get to know your returned child in a different way than you did before. That's in the best of all possible worlds, of course. The bad news is that the situation may not be as easy, or as natural, as you might expect, especially if you were already relishing your position in the Joy stage.

Here are a few tips for coping with a grown child's return.

Make new rules. When a teenage child lives at home and attends high school, there are lots of family rules, although many of them may be unspoken. The high-school senior has to ask permission to use the car, for example, or needs permission to stay out past midnight. But once a child has left home to go to college, returning after living a mostly independent life, those rules begin to seem as if they no longer apply. That's why it's a good idea to set new rules right from the beginning, to avoid intergenerational misunderstandings. Requesting that your daughter call if she won't be home in time for dinner, or if she plans to stay the night at a friend's house, is not treating her like a child, as she might insist. Instead, it's treating her like a mature member of the family, one who is considerate of your needs. It's what you would do for your husband, and he for you.

That's why it's a good idea to sit down together, as soon as possible after your child returns home, and agree on the house rules. Make sure that they are rules that everybody agrees upon, or they will have no binding ties. If "rules" sounds too harsh to your child, then call them "expectations" instead.

Some examples of reasonable expectations for parents with a returned child:

- ❖ We expect you to pay for your gasoline and your bar bills, but we'll pay for your medical insurance.
- ❖ We'll pay for your cell phone, as long as you don't send more than fifty text messages a month (or one hundred, or whatever you believe is reasonable).
- ❖ We expect you to turn down your music at midnight.
- ❖ We expect you to inform us when you have an overnight guest. (This is assuming you have already had the discussion about who is an acceptable guest and who is not—as in boyfriend or girlfriend.)

❖ We expect you to make a reasonable attempt to find a job, or to make plans to go back to school.

A good way to avoid arguments and potential conflict is to get as much as possible out in the open, right from the start. You won't completely rid yourselves of disagreement—unless your child is a combination of saint and martyr—but you'll be taking the right path toward preventing the worst of the nasty grown-child-back-home fights.

Plan family activities. Don't force the issue, but try to schedule occasional outings with your child, the way that two longtime friends would. Go to a movie, play a round of golf, go shopping, watch a favorite television show together every week. Do something that you both enjoy, and you'll probably discover that you like being together.

But don't make the mistake of pulling back from your partner, either. Just because a child is back home is no reason to cut back on the activities you had established with your husband after the child left. If you and your husband have a standing date to take a dance class at dinnertime, then your boomeranged child will simply have to fend for himself. Remember, that's what he'd be doing if he were living on his own.

Insist on a job hunt. Unless your child is seriously ill or incapacitated, insist that she find work, even if only part-time work. The odds are that you will argue less often if you feel that she is making an attempt to support herself.

Teach appreciation. Have a heart-to-heart discussion, at the right moment, about how much you'd appreciate a show of appreciation. Children of all ages tend to take their mothers for granted, but it's less acceptable when that child is nearly grown up herself. If necessary, you can give a blow-by-blow example of the gratitude process. Explain to your son that he can thank you for cooking him a meal, or picking up his dry cleaning, or gassing up the car. You might point out to him that he'd complain if you didn't do any of this, so he may as well reward you for behavior that benefits him.

Show your appreciation. By expressing your appreciation for the small things that your children do for you—no matter how trivial—

you will be setting an example for the appreciation you'd like in return. Thank them for making the bed, or doing the laundry, or unloading the groceries, or whatever it is they've done recently. If you can't think of any help they've given whatsoever, maybe it's time to have another discussion about setting rules.

You might also remember to show your grown children some affection, if only to get some in return. Just because they're almost all grown up doesn't mean they can't give Mom a hug or a kiss every so often.

Respect their privacy. Although it's your house, make sure that you allow your child some private space that is his alone. Try to avoid yelling any sentence that includes the phrase "under my roof," since that's almost a guarantee that your child's hearing will instantly fail. Remember that if you allow him his privacy, then you can demand your own privacy in return. Agree on what territory is off-limits to you, and then stick to the agreement. If his room is his sanctuary, then abide by that rule. Thus, you may not peek in drawers, look underneath the bed, or examine the inside of his closet, even when he's not at home. Privacy means privacy. The same goes for your bedroom or office, or whatever part of the house you want to be yours alone. You get off-limits territory, too.

Air your grievances. Don't bottle up what's bothering you. Let it out during an occasional family meeting. If this seems too bogus, then make an effort to have a heart-to-heart discussion over the dinner table every so often. The point is to give everybody in the family, parents and returned children, a chance to air their grievances.

Psychologists in Germany studied adult children and their parents, asking family members what the others did to please them, and what they did to irritate them. The pleasing things included offering candy and flowers, listening to each other, offering gestures of tenderness and affection, helping with errands and chores. Children were most irritated when parents were bossy, when they ignored them, and when they insisted on seeking constant approval for decisions. The researchers found that grown children were most helpful to parents when the family enjoyed being together, a rather obvious, "no kidding" finding.[43] The underlying point, though, is that you get what you give.

Treat the child like an adult. If you treat her like an adult, she's more likely to behave like one. While this is difficult to do with a child who is a college student, one with few worries or responsibilities, it should become a lot easier with a child who has a full-time job. She works hard, and so do you, so don't belittle her efforts or undermine her confidence.

Let's assume that you've reached Stage Three and you have a boomeranged child and also some major adjustments to make. But it's also likely that right around this time you'll find yourself undergoing yet another physical change, one of the most dramatic a woman can undergo, other than being pregnant. Can you guess what it is?

CHAPTER FIVE

The Great Changes in Change of Life

Maybe you're just beginning menopause, or maybe it's ten years in your future, but I'd bet that by the time your grandmother hit menopause, she had long since launched her children into the world. A generation or two ago, if a woman gave birth for the first time at the age of twenty, then her firstborn child would have been thirty when she reached menopause. Thus, mothers in earlier generations usually dealt first with the leaving of children, and only much later with the leaving of their menstrual cycle.

Now, though, all bets are off for where mothers will be in the family life cycle when they reach menopause. Some baby-boom mothers, those who had their babies in their early twenties, match the life pattern of their mothers and grandmothers and reach the change of life after the change of children. At the other extreme, some baby-boom mothers postponed childbearing until their mid-thirties, or even later. When they reach menopause, some of their children will still be at home, in high school, middle school, or even elementary school. However, a large number of baby-boom moms, like me, fall somewhere in between. We had our children in our early thirties, so we will experience the leaving of our children and menopause at about the same time.

Jessica is one such mother in the middle, a pixie of a woman. A mixed-media artist who lives in Philadelphia, Jessica had her first child at thirty, her second at thirty-two. She's in the throes of perimenopause now, while also dealing with an anorexic twenty-four-year-old daughter who lives in Los Angeles and a son who dropped out of school, came back home to live for a while, and just left home again for the second time. Jessica ranks herself high on the maternal worry scale, though she admits that her life is much calmer, and happier, without the children around. "It's much more peaceful without my kids here," Jessica says. "When they are at home, I tend to drop everything in my life to do whatever they want, and I start to ignore my husband, too. Then we fight a lot."

Still adjusting to her children's almost-exodus, Jessica is also getting used to a life of hot flashes and night sweats and skipped periods. She still menstruates at random times, usually when she least expects it. Getting used to being without children, she says, was not as difficult as getting used to all the sweating and flushing and not getting enough sleep. Missing her children, she says, is an emotional pain, the other is physical; but both seem to go hand in hand, at least from her point of view, because they're happening all at once.

Jessica and her husband, Joe, live in a charming townhouse on a quaint, tree-lined street in the center of Philadelphia. Lined with faux gas lamps and cobblestone paths, the street is so charming it makes your teeth ache. The entry of her house is paneled with leaded glass, the floors are stained oak, and the musty third-floor bathroom features old-fashioned faucet handles, labeled not "hot" and "cold," but "chaud" and "froid."

Although she lives in comfort and style, an apparent member of the bourgeoisie, Jessica's hippie history is reflected in her face and in her style. She wears her hair long, threaded with occasional undyed strands of gray, and if you look closely, just beneath her tortoiseshell reading glasses, you can see that the side of her nose sports a tiny diamond stud.

Jessica's work is displayed all over the house, but the heart of her home is in her kitchen, the place where she keeps her babies. Her precious ones are three tiny, gloriously colored parakeets. When I mention how lovely they are, Jessica begins to whisper, pointing to her favorite bird, Peri, a sixteen-year-old Creamsicle-colored creature with a private two-story cage. "She knows we're talking about her," says Jessica about the bird.

I'm not sure if birds know when people are talking about them, but

I do believe that my dog knows when I'm talking about her, so I refuse to be critical. Instead I simply smile and say, "No kidding."

Jessica's kitchen features several pieces of art inspired by Peri the bird, and partly made by Peri the bird. Just across from the oven, a framed memory box contains several of Peri's long feathers, along with five of her eggs, now dried out.

"These eggs are from Peri," Jessica says, "back when she was laying eggs twice a year. My bird is no longer fertile, just like me," she says. "She's Peri, and she's irritable and grouchy, like me. She's Peri and she's perimenopausal, and so am I; we're both growing old together," Jessica says and laughs.

Although Jessica looks youthful and hip, what with the nose piercing and the lanky hair, she's actually in the throes of menopause. But menopause no longer means that a woman is automatically "granny-ized." Just because a woman no longer needs Tampax doesn't mean she's over the hill or finished raising children or done with sex. On the contrary, transitioning through menopause is just one of several biological and social hurdles that occur in midlife, along with dealing with health issues, redefining the rules of marriage, finding a new outlook on work, deciding where to live, and reimagining one's identity, to name just a few. Most of these social changes are inspired by the last child's exit from home, and menopause is simply another facet of the process of personal transformation that baby-boom women undergo in their fifties.

Menopause may actually be one of the easier transitions, since it has become so very public. Your mother's menopause was hushed up, quiet, an unspoken secret, like girdles and sanitary napkins. It was simply not a topic to be spoken of in polite company, or any company, for that matter. But today, baby-boom menopause is out there in the open for everybody to notice and comment on. Every single detail of the process is up for public scrutiny.

Are you having daily hot flashes, sweating into your cleavage and dripping onto your waistband? Call in to a radio show and tell everyone all about it.

Have your breasts lost any semblance of perkiness, do they sag like a bag? Ask your doctor how to fix them.

Are you thrilled about having no-fear-of-pregnancy sex? Tell your story to Gail Sheehy.

There is no longer much mystique in menopause, and that's a good thing, because for many baby-boom mothers it is arriving at a time of maximum upheaval and confusion—the emptying, sporadic refilling, and final emptying of the family nest. But my research shows that it is not necessarily a disadvantage if mothers enter menopause around the time their children leave home. In fact, the **women who have the most difficulty adjusting to their children's absence are not those entering menopause.** Instead, mothers who are premenopausal, **those who have not yet hit menopause, tend to be most devastated when their children leave home.**

Why should this be so? Aren't they younger and more attractive, more energetic and healthier? Shouldn't they have it easier when their children leave, since they aren't undergoing such a dramatic transformation in their own bodies?

Actually, no.

The Timing of Menopause

When menopause and children's exodus happen simultaneously, during the same two- or three- or four-year period, women must reevaluate themselves completely, from stem to stern, top to bottom. By definition, they are undergoing three types of drastic change all at once—social and psychological and biological. First, their role as wife and mother is shifting, in a kind of social revolution. Second, their view of themselves is changing, a psychological evolution. And third, their body is being transformed, a biological metamorphosis. In a way, it is easier to do this triple-header as a whole person makeover, transforming everything all at once, rather than ever so slowly, bit by bit, over a period of ten years or fifteen or twenty.

In addition, menopause is a physical distraction that forces a woman to be extremely self-focused. For some women, menopause is all-consuming, with so many symptoms and changes and quirky difficulties that they don't have time to think of much else. It's a kind of biological wake up call that plays the same message, over and over. **pay attention to yourself.**

If your children are leaving home while that alarm is going off, you have less time and energy and motivation to focus on the departure as a loss, because you are also dealing with your own physical changes and losses. It's when your children leave long before menopause, though, that you are more likely to have the time and energy to wallow in your sorrow and regret.

Jill, forty-three, is an administrative secretary in Idaho, whose twenty-one-year-old son left a few years ago. She is premenopausal, and consumed by his absence. Although years away from menopause, Jill imagined that she was suffering from menopause-related mood swings at about the time her son left home. "I felt like someone had ripped my heart out," she says. "I could not function for a long time."

But during the same month, Jill also discovered that her second husband had been having an affair, which threw her into a different kind of emotional tailspin, also unrelated to her hormone level. "We are trying to recover and put our marriage back together," she says, "but I don't want to play games anymore. I want to be attracted to my mate again, although I don't know if that will ever be possible."

Suffering from a husband's betrayal and a son's move, Jill says that she became very depressed. "And that was way before I had to deal with menopause. I just felt like a dark cloud was following me all the time, and I was wishing I could blame it all on menopause," she adds.

For Jill, menopause would have been the perfect excuse for her misery, rather than her absent son and her philandering husband. It would have made her other life stresses more bearable, too, if only she'd been forced to focus on her own physical changes. But she was too young for menopause, and wishing for it didn't make it so.

Jill expects menopause to bring her moodiness and despair sometime in the near future, and maybe it will, eventually. Most women have their own expectations and beliefs about what menopause will be like, based in part on what happened to their mothers, or their friends, or their sisters, or what their culture says should happen.

Thus, **the way that women experience menopause depends, in part, on what they believe about it and what they think will happen.**

When you see the word "menopause," what springs to mind?

Do you think of loss? Do you believe that menopause means the loss of youth and beauty and fertility, the loss of estrogen and eggs and firm skin tone? Does it mean the loss of your role as a soccer mom, as an everyday mother who looks after children?

Or does menopause make you think of freedom? Do you believe it means freedom from pregnancy, freedom from the tyranny of Tampax, freedom from bloating and fatigue and chronic recurring crankiness and migraine headaches?

Menopause is rife with symbolic meaning for baby-boom women, many of whom have temporarily postponed it by taking artificial hormones or using all-natural remedies, like black cohosh. Most of us know that menopause means the end of reproduction, although when we read about a sixty-three-year-old Italian woman giving birth, or a sixty-five-year-old Indian woman delivering a baby, or a sixty-year-old New Jersey woman having twins, we begin to doubt even that very basic assumption. Still, our expectations of the change of life can determine how we experience it.

With Menopause, What You Expect Is What You Get

Our grandmothers didn't mention it, and our mothers skirted the topic, but as baby boomers, we embrace menopause. Indeed, baby-boom women are mostly positive about the personal changes that will come with aging and menopause, according to a great deal of recent research. In one study of American women, for example, about six in ten agreed that "the older a woman is, the more valued she is," and very few said that a woman is less attractive after menopause, only about one in ten. Only 16 percent agreed that "as I age, I feel worse about myself." About seven in ten even said that "women who no longer have menstrual periods feel free and independent."[1]

A fifty-two-year-old saleswoman in North Carolina who answered my Web survey agrees wholeheartedly that she enjoys not having to worry about periods and pregnancy, especially since she is only six years into her second marriage, to a man she adores. "The only damn thing is the dryness," she says with dismay, "I gotta use all kinds of jellies and creams to try to fix it."

This general optimism about aging is a far cry from the old days, just a few decades ago, when experts considered menopause a serious deficiency—of eggs, of youth, of the entire body. That condescending and paternalistic view of the process was, in fact, what inspired Nancy Avis to spend her entire career as a public-health scientist studying menopause in all its forms and variations.

Avis began to study menopause after she went to a conference on the topic and heard male researchers speak of postmenopausal women with contempt and derision, she tells me in a telephone interview. "They were using terms that were so sexist and ageist," she says. "It was all about deficiency and about how, after menopause, women are finished." She was infuriated by their condescension and arrogance.

"I became energized by the whole topic, because these male researchers were making statements based on nothing," Avis says. "They had just studied a few women who had showed up in their clinics to be treated for problems. I came at it from an approach of activism and feminism." She wanted to study all kinds of women so she could figure out what menopause means for the vast majority, and not just for those who seek medical treatment.

Today, Avis is a professor in the Department of Social Sciences and Health Policy at Wake Forest University School of Medicine, and she plays a leading role in one of the largest and most groundbreaking studies of menopause ever conducted in the United States. It is known as SWAN, or the Study of Women's Health Across the Nation, which began examining midlife women in 1994 and will continue to do so until at least 2010. The original study included almost sixteen thousand women, all of whom were between the ages of forty-two and fifty-two. They were Caucasian, African American, Chinese, Hispanic, and Japanese and were selected from seven cities in the United States, including Newark, Detroit, Los Angeles,

Boston, Pittsburgh, Chicago, and Oakland. All were premenopausal when the study began and still menstruating regularly, so the researchers could track the progress of menopause, instead of relying on women to remember what had happened to them and when. Avis followed the women through perimenopause, when their periods started becoming irregular, skipping for at least three months at a time, and finally, through postmenopause, when they had had no menses for twelve months.

When I ask about her own menopausal history, though, Avis laughs. "I don't really remember when I hit menopause," she says, with equal parts embarrassment and astonishment. "That just shows how inaccurate recall is! I pay such close attention to this in other women, but I don't know about myself," she says, pausing. "I hit menopause, um, maybe a few years ago?"

Part of the reason Avis is confused, despite the fact that she's an über-expert in the field, is that menopause isn't a physiological process that flips menstruation from on to off, like a light switch or a car ignition. Instead, it's a three-stage process that lasts between three and five years, at least, and ends, for the average American woman, at the age of about fifty-one.

Not only is menopause a transitional phase that takes years to complete, but its symptoms vary wildly and unpredictably.

The SWAN study shows, for instance, that Caucasian women complain about psychosomatic symptoms of menopause much more often than Japanese American or Chinese American women. White women kvetch a lot more about feeling tense, depressed, irritable, stiff, and headachy, and they are more likely to take hormones to try to cure themselves of these menopausal ills.[2] And this is just one of many recent studies trying to unravel the mysteries of menopause, at the same time that millions of American women are tiptoeing their way through the change.

Your Great-Great-Grandma's Menopause

There has been an explosion of serious research during the past decade, focusing on menopause and health in midlife, in part because so many baby-boom women are now poised to pass this biological milestone. In 1990, there were 467 million women over the age of fifty in the world, but by 2030, there will be 1,200 million, according to the World Health Organization, which issued a report called "Research on the Menopause in the 1990s."[3]

I believe that number could also be written this way: **there will be 1.2 billion women in the world over the age of fifty.** Either way you put it, that's one hell of a lot of postmenopausal ladies around the globe, thus the worldwide bonanza of new studies on older women.

In America, in addition to SWAN, there are several Massachusetts-based studies on midlife women. In Europe, there is EPIC, or the European Prospective Investigation into Cancer and Nutrition, which includes 366,521 women, ages thirty-five to seventy, in France, Germany, Greece, Italy, the Netherlands, Spain, Great Britain, Sweden, Denmark, and Norway. These women have been followed since 1992, and will be for decades to come. While the study focuses mainly on cancer, it also contains a wealth of information about menstrual cycles and menopause.

A British study is examining 1,515 women, all born within the same week in 1946, who have been studied every year since the age of forty-seven. And in Melbourne, Australia, there is an ongoing study, started in 1991, of several hundred premenopausal women, ages forty-five to fifty-five.

The spotlight on menopause is yet another baby-boom trend, where no life passage goes unexamined or unexplored. That view is a world away from how other generations looked at the change of life.

Take a stroll down menopause memory lane, and the condition becomes a serious medical problem, one that sometimes required hospitalization. In a report for the United States Census of 1890, for instance, the deputy surgeon general explained that the "excess of insanity among females as compared with males, in ratios to population, is usual in all countries and may be due to several causes, such as the effects of pregnancy and of the menopause." That information was reported in a census publication on the "Insane, Feeble-Minded, Deaf and Dumb, and Blind."[4]

Apparently, both giving birth and losing the ability to do so can make women crazy.

By the early 1900s, that view hadn't changed much. A woman doctor wrote about "the seven ages of woman," in which she stated that the peak of life was between twenty and twenty-five, and it was downhill from there, all the way "until the time of the menopause arrives." It was then, she said, that many unpleasant things begin to befall women.

First, she said, was "the accumulation of unnecessary fat," this even in the pre-Oreos era. Also, women suffered from having "pendulous breasts," as well as "heats" and "flushes," in which "the woman suddenly feels as if a bucket of hot water had been poured over her head and shoulders." They also had a "greater irritability of temper and diminished power of 'suffering fools gladly.'" Too polite to use the word "bitchy," she says instead that "the whole organism, physical, mental, and moral, is unstable, as it always is during periods of stress and change."

But not all was doom and gloom over menopause. In fact, in an age before birth control, a time in which women spent decades getting pregnant and giving birth, over and over and over again, losing that ability came as something of a relief and a blessing.[5] Indeed, as long as women retained their health, menopause was sometimes seen as an emancipation from the bondage of menstruation and pregnancy, a release from "a world of troubles."[6]

Even today, as Nancy Avis points out, women who live in parts of South Asia, where the culture imposes strict rules about menstruating women (that they be isolated or cleansed or forbidden to touch men), are thrilled when they reach menopause. In those countries, menopause is literally liberating, because women are finally free to behave like men and young girls. No more huts, no more washing, no more taboos. Even in our own, more modern culture, at least half of women who live in the United States, Canada, Denmark, Israel, Japan, and the Netherlands say they are relieved when they cross the threshold of menopause.[7]

Women react much the same way to menopause that they do to the departure of their children: with some sadness, yes, but also with enormous, blessed, glorious relief.

"Most women don't like having menstrual periods," Avis tells me.

"It's a pain, so they tend to say, 'Thank goodness that's over with.' It's upsetting, because you can't have any more children, but for women who've already had their children, it's liberating. Sexually liberating too, since you don't need contraception anymore. That part women like."

Menopause Around the World

Women in today's world experience menopause differently, depending on where they live and how they live. In the United States, France, and Sweden, for instance, menopause begins at about age fifty-one. But in India, it begins at forty-five; in Nepal, Nigeria, the Philippines, Ghana, Turkey, and China, it begins at forty-seven, forty-eight, or forty-nine.[8] This is probably due to a variety of factors. Research shows that smokers, for instance, tend to begin menopause much earlier than non-smokers. Women who smoke at least fourteen cigarettes a day experience menopause three years earlier than nonsmokers.[9] But drinking seems to postpone menopause somewhat: women who have between five and seven or more drinks a week experience menopause two years later than teetotalers. Women who have about one drink a week put off menopause for about a year later than normal.[10] Even odder, perhaps, is the fact that women who grew up poor reach menopause, on average, about two years earlier than other women. The researchers define "growing up poor" as having lived in a house with no hot water, no indoor bathroom, and no family car, the way large numbers of British women did before World War II.[11]

There are a few fairly common symptoms of menopause, at least in Western countries: hot flashes, night sweats, irritability, trouble sleeping. But not all women who report these signs are bothered by them.

One of my favorite what-bothers-you-about-menopause questions is the one about whether women are "afraid of losing their mind" while going through menopause. About one in five American women agrees with that statement, but twice as many middle-aged women in Taiwan do so.[12]

As for how life experience and culture can influence menopause, here are results of some studies from around the world.

Seven Weird but True Menopause Facts

Menopausal women in:

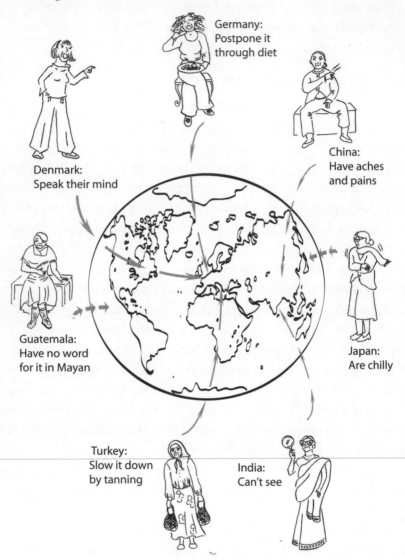

Germany:
Postpone it
through diet

China:
Have aches
and pains

Denmark:
Speak their mind

Guatemala:
Have no word
for it in Mayan

Japan:
Are chilly

Turkey:
Slow it down
by tanning

India:
Can't see

1. **In China, menopausal women don't sweat, they ache.** In
    Singapore, where women commonly begin menopause at the age
    of forty-nine, only 4 percent have hot flashes, but more than half
    say they have "muscle and joint aches."[13]

2. **In Japan, menopausal women are chilly.** Menopausal Japanese women don't get hot flashes or night sweats, either. Instead, six in ten complain of "shoulder stiffness," four in ten have memory loss or stress, and three in ten complain of "chilliness."[14]

3. **In India, menopausal women can't see.** When women in Chandigarh, India, go through menopause, only 17 percent complain about hot flushes, but a majority say that they can't see clearly.[15]

4. **In Turkey, being pale encourages menopause.** Turkish women who don't get a lot of sun start menopause earlier than the average national age of fifty-two, as do those who engage in heavy physical activity.[16]

5. **In Denmark, it's a good thing.** The Danish word for menopause means "the transitional phase," a time when women feel they can finally speak their minds, and they also feel more experienced and competent and free.[17]

6. **In Germany, vegetarians begin menopause sooner.** A study of women living in Heidelberg shows that diet influences the onset of menopause. Vegetarians hit the change sooner, but women who eat a diet especially high in fats postpone menopause.[18]

7. **You can't say "menopause" in Mayan.** In the Q'eqchi tribe of Guatemala, there is no word at all for menopause, other than one that means "no washing," since the women no longer need to be purified while they are menstruating. Also, women are rarely told about menopause until it happens, because the whole topic is taboo. If a middle-aged tribal woman complains about vaginal dryness or having no interest in sex, her husband assumes she has been unfaithful.[19]

As these studies show, many of the symptoms of menopause are ruled not by biology, but by culture. A woman going through menopause will feel what she expects to feel, based on where she lives, how she lives, and when she lives. It's not that all of the symptoms of menopause are psychological, just that **we interpret what's going on in our bodies in very different ways.** Thus, we are seeing menopause through our own cultural lens, for better or for worse. Whether we feel chilly or sweaty, blurry-eyed or stiff, all of us undergo a slow reduction in estrogen levels. In fact, only two symptoms have been proved to be directly caused by the specific hormonal changes related to menopause: hot flashes and night sweats. Oddly, researchers also agree that African American women are much more likely to have hot flashes than white American women, and their flashes are more severe and tend to last much longer, over a period of at least five years.[20]

As for the rest of menopausal symptoms, there are wide variations in who reports them and who complains about them.

Here are eleven common menopausal symptoms, at least according to American women in the SWAN study: night sweats, stiffness or soreness in joints, headaches, hot flashes or flushes, forgetfulness, feeling tense or nervous, feeling blue or depressed, vaginal dryness, irritability or grouchiness, heart pounding or racing, and trouble sleeping.[21]

Nearly all menopause researchers agree that instant menopause, triggered by surgery or chemotherapy, is often the worst, with the most severe symptoms that can last a long time.

Carrie, now fifty-nine, was thrown into instant menopause by the chemotherapy treatments she received for breast cancer fifteen years ago. Her husband is a radiologist who specializes in mammography, ironically enough, and she knew she was in trouble as soon as she saw his face as he examined her films. She says:

He called the surgeon that day, and I had a lymphectomy by the end of the week, six weeks of radiation, and then I took tamoxifen for five years.

I had hot flashes every twenty minutes of those five years, and I gained twenty pounds. My hair fell out, my skin was dry, and other things got dry, too. Talk about no sex drive! I put an air-conditioning vent right over the bed and set it on high every night. My husband was freezing, and had to wear a tracksuit every night, but I was soaking wet. I took other drugs to stop it, but nothing worked. As my husband says, "Medication is the art of selective poisoning," and that's so true. I just had to get through it, and I did.

Carrie believes that the hormone replacement therapy she took for eighteen months is what gave her breast cancer in the first place. Not only that, but after she finished the tamoxifen, she developed cataracts in both eyes. She had surgery on one side, but still can't see very well out of the other eye.

Cancer free for seven years now, Carrie is grateful to be alive, but she believes wholeheartedly that her worst-menopause-ever experience was a direct result of her breast cancer treatments.

Whether you are suffering from instant menopause, like Carrie, or just random signs of the change that you may or may not notice, think of this time of life as a biological call to arms. The call is similar to Paul Revere's, but it's not "The British are coming!"—instead, it's "The change of life is near!"

This change represents more than just a physical change of life. This era is a whole new time of life, a time of privacy in marriage, freedom in friendships, latitude at work, more time and more money and more room to be who you want to be.

The call gives women a clear and insistent message; it alerts them that now that the children are gone, **it's time to pay attention to yourself.**

Your Health, Your Insomnia, and Those Damn Extra Pounds

The midlife call to arms is not about children leaving, returning, and leaving again. It is about physical health and well-being. It is about noticing what's going on inside your body, and menopause is like a physiological wake-up call to the body.

Your body is telling you not only to focus on yourself, but to consider what it means to be growing older. That's a difficult message for many baby boomers to hear, mostly because we are a generation who refuses to believe we will ever be old. It's not that we expect to be young forever, it's just that **we expect to feel young forever,** which includes staying in good physical shape. We want to remain mentally and psychologically youthful, which to us means being adventurous and enjoying life and having fun. So we refuse to stop running or walking, even if our knees throb and our hips ache. We continue to bike, hike, climb mountains, or run marathons, or whatever it is that we've always done to stay fit and healthy.

While the words "middle-aged" and "marathon" don't seem to go together like a horse and carriage for everyone, they do for some. In fact, four in ten people who run marathons are now over the age of forty. In the 2006 Boston Marathon, two in ten finishers were over the age of fifty, which means not only that they ran 26.2 miles, but that some of them did it really fast.[22]

Let's face it, though, the majority of nearly menopausal moms are not marathoners. Instead, we're facing our own personal race against our body's clock. For us, there is no time of life, with the exception of pregnancy, in which so many bodily changes happen at once. While the list of aches and pains and bodily woes of middle age is almost without limit, there are two major health problems about which the largest number of American women complain: insomnia and weight gain. This was true in my Web survey, as well as in most medical research on midlife done over the past few decades.

In fact, one researcher called insomnia women's "overlooked epidemic."[23] That's because, in most national studies, slightly more than half of women say that they have trouble falling asleep or staying asleep, at least several times a week. During perimenopause, especially, fitful sleep is often triggered by night sweats, when women wake up drenched and unable to fall back to sleep. Many experts believe that it is the lack of sleep that causes moodiness and depression in so many menopausal women. They even refer to this as the domino effect: a woman has trouble sleeping at night caused by the hormonal changes of menopause, which makes it difficult for her to get through the day, but no matter how exhausted she is, she can't seem to catch up on her sleep. Eventually, she becomes depressed by fatigue and frustration. So it's not the menopause that causes the depression, it's the lack of sleep.

Many women tell me that they have no trouble falling asleep at night, mostly because they're exhausted after working eight or nine hours, commuting, and doing errands and housework. But then they find themselves wide awake, staring at the clock, at 3:37 a.m., unable to fall asleep again. I'm one of those who finds herself waking up at 2:00 a.m. or 3:00 a.m., covered in sweat, though the room is cool and it's wintertime. And I cannot get back to sleep, no matter what. I even went through a six-month period where I blamed the sweating on my nightgowns, throwing away one after the other, because I thought they were making me feel so hot, only to realize, after I had depleted nearly all of my nightwear, that maybe it was me and not my clothing.

In my Web survey, half of all women say they have trouble sleeping, and even more menopausal women, I find, about 65 percent, report being troubled by insomnia. As for weight gain, half of the women in my survey are also troubled by weight gain, especially after they begin the menopausal transition. It's as if no matter how much they exercise or how little they eat, the pounds keep pouring on.

A fifty-three-year-old woman in South Carolina writes that, for her, the one and only downside of the change is that "I can't lose these friggin' pounds since the memopause." She's so upset by her newly rounded belly that she can't even spell the word!

I'm convinced that there's a curse called mother weight, and many of us fall under its spell. First, we can never get rid of those extra pregnancy pounds, no matter how young or svelte or toned we were to start. Then there are years of eating quick, kid-friendly convenience foods that tend to be high in calories, high in fats, and not particularly nutritious. Also, there are years of cookie baking, brownie making, and cupcake buying that require a mother's tasting and grazing. All of this can really pack on the pounds. Even women who exercise on a regular basis while their children are young find that when they reach the age of forty-five or fifty, their former level of activity no longer seems to prevent weight gain. It's as if the pounds and the years add up together.

No wonder menopausal moms are so frustrated by weight gain: it can seem as inexorable as the ticking of the clock.

On the rare occasion that a midlife woman does defeat the weight-gain demon, though, she's bound to feel gloriously triumphant. At forty-eight, Shirley is just starting menopause, after having gained an enormous amount of weight over the years. Working full-time as a human-relations manager near her home in Erlanger, Kentucky, Shirley raised two children and didn't have much time to do anything for herself. It was only after both children went off to college that she decided she'd had enough of feeling like a whale.

Rather than look like a whale, she decided to swim like one.

"That's when I got serious about fitness and began swimming regularly," she says. "I lost thirty pounds and dropped four sizes, and three years later I am still swimming and have not gained back a pound, and I eat much healthier than before. For the first time in a while, I feel comfortable in my own skin, and this has given me confidence and a sense of well-being." Although her daughter came back home to live for a while until she can start graduate school, Shirley hasn't given up her swim habit, going so far as to work part-time as a swim coach, along with her regular job.

"Empty nest is awesome, once you get through the initial shock," Shirley concludes.

Although enormous numbers of women in midlife struggle with silent weight gain, it's not until the children leave home that many take the initiative to do something about it. With all of that soccer-team fund-raising and basketball boosting and cheerleading-squad supporting, some moms never find the time to engage in their own strenuous physical activity. It's almost as if watching the children exercise becomes their own, a case of exercise by proxy.

Unfortunately, as rewarding and uplifting as that may feel, it doesn't get rid of extra pounds. That's why some mothers feel enormously liberated when they begin their own athletic program after the children are out of the house.

Few mothers are oblivious to their own weight gain, or to their lack of sleep. In fact, some are actually hypersensitive to their own physical state, magnifying the signals that their bodies send out. These women notice every twinge, every sneeze, every ache; for them, menopause can seem like a terrible tornado of symptoms. Psychiatrists call this trait "sensory amplification," and they say that a small proportion of women suffer from such hypersensitivity. They measure this attribute with a simple test, similar to this one.[24]

ARE YOU HYPERSENSITIVE?

Think about how well these five statements describe you:

0 = Not at all   1 = A little   2 = Moderately   3 = Quite a bit   4 = Extremely well

1. Sudden or loud noises really disturb me.

    0   1   2   3   4

2. I'm really uncomfortable when I'm in a place that's too hot or too cold.

    0   1   2   3   4

3. I can't stand pain the way other people can.

    0   1   2   3   4

4. I'm often aware of things happening in my body.

    0   1   2   3   4

5. I always notice hunger pangs in my stomach.

    0   1   2   3   4

Your score should range from 0, if you answered all 0s, to 20, if you answered all 4s. If you scored below 10, you don't notice your bodily symptoms all that often. If you scored between 10 and 15, you are close to being an amplifier, but not quite. And if you scored 15 or higher, you are probably hypersensitive to what's going on inside you. This doesn't mean, by the way, that you're also depressed or anxious, just that you are really in tune with your bodily signals, and probably always have been. It might even mean that you will be more likely to notice the onset of a serious disease, because you pay such close attention to your body and to the messages it sends you.

No matter how you score on this sensory amplification test, experts agree that women are generally more in tune with their bodies and the state of their own health than men are. This is probably due, at least in part, to the fact that women have been forced to pay attention to their monthly menstrual cycles for decades. Perhaps that's why women of all ages tend to report more health problems than men do. That's just one of many gender differences in health commonly accepted by most social scientists.

Seven Health Truths for Women

1. When asked about their health, women say they have more health problems than men do. This includes temporary problems, like the flu, headaches, and aches and pains, as well as chronic illnesses, like asthma, diabetes, and arthritis.
2. Women spend more days each year in bed due to illness than men do.
3. Women see doctors more often than men do, about six times a year, compared to four times a year.
4. Despite having more health problems, women live longer than men.
5. The more friends women have, the healthier they are.
6. Women who work are healthier than those who don't.
7. Women who are optimistic are healthier than those who aren't.[25]

Although women complain about their health more than men do, women manage to live longer, almost as if noticing what's wrong helps them deal with and overcome the problems. Also, women make more of an effort to maintain their health, researchers find, like taking vitamins, seeing doctors, and limiting drinking and other kinds of risky behavior.

Healthy women also have more friends, are more likely to work, and are more optimistic than sickly women. But we don't know what comes first, the good health or the good life. It's certainly possible that having close friends and satisfying work makes women feel healthy; but it may also be true that women who are healthiest are better able to maintain friendships and hold a job than women who suffer from poor health.

Not only do women pay close attention to their own symptoms, but as family caretakers, they also tend to be responsible for the health of everybody else in the family. Claire, a mother of three from India-napolis, was struggling with arthritic pain in her feet the year after her youngest child left home. But she also had to deal with her in-laws, who were both suffering from Alzheimer's and had moved nearby so she could care for them. In addition, two of her three children became de-pressed and had to move back home, and her husband was diagnosed with heart disease at about the same time.

It was Claire's job to notice not only her own health problems, but those of everybody else in her family. She might just as well put on a nurse's uniform and comfy white shoes so that she can minister to everybody's health needs. It's too bad that she already has a full-time job, as a third-grade teacher.

"Some days, my head is aching from all the running around and worrying I have to do for my family," Claire says. "The only good thing is that it distracts me from my feet, which are almost always stiff or sore. But I really don't have the time to deal with my own aches and pains," she adds.

Claire would probably rate her own health as fairly good, which also tends to reflect a sense of well-being. Experts who study women's health usually ask women to rate their own physical health this way: do you consider your health to be: poor, fair, good, very good, or excel-lent? It turns out that this simple self-evaluation is often strongly tied to many other aspects of women's lives. Women who think of themselves as in very good or excellent health, for instance, also tend to say their marriage has fewer problems and is more rewarding, as is their relation-ship with their children. They say their husband appreciates them more, that he shares in housework, and that he's easier to get along with. They get more pleasure from their children's accomplishments and from see-ing them mature, they enjoy doing things with their children, and they feel that their children have changed them for the better.

Of course, there's a chicken-and-egg problem here, since we don't know if women who have better marriages and stronger ties to children stay in better health, or if being healthy is what makes women perceive their marriage and maternal duties as more satisfying in the first place. In all likelihood, both are probably true.[26]

But it is surely a universal truth that when women in midlife look at themselves from the neck down, they see all kinds of changes, most of them due to aging and most of them disturbing. Doing this "how do I look?" review is an integral part of most women's lives, but it becomes especially pressing during the change of life, when a woman is reminded almost every day that her body is growing older. In my survey, I ask women if they are afraid of growing old, and four in ten say they are.

As one woman put it, rather bluntly, "I don't feel pretty anymore."

But what's odd is that the women who are most likely to fear aging are those still going through menopause, not the ones who are older. As soon as women finish menopause, in fact, fewer say they are afraid of getting old, and by the time they reach their sixties, just one in four women is still worried about aging. It's as if, at some point, we accept what is happening and decide to embrace it. (While a great many midlife women decide to embrace graceful aging, most of us refuse to give up coloring our hair!)

A majority of menopausal Australian women don't worry all that much about getting old, either. Most are not at all worried about being too old to have children, being less physically attractive, or seeing their children move away, according to a study in Melbourne that followed women over a five-year period during menopause. The researchers conclude that the menopausal transition doesn't cause women to feel a devastating increase in anxiety about aging. They conclude that "women see the relevance of menopause as a time to focus on future opportunities for self-accomplishment and positive changes."[27]

It's a matter of looking at the menopausal glass as half full, and not half empty.

The Bitchy Factor

There's no question, though, that going through menopause is no picnic for many women, especially when they have no other distractions in their lives. The slow loss of estrogen may lead to specific vasomotor symptoms—hot flashes and night sweats—among some women, but women all over the world blame menopause for a range of other problems and afflictions. These symptoms are worst during the three or four or five years it takes to get through perimenopause. Think of perimenopause as a kind of fun-house tunnel that leads, eventually, to postmenopause, which is the light at the end of that tunnel.

American women complain about five major types of problems during perimenopause, according to a comprehensive study done in Seattle that required women to keep a diary of their symptoms for three years. The five types of problems include:

1. Vasomotor symptoms: night sweats, hot flashes, trouble breathing, and heart palpitations
2. Somatic symptoms: nausea, headaches, dizziness, painful breasts, fatigue, and constipation
3. Neuromuscular symptoms: backache, numbness, joint pain, and vaginal dryness
4. Insomnia
5. Dysphoric mood: nervousness, panic, irritability, mood swings, forgetfulness, depression, trouble concentrating, tearfulness, and weight gain[28]

The good news, though, is that for most women, many of these troubles vanish after a woman has stopped menstruating for at least a year.

Still, the dysphoric mood category is troubling, because if menopause does lead to depression, then that's a much more difficult problem to cure than hot flashes or joint pain. Also, if perimenopausal women are in danger of becoming depressed at the same time that their children are fleeing, that one-two punch could make this time of life that much more painful and difficult.

But experts are in agreement that this rarely happens: **menopause does not cause depression.**

A few women become depressed during menopause, but the numbers are quite small. In the SWAN study, for instance, Caucasian, Hispanic, and black women were much more likely than Chinese American and Japanese American women to say they felt symptoms of depression. About 16 percent of perimenopausal women felt irritable at least six days a week, 15 percent reported mood changes that often, and 14 percent felt blue or depressed at least six days a week.

When the researchers looked more closely at these unhappy women, however, they found that such women tended to have other complications that were more likely to explain why they felt so rotten. Such women tended to say that they were in moderate or severe pain from other health problems, that they didn't have many friends, that they were struggling financially, and that they'd had to face at least two upsetting life events, such as divorce, legal troubles, or being forced to move. But children leaving home, it turns out, wasn't included in the "upsetting life events" category, since it was not related to the onset of depression, according to the researchers.[29]

Looking at that list, it's difficult to figure out who wouldn't be depressed under such awful circumstances. While some women are more prone to depression than others, due to genetic predisposition or a chemical imbalance, it's also true that stressful life events and really bad luck can mean the difference between feeling okay and being clinically depressed.

Indeed, a wave of other studies is confirming this somewhat obvious conclusion: **it's not menopause, but the stress and strain of bad luck and poor health and financial pressure that make women depressed**.

Professor Nancy Avis is convinced that this rings true. "There is no evidence of higher rates of depression among postmenopausal women," she says, or that "perimenopausal women suffer from a sense of loss." The only exception to this rule, she feels, is among women who undergo surgical menopause, by having their ovaries or uterus removed. In this situation, one that's often extremely stressful and usually occurs before natural menopause, women tend to be more distressed and are, in fact, more vulnerable to depression.[30] That's probably because the procedure is the result of a serious health problem, and because it occurs unexpectedly, as well as unnaturally.

Wendy contracted uterine cancer at fifty-one and had a hysterectomy at the same time that her youngest son left home, for example.

There's no question in her mind that it was the operation, and not her son's departure, that threw her into a two-year-long spiral of depression and uncontrollable sadness. "I felt lost, sad, upset, depressed, and scared," Wendy says, a feeling that she did not experience when her oldest son left. The depression and sadness were especially upsetting, since she had been married to her second husband for only a few years. Refusing to bow down to despair, Wendy saw a therapist, who prescribed antidepressants, and after a time she got herself back.

"I now enjoy traveling with my husband and I have more time for myself. I have begun modeling, which I had given up due to my career," she adds. Wendy, a brave midlife soul who lives in Austin, Texas, poses for drawing classes at a local art school.

Now fifty-five, she has come to a place in her life that feels so sweet. "I am more than just someone's mom," she says. "My children are still very important to me, but I can fill the void with new ideas. I can now work like I don't need the money, dance like no one is watching, and love as if I have never been hurt."

Changing the Change for the Better

It's safe to assume that finding yourself without children at home and being menopausal is not such a bad thing. If you find yourself struggling, though, here are ten suggestions for getting through menopause in the least traumatic way possible.

Exercise. Unfortunately for those who tend toward couch potatoism, the facts are in: getting regular exercise reduces the complications of perimenopause. Women who don't exercise feel less healthy and gain more weight than those who do.[31] It's an elaboration of the obvious, but it's also proof that common sense makes sense. One study even shows that more active women report fewer problems with menopause and the ones they have seem less severe than those of sedentary women. They also have higher self-esteem and are more satisfied with their lives, a kind of psychological bonus of regular exercise. Getting regular exercise means doing some kind of physical activity at least three or four times a week for forty-five minutes to an hour.[32]

Even if you take up racewalking or lap swimming, that doesn't mean you'll never have a hot flash or a sweaty night again. But it does mean that your flashes won't be as bad and that your sweats won't last as long.

Win the lottery. Money can't buy you love, but it can buy you a relatively stress-free life. Women who live below the poverty line, and those who suffer from severe financial worries, tend to suffer more when they go through perimenopause. If you've tried to win the lottery but can't seem to manage it, then you can try to improve your financial situation. Get out from under credit-card debt, and if you are addicted to spending, cut up all your cards and throw away every offer for new ones. Work out a budget, and stick to it. Find a financial consultant, or look for free financial counseling at a local church or civic organization. You can't squeeze money out of a stone, but you can organize whatever you've got more efficiently.

Remember your history. If you've had a previous bout of depression, including postpartum depression, or you used to have bad premenstrual symptoms, you are much more likely to suffer from depression when you go through menopause. If you find that you are feeling deeply blue and very sad, take concrete steps. See a therapist and ask your doctor about taking antidepressants. Don't be ashamed to take this step; remember that such drugs often work. You won't have to take them for the rest of your life, just as long as you need to get you through this rough menopausal patch.

Be wary of hormone therapy. Most midlife women have read about the possible dangers of hormone therapy, such as increased risk of breast cancer and heart disease. Taking estrogen will certainly reduce your menopausal symptoms, in part because it tricks your body into believing it's not time for menopause yet. But hormone therapy simply postpones the worst symptoms of menopause, and as soon as you stop taking it, the symptoms begin right where they left off. So hormones are not a cure, they're just a deferral, a rescheduling of the inevitable.

Go natural. There's no solid evidence that natural remedies for menopause work, but they can't hurt, either. Some women swear by their all-natural antimenopause vitamins, which include Saint-John's-

wort, vitamin E, black cohosh, ginseng, evening primrose oil, moth-
erwort (great name!), red clover, and soy products. Unlike synthetic
hormones that mimic estrogen, they won't increase your chances of
contracting breast cancer.

Try antidepressants. Some gynecologists have begun to pre-
scribe low-level doses of antidepressants for menopausal symptoms—
not for depression. It turns out that a few of these drugs seem to
alleviate problems such as hot flashes and night sweats, at least for some
women, although nobody knows for sure why this is so.

Try vaginal inserts. If vaginal dryness is driving you crazy and
you don't want to start taking artificial hormones, there are other options available. Several products containing very low doses of artificial
estrogen, including pills and creams, can be inserted into the vagina to
relieve dryness. They basically fool the vagina into believing that menopause is not happening.

If this works for you, it's one of the best things to happen to midlife
sex since Viagra and a child-free house.

Make friends. In another belaboring of the obvious, experts find
that having a group of good friends helps reduce many of the negative
psychological side effects of menopause. I can vouch for this tip. I call
my friend Kate "Kvetch Central," since she's someone I can rely on to
listen to my complaints and to take them seriously. No matter when
I call or how stupid my problems are, Kate respects and honors my
complaints. As long as you have one or two Kates of your own, you will
surely get through a little perimenopause.

Join a menopause group. There are many such groups that
focus specifically on menopause and women who are going through the
change. Sarah, a woman who answered my Web survey, joined a menopause group for business executives. She attends the group's monthly
meetings, which sometimes attract as many as five hundred members,
she says. "We feel mentally happier, because we've had financial difficulties and experienced tragedies, but we know how to deal with it all.
We no longer struggle, and things that used to bother us don't anymore,
since we finally know what's important in life. We don't waste time trying to please other people and we don't do things we don't want to do.

The fifties are the best time in our lives," she continues, "since we're young enough, healthy enough, and experienced enough to know that life has never been better."

Work on your marriage. As long as you're in the market for distractions, working on your marriage is a good way to take your mind off the sweaty flashes and crankiness. If you put in the effort, you might even elicit some sympathy from your mate, who's had to stand by and watch the changes wrought by the change.

Now that we're on the subject of marriage, it's time to take a close look at your own. After the children leave home, many marriages are transformed. They aren't the same as before the children were born, nor are they exactly like what they used to be when the children were at home. Instead, many marriages become a new creation in the post-parental years. Often it's one that's either stronger and better or weaker and ailing.

Which one is yours?

CHAPTER SIX

Making or Breaking Marriage

A family is like a circus troupe, performing stunts under the big top for decades. There's Mom, juggling chores and work and hot flashes. There's Dad, clowning around in his big shoes. And there are the precious children, running around in circles, the star attractions, bouncing basketballs, riding bikes, doing tricks with the dogs.

It's stressful but sweet, lovable but distracting, and above all, it's supremely and incredibly entertaining. Eventually, though, the children outgrow the circus. They leave, with the intention of someday starting their own family circus.

Then it's just you and your partner. The two of you are the only stars of the show now, standing alone in the harsh, bright circus light.

Just the two of you.

At first you miss the presence of your little sideshow attractions. You're dazed, and a bit afraid, too, because you can't figure out what will happen next.

How will you and your mate be as entertaining, and as entertained, if it's just the two of you? What will you talk about, for instance? Many of your former topics of conversation no longer apply. You don't need to figure out who gets the car when or who attends which school events. You don't have to assuage your son's anxiety about finding a prom date or argue with your daughter about missing her curfew. All of the former child-oriented discussions and arguments and plans are mostly over, or at least put on hold for a while.

What do you do together, now that you can do anything at any time? It's almost as if you're newlyweds again, only with a lot more wrinkles and cellulite, as well as a much-reduced sex drive. But you also share years and years of companionship and troubles, heartaches and joys, disappointments and triumphs. Ideally, all those years together should form a solid foundation of love and support on which you will build the rest of your married life.

But in marriage, as in life, the ideal path isn't the only one.

Take my own marriage. When my youngest child left home, my husband and I talked about the dog. We discussed who would feed her, who would let her out, who would take her to the monthly vet appointment she needed. We imagined what our son, or our daughter, might be doing at the moment we were thinking about them. We talked about our work and our exercise plans for the weekend, and whether we'd go to a movie on Sunday afternoon. But those discussions didn't take very long, nor were they particularly engaging. We ignored the obvious, like the fact that we should try to go on a date together, or take up a sport or hobby together, or go away for a weekend together. These kinds of togetherness "shoulds" just didn't interest us.

We didn't do them before our kids left, so why should we start now?

Because we needed them, that's why. It soon became clear that we had lost the ability to show mutual consideration and respect, as if we'd forgotten how to speak a language we once knew. We were a kinder and gentler couple twenty-two years ago, before we had children. But those days were long vanished. Indeed, it seemed as if the harsh way we treated each other, spoke to each other, touched each other was out in the open for the first time in ages, no longer obscured and shielded by the commotion and distraction that children provide.

Our shaky marriage was all we had left under the family-circus big top. We were the only remaining stars, but we were wobbly on our feet, damaged by years of neglect for each other and for our marriage. We had no clue what we should do next.

Many couples are like us after their children leave. They become partners without being parents, and they're confused and uncertain about what that means. "Just the two of us, building castles in the sky," as Bill Withers's 1980 song lyric goes. "Just the two of us, we can make it if we try."

But it's the "trying" part that so many couples forget to do, and for some, it's no longer something they are able or willing to do.

Yet other couples find themselves in hunky-dory shape when the kids fly away. They have paid attention to their relationship all along, and they're able to pick up right where they left off, before they had children, when they were a couple and not a family.

Wives in my Web survey who are lucky enough to have such marriages say they are relieved that they get along so well with their husbands. "We're still good friends," they say, sometimes with amazement.

Once their children are gone, these wives report that their married life improves enormously. Many say they're thrilled and delighted to find there's less tension and stress without the children at home. They claim that while they used to argue constantly about their son's trouble-making or their daughter's grades, now that they no longer have the children to fight about, there's less conflict. Wives adore getting more attention from their partners once the former little ones have shut the door and walked out. Husbands appreciate getting more wifely attention, too, according to their wives, who sense that their husbands have been jealous of the children for years, because the kids hogged most of the family limelight. Many wives agree that once the children are gone, hubby becomes priority number one again, the way he was before the kids were born.

"We still feel close and we're still in love, but now we don't get distracted by the kids," says one of these happy wives. "And my husband loves having all my attention." Another confesses that "it's exhilarating to come home in the afternoon and leap into bed with my husband."

That is an empty nest filled with middle-aged sex.

Not all marriages, of course, are hearts and flowers and midday sex after the fledglings have flown. One woman says that her husband decided, on the second Thursday in September, right after their youngest son had left for college, that something was missing. "So he walked out the door, and we separated," she says.

"We spent so many years taking care of everyone else that we have forgotten to take care of each other," another unhappy wife confides. "For me, it feels more as if I'm living with a roommate than a husband and lover. There have been too many years of indifference for me to relight how I felt."

Her image is nearly perfect: a marriage is like a bright light for two, and both partners must constantly tend the flame, or else it goes out. And it becomes increasingly easy to tell if the light is no longer lit once the children's own vivid lights have moved on.

It's not all that difficult, in fact, for couples to figure out if their conjugal flame is alive or if it has been snuffed out for good. It's a matter of being able to see each other, to listen to each other, to be in tune with each other in a way that was difficult to achieve when the children were clamoring for attention.

Do you praise each other? Do you offer each other compliments and encouragement? Do you really listen to each other? Do you provide sympathy and support and strokes of affection for each other? Do you worry about each other's health and well-being? Do you notice signs of sadness or anxiety or when something's just not right?

I'd have to say that my own initial answers to these questions are, mostly, "no." It's as if my husband and I got out of the habit of being considerate to and thoughtful of each other. We had grown used to giving commands, managing all the tasks required to keep the circus going, instead of enjoying each other, with affection and comfort.

But marriages like ours may be in the minority, according to my Web survey. In a group of seven women I interviewed in Connecticut, for example, just one said that her marriage was worse after the children left home. She was the only one whose son had come back home to live, which may have had something to do with her marital blues.

I met these women in a sprawling contemporary home set on a lush, manicured property that included a perfect lawn and a perfect garden, as well as a tennis court and swimming pool. Inside, the dark hardwood floors gleamed with polish, and the marble floor in the vast kitchen was so shiny it could have been used as a makeup mirror. The guest bathroom was covered in narrow strips of mirror, mirrors from floor to ceiling, so many mirrors that you could see all of yourself as well as infinite reflections of yourself.

This is the House That Failing Feet Built, owned by Rosie and her husband, a monstrously successful podiatrist.

Rosie and her six friends, all in their fifties, agreed to meet me on a late summer afternoon, since a few work full-time and one takes an afternoon class. But they also spend a great deal of time playing tennis and going out for lunch, a July indulgence. They are the sort of women who, when they tell me they go out clubbing with their husbands, mean that they spend a lot of time at their country clubs. Many wear diamonds, thick encrustations of faceted stones, around their necks, on their wrists, in their ears.

The only one who isn't drenched in stones, oddly enough, is Denise, who owns a jewelry store with her husband.

As the women describe themselves and their marriages to me, it's clear that for most, the disappearance of children reduced the daily stresses and strains on their unions. It wasn't until the children were gone, they say, that they noticed how much more relaxed they were with their husbands, and how much less they argued. It's enormously liberating, they say, to be freed from the relentless Battle Over the Children.

One of the most vociferous on this point is Lenore, fifty-six, who has four sons. Lenore is small, the kind of woman who would never be seen in public unless she was wearing a perfectly coordinated outfit. And she is, right now: a navy-and-white suit, with matching navy heels and a white-and-navy handbag. Lenore and her husband of thirty-three years work together in their family real-estate business, along with two of their sons.

"Our marriage has definitely improved, because we always fought over the children. Now that they're not here, there's just not as much to fight about. We play golf and we take trips together, and we enjoy traveling without the children," Lenore says.

"Before, I used to do everything in the kitchen. But now my husband has become a big vegetable gardener, and he's into cooking and preparing his own vegetables," Lenore adds, blushing deeply at the idea that her husband is doing more cooking than she is.

Denise, fifty-three, wears girlish jeans and a blue, sequined tank top.

She met her husband when they were both nineteen years old and says that people make fun of them for being so lovey-dovey at this late date. "We are soul mates," she says, with some pride. "We really enjoy each other. There is so much ahead for us, traveling and having fun together, having grandchildren. We feel just the way we did when we were young, only we've had lots of life experience."

Annette, fifty-two, agrees with Denise that her marriage has improved since her two children left home. She and her husband, she says, are reveling in their luxurious solitude. "We are on a honeymoon," Annette exclaims, "it's wonderful. We learned that we don't have to be with our children all the time, and we aren't. For the first time, we are going away without them. Now when they come home to visit, we're happy, but when they leave, we say, 'Thank God!'"

These women agree that they've led what they call "charmed lives." As Kathy puts it, "we are financially blessed, and we are very happy and secure in ourselves and with our lot in life. It's pretty nifty."

Now fifty-nine, Kathy is a petite blonde who adores her second husband. Her life would have been hellish had she stayed in her first marriage, and she's grateful that she got out when she did, about fifteen years ago.

Rosie, though, was not so fortunate. She sits quietly while her friends crow about how well they get along with their husbands now that the children are gone. At fifty, Rosie is tall and gaunt, and wears cargo pants with flat, jeweled sandals. She considers herself strong and healthy and ready to see the world now that her boys are grown. But her husband, the foot man, believes that her child-raising job is done, so she's somewhat useless. He refuses to travel with her now that they're free, so Rosie has done some Internet research and found a woman's group that sponsors trips for women who want to travel alone. If she can work up the courage, and persuade her husband to foot the bill, Rosie hopes to visit India and China, on her own.

Finally, there's Sue, a thickset woman who owns a handbag company that manufactures copies of designer products. She and her husband have never spent much time together, since Sue always traveled a great deal. But now that their children are gone, she says, "he has become more considerate. If he knows I'm going to be home alone, he'll leave work early to spend time with me. We're together more now, and we go to our place in Florida, and we socialize with friends."

Is Marriage Like a Smile—Or Is It Downhill All the Way?

Most research on marriage shows that my husband and I are not alone in our confusion about how to rearrange our relationship in the postparental stage. It's not that we're miserable, and neither are many other longtime married couples. It's just that most of us are not nearly as smitten with each other as we were a few decades ago.

It's a standard operating belief among experts that marital satisfaction decreases over time. The only questions are these: How fast does happiness with marriage decline? For what reasons does that happen? And does it ever get better?

Until recently, social scientists believed that once the honeymoon period was over, after the first three or four years of marriage, wives and husbands tended to say that they felt less and less happy about their marriage as the years passed. The theory went that contentment with marriage declined as soon as children were born, it reached a low point when children became teenagers, and improved slightly when the children left. If this is the case, the shape of marital satisfaction is a U-shaped curve, because if you graph couples' happiness over the years, the shape looks like a large U, or a smile.

The logic of this approach is simple and almost elegant, like an equation:

Marriage + Children + Stress + Less Time Together = Less Happy with Marriage

Marriage − Children + Less Stress + More Time Together = Happier with Marriage

Thus, it seems to make sense that wives and husbands should be happiest about their marriage at the beginning, then less and less so, until later, if they are still married, it goes up again. Graphing the life of a marriage, according to this theory, it should look somewhat like this:

Is Marriage a Smiley?

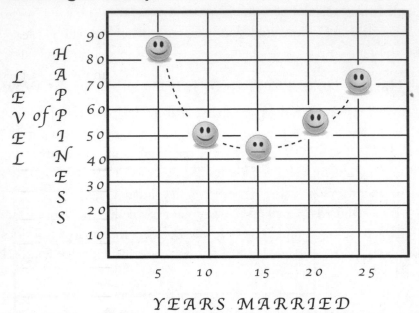

On the magic day that children leave home, so the experts believe, couples find renewed vigor and affection and love for each other. One group of researchers even stressed that all of the children have to be gone for the effect to take hold, and that an empty nest is almost guaranteed to improve marital satisfaction. And this is especially true, they say, in the first year or two after the children leave, which they refer to as "the euphoria stage." They figure that mothers, in particular, are greatly relieved when their children go off into the world, in part because they find parenting so much more stressful than fathers do.[1]

More recent studies, however, demonstrate that this U-shaped curve might not really exist. In fact, the news about marriage could be worse, much worse, than that.

Most couples become less happy about their marriage as time goes by, and there is not an upswing at the end. This fact shouldn't come as a surprise, since about four in ten first marriages end within fifteen years, a divorce rate that has gone down only slightly in the past decade or so.[2] What's surprising, though, is that even couples who don't divorce complain that their marriage is not as good as it used to be.

This marital fact of life doesn't change much when children leave. So the graph isn't a U-shaped curve, it's more like a downhill slide, starting on a high note, but going lower and lower and lower as time goes by.

Or Is Marriage a Downhill Slide?

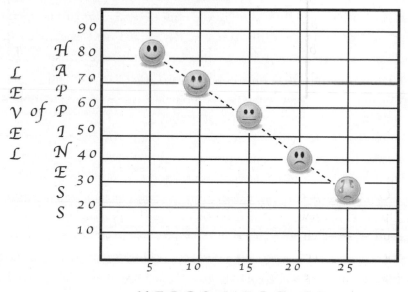

The high point of marriage is at the beginning, in what is known, quite obviously, as the Honeymoon Effect. Right after the wedding, most couples are high on the brain chemical associated with passionate love. It's called phenylethylamine, or PEA, and the body produces it when people fall in love and are deliriously blissful about being together. Eventually, the level of PEA in the brain diminishes, or else the brain's neurons become adjusted to the effects of so much PEA—experts can't really decide which is most likely. Whatever the reason, the newlyweds' initial blast of chemical blissfulness and well-being goes away over time.

After that, most couples experience "relationship disenchantment," the period during which the brain chemistry of love has worn off, and they come down to earth. After couples have children, though, marital satisfaction tends to plunge even farther down the scale. The thrill is gone, the passion dies down, and marital satisfaction goes the way of middle-aged boobs and bellies—down, down, down.[3]

The problem with studying married couples, homosexual partners, or significant others who live together is figuring out a way to find out just how happy they are together. Most of us know from experience that one day we feel thrilled to be with this person, happy to be spending our lives in tandem. But the next day, or the next week, we can't believe we've yoked ourselves to this fool and wonder what we were thinking when we did so. It's this kind of "what was I thinking?" moment that stops us in our tracks and makes measuring something as complex as marital satisfaction so difficult.

It turns out, though, that this feeling of marital dismay is completely normal. Each marriage is unique, with a life course and a path all its own. It meanders up and down, this way and that, depending on what's going on all around it. For this reason, researchers like Debra Umberson at the University of Texas in Austin believe it's crucial to study the same marriages over time to see how they develop and change.

Because no two marriages are alike, "it's important to look at how individual marriages change over time," she tells me in a telephone interview. "You can't compare apples and oranges to see how marriages change, which is what you do when you look at different people's marriages at one point in time." Thus, it's foolish to compare the marriage of a young couple married ten years with that of an older couple married twenty years with that of an even older couple married thirty years, "because they grew up in different times and with different values," she says. "Their marriages have a character and flavor unique to the couple and their place in history." But that's just what some researchers do when they ask people of all ages, at one point in time, how happy they are with their marriage, and then compare young couples with middle-agers and older couples.[4]

Umberson stresses that this approach is misleading. It's much better, she contends, to study a group of forty-year-old couples until they become sixty-year-old couples, to gain a true understanding of the life course of marriage over a twenty-year-period. Of course, doing such a study will take two decades, a luxury of time and expense that many researchers simply don't have.

That's why Umberson cites the results of a major national study of about three thousand people that began in 1980. The researchers who created and maintained this study called it "Marital Instability Over the Life Course," and they interviewed wives and husbands five times between 1980 and 1997. Consequently, they have detailed pictures of the life course of thousands of marriages, some that ended and others that did not.[5]

It's from research like this that Umberson concludes that **as couples age, they grow more accustomed to each other, and more accepting of each other's flaws.** That annoying habit he has of rearranging things in the refrigerator, or her habit of eating pretzels in bed, becomes less troublesome over time. Still, they're no longer on a thrilled-to-be-in-love high, and not nearly so happy about their marriage as they were at the beginning. They are, however, slightly more comfortable with each other.

"In some marriages," she tells me, "people learn to live with each other; it's almost like a merged pathology. If a woman and man are matched, it doesn't really matter if they're dysfunctional. It doesn't matter if you're controlling and domineering, as long as your partner happens to be a submissive person." Umberson goes on to offer this example:

> I interviewed a woman with real mental health problems. She liked to stack big piles of things in front of all the doorways inside her house. Her husband loved her, though, and he just thought she was quirky, so he'd walk around the piles, and he didn't mind. Then his eyesight started to go, and he began to use the stacks of books to help him get around in the house. Their marriage worked because he could live with her mental illness. People stay together and they work things out, even though it may not be a blissful relationship.

Umberson is fascinated by marriage, she tells me, for two reasons. First, because hers didn't last very long, and second, because she grew up in a house where her own parents "were miserable for twenty-five years." But what's most amazing to her, she says now, is that after watching her parents suffer through decades of wretched unhappiness, "things turned around for them, and for the last twenty years, they've been best friends. But this is not what happens to most people," she hastens to add.

Umberson also believes that as women and men age, they become slightly less "emotionally reactive," which means they don't fly off the handle so much. A middle-aged wife won't scream and yell as much as she would have a decade earlier, when her partner takes a two-hour nap in the middle of a busy Sunday afternoon. And he won't become as furious or as sullen when she forgets to fill up the gas tank, in part because they've learned to temper their anger and irritation. They don't fight less often, they just fight better, she believes.

Despite acknowledging the potential benefits of long-term marriage, Umberson is in the marriage-gets-worse-over-time camp. In all of her research, couples say that, on average, the number of positive marital experiences decreases the longer they've been married, and negative ones rise. So they are less likely to feel loved or listened to, and they tend to have trouble sharing private feelings and worries with each other. In addition, she concludes, they grow gradually more bothered or upset by their marriage.

It's this kind of minor ratcheting up, of secrets and complaints, that can poison a once-solid marriage, invisibly undermining it like carpenter ants infesting a porch.

She adds that children increase the stress and strain on marriage, not only as soon as they're born, but when they're almost grown, too. As long as the kids are home, she says, they have an adverse effect on how wives and husbands feel about each other.[6] While children make life more wonderful and worth living, they also make marriage a lot more difficult.

Children coming and going are just two of many major life events that can strengthen or weaken marriages, she says. Another is losing a parent, for example, or losing a job, or when one partner suffers from a serious illness. That's why it's so difficult to predict upturns and down-turns in marriage, according to Umberson.

"Losing a parent often has a negative impact on marriage. But for some it gets stronger, like when a wife says, 'I admired the way you supported me when my father died.' But every major life event means different things for different people. If a spouse becomes extremely ill, it can make the marriage stronger or it can make it weaker," Umberson tells me.

When a spouse retires, that, too, can alter the marriage for better or worse. In fact, it turns out that **most marriages become less happy for both wives and husbands after one retires.** It seems that couples fight more often when one retires and the other doesn't. But if both retire at about the same time, the marriage suffers least, according to a three-year study of couples between the ages of fifty and seventy-two conducted in upstate New York.[7]

Although couples who have weathered many marital storms may grow less thrilled about each other over time, some learn how to argue more effectively. The longer couples have been married, experts say, the more adept they become at diffusing their disagreements, in part because they have so much practice at it. It's like this:

Long-Term Marriage = Expert at Arguing

One group of researchers compared couples married fifteen years with those married at least thirty-five years by studying their conversations. It turns out that the long-married wives and husbands were better at dealing with their emotions than the couples who hadn't been married as long. Older couples expressed fewer negative emotions and more affection for each other while arguing, almost as if they were doing so on purpose. Even when they were being critical, the older couples tended to interweave their comments with affection and humor.

So a wife may say, "You are really a dope for trying to bake the casserole without turning on the oven," to her husband; she might also add "sweetheart" to the criticism, softening it somewhat.

These researchers also discovered that wives of all ages expressed more emotion, both positive and negative, than husbands, who tended to be more defensive and to stonewall. When wives get mad, they show it, letting it all out in a righteous tirade. But when husbands become angry or upset, they tend to close off their feelings and hide behind a fake, everything-is-fine facade. This is the "no, I'm not mad that you dented the car" approach, which is fairly transparent to any wife who knows her husband well, especially if she recognizes the gritted teeth or the clenched jaw.

These researchers developed a system so that every time wives and husbands expressed a negative emotion, they noted if it was anger, sadness, contempt, disgust, belligerence, bossiness, or whining. On the positive side, they also kept track of how many times couples expressed joy, respect, interest, affection, humor, and validation while talking to each other.[8]

It comes as no surprise, perhaps, but they found that happy couples expressed more humor and affection and validation to each other, even while arguing. Unhappy couples showed more anger, contempt, sadness, belligerence, and bossiness, and wives in such couples expressed their negativity more often and more vocally. In other words, wives in unhappy marriages screamed and hollered. This was true even among some middle-aged and older couples who had been married for quite a while, the researchers say.

Also, it turns out that wives and mothers, especially, are no strangers to anger. In fact, wives tend to wallow in anger and rage and recrimination, much of it aimed directly at husbands.

A great deal of research shows that mothers report more psychological distress than women the same age who are not mothers, and that they are angrier, too. A telephone survey of a large number of Americans over the age of eighteen asked specific questions about anger. Pollsters asked women of all ages how many times during the prior seven days they had felt annoyed with things or people, felt angry, or actually yelled at someone.

Who are the angriest Americans?

Parents are angrier than nonparents, and mothers are angrier than fathers. Not only that, but mothers' anger increases with each extra child in the house! Also, those struggling financially are angrier than those who are not, divorced people are angrier than the married, and younger adults are angrier than older folks. It seems that there's a lot of anger out there.

And mothers feel angrier than just about everybody else, according to these researchers.[9]

Maybe, just possibly, that's why moms are so thrilled when their children leave home—it's because they can finally take a vacation from all that anger.

How to Measure a Marriage

It's relatively easy to ask people how angry they are or happy they are, how often they have sex, or even how often they think fondly of each other. You can also sit around and listen to their conversations, code the words they use, and try to figure out if what they say is constructive, helpful, and loving or nasty and negative.

But is there any way, really, to accurately judge a marriage if you're not the one in it?

Social scientists insist that they can, since so many of them are determined to try to figure out which marriages are happy and healthy, and which are sad and ill fated.

One of the simplest ways they do so is to ask people the following basic question.

Is your marriage:
o Very happy?
o Pretty happy?
o Not too happy?

Most wives and husbands could pop a pencil into one of those empty circles and give a quick answer to this kind of straightforward inquiry. Slightly more than half of married couples, when asked this question, say that their marriage is "very happy." But there is a fundamental flaw in the question itself, as Umberson points out, one that makes the conclusion—that half of marriages are very happy—seem close to meaningless. "It's a biased measure, because everyone knows they are supposed to be happy in marriage," she tells me. "It's much better to ask about how much you feel loved and listened to by your spouse, so that you're asking more about behavior than attitudes. It's like, if you ask about children, people feel too guilty saying they don't like their children or they hate being a parent, but if you ask them what they find about their children to be stressful or annoying, they'll tell you."

That's why Umberson believes it's important to look at several attributes of a marriage, which she calls the positive and negative qualities of marriage. The positive qualities of marriage, or the pluses, include how satisfied you are with it, if your partner makes you feel loved and cared for, how willing your partner is to listen when you need to talk, if you can share feelings and worries with your partner. The negative qualities of marriage are how often you are bothered or upset by your marriage and how often you have unpleasant arguments with your mate, according to Umberson's research.

Her theory is logical, and it also seems intuitively correct.

Other researchers have different, and more elaborate, methods of getting at the complex question of "How good is your marriage?"

One group of marriage experts insists that every marriage contains five qualities. First, there's **divorce proneness,** how often you think or talk about your marriage being in trouble. Second, there are **marital problems,** which include how often you and your partner become angry, easily hurt, jealous, critical, moody, or give each other the silent treatment. This also includes how domineering and irrational you are, and if one partner stays away from home, spends money foolishly, gets drunk or takes drugs, or gets in trouble with the law. Third, there are **marital disagreements,** which include how often you have verbal arguments or physical fights. Fourth, there is **marital happiness,** including the strength of your love for each other, the amount that you understand each other, how often you agree about things, how happy you are about your sex life, if you are faithful to each other, and how often you do things together. Fifth, there is **marital interaction,** how often you eat together, shop together, visit friends, go out, and do projects around the house together.[10]

That's only one example—and there are dozens, if not hundreds, of ways to measure marriage. In another major national study, for instance, researchers asked married couples over the age of fifty how happy they are with their marriage, how often they disagree, and how often they do household chores. It is probably no surprise that **the happiest marriages are those in which couples share a great many activities, including the chores.** And, also no surprise, wives are happiest if they view themselves, and their husbands, as each doing a fair share of the chores and the grunt work.[11] A husband who does the dishes, folds the laundry, and cooks the dinner makes for a happy marriage, apparently (as if you didn't already know that).

With all of this in mind, here's my simple adaptation of two ways to measure marriage. Think about how often you do or feel the following about your own marriage. Then answer these questions, as honestly as possible.

FIGHT CLUB TEST

Is your marriage a constant battle, like a new version of the Hundred Years' War? Did you declare a cease-fire long ago? Or do you live in near-complete harmony and tranquility? To find out, answer these questions.

How often do you argue or disagree about the following:

I = Almost every day   2 = Sometimes   3 = Occasionally   4 = Never

1. Doing dishes
   - 1   2   3   4
2. Cooking
   - 1   2   3   4
3. Cleaning house
   - 1   2   3   4
4. Spending time together
   - 1   2   3   4
5. Spending money
   - 1   2   3   4

6. Children

    1   2   3   4

7. Vacations

    1   2   3   4

8. What to watch on television

    1   2   3   4

9. Sex

    1   2   3   4

10. In-laws

    1   2   3   4

SHARING SCALE

Do you have an "every man for himself" kind of marriage, one in which you do your thing, he does his, and never the twain shall meet? Or are you more cooperative, abiding by the kindergarten rule of sharing? Answer these questions and you'll find out.

How often do you:

1 = Never   2 = About once a week   3 = A few times a week   4 = Almost every day

1. Talk to each other for at least fifteen minutes?

    1   2   3   4

2. Go out for dinner?

    1   2   3   4

3. Exercise or walk together?

    1   2   3   4

4. Have sex?

    1   2   3   4

5. Go out with friends?

    1   2   3   4

6. Talk on the phone?

    1   2   3   4

7. Go grocery shopping or do errands together?

    1   2   3   4

8. Cook together?

    1   2   3   4

9. Worship together?

    1   2   3   4

10. Sit quietly, watch television, or read together for at least fifteen minutes?

    1   2   3   4

Add up your scores for both the Fight Club Test and the Sharing Scale. Your number should range between 20, if you answered all 1s, to 80, if you answered all 4s. If your score is 60 or higher, your marriage is probably in great shape, at least according to the numbers. If it's between 40 and 59, your partnership is middling, and if it's lower than 40, you may have some major marital problems. But you probably knew this already, or you may have suspected it.

If you had taken this test right after you were married, do you think your score would have been different? It probably would have, and it would also have changed again, for the worse, after your children were born. When they were teenagers, your score might have been even lower. Now that the children are gone, or almost gone, your score might be slightly higher, or not. If your memory is decent, and not too colored by time and distance, you could try to create your own personal marriage graph. If you do so, you might be able to figure out if the shape of your marriage is more like a smile, looking like that U-shaped curve, or closer to a downhill slope.

The Second (or Third) Time Around

If you are remarried, then you'll have not one, but two or three marriage charts to work on. Presumably, none of the ones that ended in divorce was a smiley-face marriage. It's more likely that it was a disastrous downhill plunge. But even if you are now in a much better marriage, your ratings are, by definition, more complicated, because you have to factor in the ages and stages of your children as well as the children your partner brought into the marriage.

In any case, whether you are married for the first, the second, or the seventeenth time, you will eventually experience the leaving of your children, his children, and all of the miscellaneous children in the family. That's when complications arise, since remarried wives must deal with the departure, and occasional return, of stepchildren as well as biological children. As I mentioned earlier, children in stepfamilies are more likely to leave home early than those who live with both biological parents, and they are much less likely to return home. "There are more stressors associated with a blended family, particularly when children are involved, and there are more challenges, too," says Kristi Williams, a sociologist at Ohio State University who specializes in research on marriage. She explained her views to me in a telephone interview. "Remarriage is a complex array of benefits and costs, in terms of women's physical health and psychological well-being. How big those costs are depends on the age of the children from both partners, when they remarry, and what their living arrangements are," she continues. And because the whole thing can be impossibly complicated, there really is no way to predict what will happen to an individual marriage; there are only vague generalizations about types of families.

Thus, Williams's research shows that single women and single men tend to be more depressed, on average, than married women and men, and they are also less satisfied with life. But—and this is a big qualifier—**those who are in unhappy marriages are even more depressed and miserable than the unmarried.** As a general rule, then, it's better to leave a bad marriage than to stay in it, she says.[12]

Jody, fifty-five, from Lehi, Utah, learned that lesson the hard way. She stayed married to her first husband for fifteen years, and at least five were years in which she was sad and desperate to escape. The day Jody told her husband she wanted a divorce, she says, was one of the happiest of her life. Not only that, but she found a new man soon after, and has been married to him for thirteen years. Both Jody and her new hubby entered their second marriage with three teenagers, and both had to work hard to blend her children and his children into "our children." It was, she says, somewhat like living in an unscripted version of a television sitcom, only none of her teenagers was quite as witty or charming as the ones on the screen. "Starting a marriage with six teenagers underfoot was quite a challenge," she admits.

There were times, many times, when Jody couldn't believe she dove into a double-wide, double-size family to be a wife once again, after ridding herself of the first husband. But eventually it all worked out. And this year, for the first time, Jody says, all of the children are out of the house. "We are finally having our honeymoon years," she states with glee. "It's just the two of us, and we are loving it."

Because she had a hysterectomy at the age of forty-five, though, Jody's sex drive is shot, and her sexual pleasure has waned to the vanishing point. Still, Jody is lucky in one respect. "I never defined myself in terms of my children or their accomplishments," she says. "So I am still the same person I was prior to becoming a mother, but with way more experiences that have refined and defined my personality and my character. The most important thing I have learned is that Life, with a capital L, is always waiting with opportunities for growth, change, improvement, excitement, comedy, and drama, no matter how far along you are on the path. I realize that I will always be me, no matter how old I get."

For Jody, then, getting married again became an opportunity to leap into a new Life.

When Caitlyn married her second husband, she took a very different route, using her new marriage as a chance to start over. She also figured out a way to postpone her empty-nest years for two more decades!

Caitlyn had divorced her first husband, in Maryland, at the moment their daughter left for college. When she remarried a few years later, she moved to Connecticut, got pregnant, and gave birth to a midlife baby. Her girls are now thirty-three and eighteen, so she is finally without a child at home, for the first time in more than three decades!

Naomi's divorce and remarriage took yet another path to ultimate happiness. Naomi married her high-school sweetheart, whom she helped put through law school while also having two babies. A pretty woman with blond hair who's not afraid to flaunt her diamond necklaces and bracelets, she's cheerful while she's describing the pain of the breakup of marriage number one. She was not yet forty when her husband decided that she wasn't paying enough attention to him because she was teaching full-time and going to school at night to get her master's degree. He decided that his legal secretary paid him much more, and better, attention, so he ditched Naomi and their family. Naomi was left with two youngsters and a wounded heart.

Almost immediately, though, she ran into an acquaintance, also divorced, a man who was her first husband's college roommate and who had actually attended her first wedding. "I met my second husband on the day I married my first husband," Naomi says, with a firm belief that they were fated to be together.

Indeed, the couple have been married for twenty years now, and she's convinced that her bad first marriage was the route she had to take to get to the nearly perfect second one. Her new hubby is "very nurturing and kind and sweet" and doesn't mind when the children come home to live for a while, as both have done from time to time. This makes him an exception to the stepfather rule, which usually prevents children from boomeranging back into a household that includes a stepparent.

"When our children left," Naomi says, "our marriage became more carefree. We were relative newlyweds when that happened, together only for a little bit of time. I was a little sad, but we suddenly had more closets and more freedom and more room and cleanliness," she crows.

The Three Marriage Paths

Whether you are remarried or still on your first husband, you are likely to look at your marriage in a new way once the children are gone. At that moment, most marriages tend to wander down one of several different paths, each in its own fashion and at its own pace. The process is slightly more complicated, of course, if parents are in a second or third marriage when children leave. Still, it's clear that most first marriages, as well as most second and third marriages, fall into one of three camps after children leave.

Half of marriages improve, getting better after the children leave; they are **Upswingers.** About one-third of marriages don't change all that much when the kids are gone; they're the **Even Keelers.** Finally, about one in ten marriages gets worse when the children no longer live at home, and those are the **Downsliders.**

Upswingers

These couples find themselves thrilled to be on their own again. This is true in part because they always made a real effort to find time to work on their marriage when their children were growing up. Even if they put their relationship on hold for a while, they always knew that one day they would be just two again, and most Upswinger wives say that they have always looked forward to this time. Half of marriages, 53 percent, are in this healthy zone, according to my research.

"That sounds just right," agrees Umberson. "Partners say their marriage gets better because they have more time together and less stress, so it's a boost. But I wouldn't expect every marriage to improve," she tells me.

Lori, a fifty-four-year-old high-school teacher who lives in Hartford, Connecticut, is lucky enough to be part of an Upswinger marriage. She is remarried, and her second daughter, from the second marriage, just left for college. "My husband really thought I was going to go into a depression when our daughter went away. But I'm happy for her because she's so happy where she is, and that means I can focus on my husband more. I pay more attention to him, and he likes that, and I like how we are more playful with each other. We can be spontaneous if we like, too," Lori says.

Lori's marriage improved after their daughter left, and she feels closer to her husband, she says, although she still misses her daughter. "I miss having her here physically, giving her a hug and sharing her everyday experiences, watching *American Idol* together, just doing everyday stuff," Lori sighs. Nevertheless, she confesses that she and her husband are suddenly "more focused on pleasing each other, and I have more energy, since my mothering responsibilities have decreased."

It's as if all of the time and energy and love that Lori used to funnel to her daughter has been diverted, as if by a giant, unseen dam, toward her husband. And he's thrilled that he's flooded with all that attention.

The same thing happened to Beth, whose nineteen- and twenty-year-old daughters have been gone for a year. She works full-time as a meeting planner and explains that her life formerly revolved around her girls, but now has shifted back to her husband. "Our relationship got put on the back burner when we were raising our daughters, but now we have each other's undivided attention, and we LOVE planning where and what we are going to do with each other next," she says. "We come and go as we please, and we are ENJOYING our time together as a couple. Now that the girls are out of the house, I am concentrating on doing things for myself and with my husband!" She writes in CAPITALS and with lots of "!!!," as if she's her own best cheerleader. And she is.

At forty-seven, Joanne lives in Holland, Michigan, and is a mother of four children, all in their twenties. She believes that her strong marriage "became even better when I could focus on my partner without frequent interruptions. My husband and I are best friends, and we greatly anticipated this phase of life." She continues that while she loves her children dearly, she's also thrilled and ecstatic that they're finally gone.

Even Keelers

These marriages keep on trucking when kids leave, and don't really change all that much after the children are launched into adult life. About one-third of marriages, 36 percent, fall into this category.

Having an empty nest "can affect you as an individual, but not your relationship," Umberson explains to me. "Or, maybe it's a wash, with the costs and benefits changing, so that it evens out in the end," she notes. Anyway, "it would be weird if everybody said it changed for the better."

Sally, fifty-two, has two children in their late twenties, and she says that her thirty-year marriage didn't change when the kids left home, although she went through a phase when her daughter moved out, then back in, then out again and in again. Sally lives near Buffalo, New York, and manages a preschool program for inner-city children who live below the poverty line.

Sally describes her current life as "pleasant and serene and calm. We can do what we want, when we want, and we have so much less to worry about." She wishes her two good friends lived closer, but they don't, so her husband is really her only close friend.

Sally's had health problems lately, including sleep apnea and nodules in her lungs that had to be removed surgically. Her husband takes care of her, and she knows that she can count on him if she's not feeling well or if she's overwhelmed by work. "My husband and I always had a strong relationship from day one. We have always made time for each other, even when the children were at home. We knew that once the children were gone, it was going to be just the two of us, so our relationship had to come first," Sally concludes.

Her marriage is a solid marriage that stayed that way, even after the children were gone.

Likewise, Brandy's marriage was fine before, and stayed fine after the kids left. Now fifty-four, Brandy has two children and works full-time as a receptionist in a financial firm near her home in Memphis. Her marriage didn't change, she says, because she always knew that "there was more to me than carpool mom, soccer mom, cheerleader mom, choir mom, maid mom, and cook and driver mom. My husband and I are loving that it's just the two of us in this big house. It reminds me of when we first got married."

Other moms I interviewed echo that sentiment, feeling as if they suddenly live on a vast estate once the kids are gone. It's not that these women live in gigantic McMansions, bouncing around in five-thousand-square-foot homes. It's just that when any space that used to house four or five or six people becomes a home just for two, it can seem palatial, even if it's not all that big. My own split-level home contains barely eighteen hundred square feet, but now that our two children are gone, it feels spacious, overwhelmingly so. My husband can be downstairs and I can be upstairs, and we can't see or hear each other. It feels luxurious, somehow, even though we've lived here, in our gradually deteriorating nest, for more than twenty years.

Downsliders

Finally, there are marriages that don't survive the children's exodus. It's as if the relationship has been deprived of vital oxygen and is no longer able to breathe. These marriages get worse once the children are gone. It's likely that wives in such marriages were so focused on the children that there was nothing left over for their partnership. Or they may have been living the cliché, waiting for the children to grow up before getting a divorce. About one in ten marriages, 11 percent, are in such dire straits, according to my Web survey.

"These are marriages that placed more emphasis on children, and it's all they had in common," Umberson tells me. "Once the children are gone, it seems more acceptable to acknowledge that you don't like your spouse, because you aren't as tied to the quality of the marriage after they've left. You are liberated to be miserable," she adds.

Jeanne, fifty-six, of Clearwater, Florida, would certainly agree. She and her husband have had no sex in almost two years, she feels constantly irritated and aggrieved by him, and she longs to divorce him, have an affair, and remarry. Very soon, in fact. "My entire life was based on my children and living for my home. But I now find that I could care less about being in a marriage and would like to pursue a new relationship with someone else," Jeanne says.

Lucy, fifty-four, of Glendora, California, understands what Jeanne is going through. She has only one daughter and is in a second, seventeen-year-long marriage. She works fifty-five hours a week as an elementary-school teacher, though she's paid to work only forty hours. In addition, her daughter is sick with fibromyalgia and hypothyroidism. Lucy gets no comfort or help from her husband, she says, nor do they spend much time together. "I had hoped my husband and I would be more involved in each other's lives, and go away for weekends and have spontaneous sex. And I am disappointed that those things didn't happen, although I feel like I tried to encourage them. I have a committed relationship with my husband," she insists, "but I am often lonely."

Although only one in ten wives feels that the last child's exit leaves a shallow and unhappy marriage, theirs is the most devastating response to the empty nest. And what they say about their lives and their love is often heartbreaking.

Stephanie, a forty-five-year-old secretary in Chicago, says that "our marriage was already doomed when my daughter left." The proof: as soon as the girl began college, "I started sleeping in her bed."

Because Stephanie and her husband are having serious financial problems, she's unable to leave her husband yet, and finds herself "doing many things by myself, for myself. I get on the train and go to the zoo or to the library in the city. I go out to lunch or dinner alone. I prefer my own company," she concludes.

Other wives who acknowledge that their marriage got worse when the children left make comments like these:

- ❖ "I've discovered that we don't really know each other and we have nothing in common."
- ❖ "I'm weary of his bull."
- ❖ "We don't enjoy each other's company."
- ❖ "He really irritates me."
- ❖ "I've grown more intolerant of my husband."
- ❖ "We watch separate televisions."

Husbands are not innocents in this game, of course. One husband whose three children left a few years ago tells me, with only thinly veiled contempt, that his wife has become "brain-dead" now that the children are gone. "She has no life now," he adds, with undisguised disgust.

It's clearly his belief, and perhaps his wife's as well, that her purpose in life is over. Since he always earned the family's income and she stayed home with the children, it seems clear that he's been itching to fire her, as he would any temporary employee who'd finished the job at hand. It's no wonder that wives with husbands like this feel distraught and anguished about the state of their marriage when the children leave. That's because the marriage itself is effectively over.

In addition, the insidious apathy that divides such couples looms large once the children are no longer around to disguise it. For some wives, this comes as a terrible shock, but others have known all along that it was there, waiting in the wings, like a lurking cancer cell or a toxic virus.

Once the children are gone, wives in such marriages often say that they are actively reevaluating their lives, trying to figure out if they want to stay married. They wonder "how I want to spend the next half of my life," and if it should be with the man they live with. Some say, "We no longer know how to relate to each other," and "Our life is boring." Others admit that they've lost sexual interest, or that they have no clue what to do or where to go next.

For these wives, the empty nest is a wake-up call to repair, restore, or retrofit their relationship. And sometimes that means throwing it out and starting all over again.

Gina, forty-seven, moved out of her house after being married for twenty-three years, just a month after her son started college. At about the same time, she lost her job and began a new career as a masseuse. It was all incredibly traumatic, she says, "and I became seriously depressed right before I gathered the courage to tell my husband I was leaving."

Trudy, a gutsy mother from Connecticut, divorced her husband when the last of their four children left home. She also fled the country and moved to Sweden for a while, all by herself, calling it a sabbatical year, although she was not a college professor, but a registered nurse. "It was a great learning year for me, all about making decisions for myself, discovering just what I wanted in life, experimenting with a lot of 'Why not try this?' or 'Why not try that?' It was a very good year." Soon after she returned home, Trudy found a second husband.

The empty nest can trigger divorce, certainly, among Downsliders. The odds of divorce are relatively low, but it turns out that about one in ten couples divorces after their children leave, according to national statistics. That's about the same proportion of Downsliders I found in my research—and not a coincidence.[13]

The briefer the marriage, the more likely is divorce, experts say. Thus, a couple married for twenty years when the children leave is more likely to divorce than another who've been married for thirty years. What gives longer-lasting marriages immunity from divorce is not just that they have survived the risky years—when their children are young—but also because they have a growing financial and social investment in their children and in their homes and in each other.[14]

Still, as baby-boom women progress through midlife, the likelihood that they will remain in a first marriage grows slimmer. Some experts predict that by their early fifties, about one-third of baby-boom women will be unmarried, because they will be either divorced or widowed or never married. And by the time they approach their late sixties, fully half of baby-boom women will no longer be living with a mate.[15]

For this reason, it's a good idea to look at how single mothers cope with their children's exodus.

Single Moms Survive

In a way, kicking out the kids is both more difficult and easier for single mothers than it is for married moms. When a single mother's children leave home, her nest is much more empty than that of a married mother who still has a husband at home. But while launching her children into the world catapults a single mother into a solitary life, it also gives her a chance to date and socialize without the presence of resentful or meddling teenage children.

For one single mother of five, facing an empty nest was thorny and troublesome, but only at first. Vivian divorced her first husband while four of her children were still at home, and she confesses that she was scared to face life as a single woman after they were gone. "For the past twenty-eight years I've had children who needed me," she says, but now that she's alone, she's worried about what comes next. "When my two youngest became more independent, and started to do things on their own, I felt lost and alone," Vivian says. "I realized that I needed to find myself, and to figure out what will make me happy again. And that has to be something that doesn't involve my children," she adds.

On the plus side, now that her children are out of the house, Vivian has started to invite her dates over before they go out, for coffee or a drink. It's something she never, ever did while her kids were still home. "I was afraid of what they'd think of him, and what he'd say to them, so I just didn't bother," Vivian says. "Mostly, I didn't socialize at all, because it was just too complicated."

Because single mothers' lives change so drastically when their children leave, they are at risk of being distressed and upset when the children are gone. Indeed, I find in my Web survey that single mothers are more likely than others to say they feel empty, while also feeling a need to move on with their lives. Many more say they look forward to fashioning a new life for themselves, which they hope to do by moving or getting remarried or finding a new job, or all of the above.

It's almost as if single moms are itching for change, any kind of change, so desperate are they to reinvent themselves and their lives. Indeed, they're just as eager to do so as their children are to begin their own adult lives. Single women, I find, are also much more identified with their work than are married moms, and it tends to be a more important part of their identity and their sense of themselves. Mothers who must work to support themselves and their children are connected by necessity to that paycheck in a way that some married mothers are not.

Life can also become easier for single mothers when the children flee, because their sexuality comes out of the closet. Once the kids are gone, single mothers are liberated from sexual sneaking and tiptoeing and hiding the part-time lovers they are lucky enough to find. **More single moms than wives report that their sexual desire increases once the children leave home.** And more single moms than wives say that they have sex more often when the children are gone.

"Much more of my sex life takes place at my apartment now," says Marilyn, a single mother from Chicago who has two college-age children. "Neither the man I see nor I was comfortable with having that part of our relationship made so obvious to my daughters," she adds. "It's really freeing and sexy to be able to do it on the couch," she admits with a laugh.

Another reason that the empty nest can be easier for single mothers is that they've had practical experience with it for years, like having endless trial runs for the final move out. This applies mostly to mothers who've had some form of joint custody, since they've had to get used to relinquishing the children to a former husband on a regular basis. Here's how Marilyn explains it:

> I experienced the real trauma of children leaving home when my husband left me. In that first year, the girls were thirteen and eleven, and he kept to the terms of the agreed-upon custody schedule. The girls had dinner with him three nights a week, and spent every other weekend with him. That was when I felt alone and empty, having to go cold turkey from a real family life to what felt like desertion.

By the time my oldest daughter went off to college, though, I had learned to enjoy the alone times, and I had rediscovered the importance of friends. So preparing myself psychologically for my children to leave for college was not a huge break or a great surprise. The worst part was the first couple of weeks, when I had to deal with their homesickness, wanting to be understanding but also wanting to encourage them to stick it out.

Cindy, an office manager in Cleveland, had her first son when she was nineteen, and a second son nine years later, divorcing her husband soon after that. But she was not overly traumatized when the boys left home, she says, although "I defined myself as being someone's mother for most of my life." Her secret, she says, was not relying on the children for her reason for being. "I've seen many divorced moms do that, and I didn't want to hang that on my kids. I love my boys, and I enjoy spending time with them, but I never wanted them to feel responsible for my life or my loneliness or my social life," Cindy says.

As for being a single mother, well, it's clear that the role is one of the most difficult jobs ever invented. Surprisingly, though, all divorced mothers are not necessarily depressed and miserable because they are single. In fact, research shows that **the women who divorce when their children are younger than the age of five are much worse off than women who divorce later on.**

"The effect of divorce on parents depends on the life course stage in which it occurs," Kristi Williams tells me. For moms of preschool-age children, divorce is associated with increased psychological distress, but not for mothers of older children, Williams says. Divorced moms with babies and toddlers suffer from greater financial stress and they are more likely to have drinking problems, according to a national study of five thousand American men and women conducted by Williams over a five-year period.

After a divorce, both wives and husbands are likely to become depressed and less happy about their lives, she notes, especially if they have at least one very young child. She believes that although divorce is stressful no matter when it happens, it is truly worst and most intense when the children are babies. There is so much work involved in caring for little ones, and doing it alone is almost unbearably upsetting and difficult, she says.[16]

Still, there may be subtle and hidden benefits to divorce, ones that have not yet received the attention they deserve.

In a huge study of ten thousand baby boomers in Wisconsin, for instance, social scientists compared divorced mothers with similar women who were married, and discovered that although the divorced moms had lower household incomes, they also seemed to have a few psychological advantages. Divorced women, it turns out, are more intelligent and open to new experiences, meaning they are adventurous and open-minded and less likely to be neurotic and anxious than wives. The researchers were surprised to discover that, among women at least, there are few differences between divorcées and wives in terms of psychological well-being. In fact, they say, the divorcées are more independent and more likely to value their personal growth, and to challenge themselves in ways that wives simply do not.[17]

Another study shows that divorced women's health improves after the divorce, probably because it tends to go downhill so fast before divorce, when they are living in terrifically unhappy marriages.[18]

This leads us to the best news of all for divorced moms: **wives in bad marriages are more depressed and unhappy than are divorcées.** A bad marriage is defined as one in which wives say that they don't feel loved or cared for, that their husband does not listen to their worries, that they fight often, and that they are stressed rather than helped by marriage, according to Williams, who conducted the research. She concludes this way: **it is better for a woman's health and well-being to leave a bad marriage than to stay in it.**[19]

Her advice then, worded in an academic fashion, is this: "Women who are in unhappy marriages will reap more benefits than costs by leaving the marriage than by staying." But what she means is this: get out while the getting is good.

Many former wives who have decided to divorce probably sensed this fact, somewhere deep down. Some actually say that they recognized the moment that they knew it was time to leave.

Lisa left her husband in her early forties, when her three children were in high school. She understood when it was, exactly, that she should have left, but overstayed that moment by two years. "I stayed in a very unhappy marriage for my children, and did no one any favors by it, especially myself," Lisa recalls. "My ex-husband made me feel worthless and belittled me," she goes on. "He tried to alienate me from my family and friends, and he convinced my daughters that all of our problems were my fault. It was then I knew I had to leave him. When I finally left him, it was the smartest thing I ever did."

Lisa sells appliances at Sears, in the small Pennsylvania town where she raised her children, all of whom are now gone. She has a new boyfriend, whom she describes as "a friend, a lover, and an equal, and I appreciate all that I have."

She just rewarded herself for making all the right choices with a gift from Sears, bought on the installment plan. "I wanted a hot tub for years, so I bought myself one! And my boyfriend says I deserve it," she adds.

But what about the many wives, some of the Even Keelers and most of the Downsliders, who might like to improve their marriage but don't know how?

Becoming an Upswinger

The relentlessly cheerful and upbeat marital self-help industry assures us that we can all have the marriage of our dreams after the children leave. We can "revive" it, "rejuvenate" it, "reinvent" it. Anything that begins with "re-" is what's possible to do to and for our marriage. We just have to "work for it," and "believe in it," and blah, blah, blah. Perhaps the only nugget of truth in all of the fix-your-marriage blather is that both partners, wife and husband, have to want to do something about the marriage for anything at all to change.

Not only does it take two to tango, it takes two to tinker.

Most wives and husbands have some intuition if their marriage is less than ideal, or if it's actually rotten to the core. Experts who study the quality of marriages have recently changed the way they study these marital unions. A few decades ago, researchers simply asked couples how happy they were and how well they got along. With this method, they discovered the more-than-just-a-little obvious: that wives and husbands in unhappy marriages tended to be more depressed, more anxious, more distressed about life, and less optimistic about their future. No kidding. I'm not sure they needed to study hundreds of couples for months and years at a time to figure that out.

But now, many researchers have become wiser and more sophisticated. These days, experts who study marriages invite couples into a laboratory for hours at a time. They make sure that the couples haven't spoken to each other for most of the day, and then ask the pair to discuss three topics with each other at length: what they did that day, a mutually agreed upon problem, and something that gives them both pleasure. The experts videotape the conversations, so they can code not only what the couples say, but how they say it, examining both verbal and nonverbal behavior. In this way, researchers have discovered how couples argue and the ways in which both happily married and unhappily married pairs argue and listen and try to figure things out.

A study like this provides a window into couples' private lives; it's like bugging the family room to find out how couples really talk to each other when they are alone. Although you'd think that wives and husbands would be on their best behavior while chatting in front of a camera and a one-way mirror, what's remarkable is how genuine these conversations are. After just a few minutes, spouses tend to forget they are under a microscope, and they laugh and chat, yell and rant at each other as if they were speaking in the most soundproofed, private space ever invented.

And here's what these authentic discussions have revealed: there are at least nine signs of trouble, indications that a marriage will probably end in divorce a few years down the road. According to psychologist John Gottman, of the University of Washington, who analyzed hundreds of these conversations, you might end up divorced once the children leave home if you:

1. Criticize your partner often
2. Speak to your partner with contempt

3. Are defensive about your position when challenged by your partner
4. Disagree with your partner a lot
5. Find that your partner becomes very defensive with you
6. Realize that your partner speaks to you with contempt
7. Notice that when you argue, your partner often shuts down, pretending that everything is fine, but leaves the room in the middle of the conversation
8. Believe that if your partner does something thoughtful for you, it's a fluke or an accident
9. Tell yourself that every mistake your partner makes is because he's like that and attribute all his flaws to something bad in him[20]

The more of these that seem true for you, the more likely it is that you are in a troubled union. Research shows that couples who end up divorced are those who get locked into a kind of inevitable cycle of doom. This four-part cycle begins with **criticism,** which leads to **contempt,** which turns into **defensiveness,** and finally becomes **stonewalling.** Stonewalling is the particularly male habit of refusing to discuss a problem, or even acknowledge that it exists, but pretending instead that nothing is wrong. Criticizing, the researchers say, is more characteristic of wives.

This doesn't mean that happily married couples don't argue. On the contrary, all couples have disagreements, bad fights, and troubled times. It's just that those who are happily married focus on the positive, believing that a nasty comment or an unkind word is just a temporary glitch, a bad day or a bad mood. But those in unhappy marriages zoom in on the negative, believing that the partner is a nasty person, and therefore unable to change.

If he says with irritation, "Stop interrupting me," there are two ways a wife could respond to such a statement. A happily married wife might answer, "Sorry, what'd you say?" ignoring his tone and focusing on what he's trying to say. But a wife in a bad marriage is more likely to come back with an angry retort, such as, "I wouldn't have to interrupt if you'd give me a chance to say something." She is focused on the irritation and annoyance in her husband's voice, rather than on the message he's trying to convey.[21]

It's from research like this, in fact, that marriage researchers have come up with a few taboos, ways never to start a sentence while arguing with your partner, angrily or otherwise.

Try not to begin any discussion with phrases such as:

❖ "You always . . ."
❖ "You never . . ."
❖ "Never mind . . ." (while walking away)
❖ "I hate it when you . . ."
❖ "It's not my fault . . ."
❖ "I'm not discussing this now."
❖ "I hate you, because . . ."
❖ "You're a moron, because . . ." (and so on)

If both partners agree that the marriage needs some work, in the same way that the house needs to be repainted or the car needs to be serviced, then here are a few suggestions. As long as the children are gone, you will have more time and more space and more incentive to get along with the person you'll be living with for the next few decades. Not all of these suggestions will be right for you, and not all of them may work, but even if you try one or two, you'll probably be better off than you were before.

Share secrets. Marriages work best when partners feel close to each other. The way to feel close to someone, anyone really, is to share secrets and intimate thoughts and feelings. That's why some women feel so close to their hairdressers or their manicurists: because they confess secrets while being beautified. When we expose ourselves to someone else, we leave ourselves vulnerable, but we also bridge the gaps that keep us apart. It's especially important, by the way, to reveal not only the good parts, but the bad and the ugly bits, as well. Confession is good for the soul, and for marriage, too.

Air your complaints. It's fine to explain to your partner what's really bugging you. In fact, if you don't, that's just another secret you are keeping, which is a bad thing. The trick, though, is to share what bothers you but to do so without criticizing or belittling. This is much harder than it sounds, so don't worry if you have trouble when you try. If it's any consolation, couples pay big bucks to marriage counselors to learn how to do this very thing.

Be a team. Just because the kids are gone doesn't mean you have splintered into a "do whatever you want" family. You are still a team, a dyad, a dynamic duo. And if you think of yourselves that way, it will help you not only when you face the world, but when you face each other, in the privacy of your own home. Even when you argue, remember that you are in this life together, and not apart.

Don't bail. If you find yourself arguing, don't quit in the middle by leaving the room or refusing to speak. This advice goes double for men, who tend to be the primary stonewallers in the family. If your husband tends to do this, find a way to remind him, gently, that you'd prefer him to stick around. Try to reward him, if he does, by expressing your gratitude and refraining from any kind of criticism, at least for a few minutes.

Show affection. Even if you don't feel it, give your partner a hug or a kiss. Offer praise. You'd do this for your children, and even your dog, right? So try to offer him even a small token of affection.

Learn how to fight. You can't avoid it completely, so don't bother trying. Instead, learn how to do it well, without hurt feelings and miscommunications. And avoid the Big Four: criticism, contempt, defensiveness, and stonewalling.

Forgive and forget. Learn how to move on, from whatever problems you've had in the past, to potential pluses in the future. It seems overly cheery and optimistic, but it will work if you really mean it.

Have sex. Even if you're not in the mood, agree to have sexual relations. If you're anywhere near menopause, it's likely that you are not now, nor will you ever again be, in the mood, but that doesn't matter, because eventually you'll get there. There are no longer children around to interrupt or eavesdrop or notice, so take advantage of your newfound sexual liberation. If you don't understand how this could possibly help your marriage, you really should read the next chapter.

CHAPTER SEVEN

Sexuality: All My Doors Are Open

Good sex is the key to a good midlife marriage.

While it's true that women's sex lives are altered in midlife—both by menopause and by children leaving home—sex is still very much on our minds, the way it always has been. As baby boomers, we led the sexual revolution of the 1960s and 1970s, and we've always prided ourselves on our open-mindedness about all things sexual.

Or at least that's what we like to tell ourselves.

In any case, midlife sex is out of the baby-boom closet, in the same way that we broke the honesty barriers over menopause. As the first generation to reap the sexual rewards of the birth-control pill and, now, of erectile-dysfunction drugs, baby boomers refuse to allow sexuality to go gently into that good night. We still consider ourselves sexy, and don't tell us otherwise. We know we no longer look twenty-something, or even thirty-something, so we tell ourselves that fifty-something can be hot and sexy. And we try really hard to believe it.

We may, at times, admit that we are in the past-the-prime sex life years, but we don't hide our graying and paunchy midlife sexuality under a barrel. (Though it may be hiding under a barrel-type belly.) That's why we love to read books, magazines, and newspaper articles about previously untold glories of a midlife ripe with erotic sensuality. Much of this attention tends to be amazingly cheerful and optimistic, and a great deal of it seems out of proportion to the truth about middle-aged sex. In fact, the headlines usually read like Pollyanna on Prozac: "The Good News about Midlife Orgasm!" or "Older Women Hooking Up with Younger Men!!" or "Why She's Sexier Than Ever at 65!!!"

Ha!

These are fairy tales for the fairly older, and they might as well conclude with, "and they had sex happily ever after. The End."

But just as fairy tales are rarely true—the princess doesn't always get the prince, and the ogre doesn't always get vanquished—the reality is that menopausal women have sex lives that are usually as good, or as bad, as they were before the onset of the change of life. Only there's a bit less of it all around.

Most middle-aged women of the baby-boom generation have had average sex lives that are still average. They have sex once or twice a week, maybe, and they have orgasm some of the time, or much of the time, though not nearly as often or as earth-shattering as when they were younger. Thus, many of the hotly hyped stories about midlife sexuality focus on sexual outliers, those few people who fall on the extreme end of the sexual spectrum, who are especially unique in their sexual prowess and ability and desire. They are fascinating *because* they are so different, because they retain the ability to have multiple orgasms, or because they keep their smooth skin and svelte good looks. These sexual outliers are the ones who look like Jane Fonda, or the one who actually is Jane Fonda.

At the age of almost seventy, Jane Fonda still looks fabulous, but that's because she also looked fantastic in her twenties and marvelous in her forties. After all, she's the one who played Barbarella to perfection, the womanly outer-space stripper from the science-fiction classic, so of course she still looks way better than most of us. That's why she was a movie star in the first place!

The truth is that **most of us are not Jane Fonda now, nor were we ever Jane Fonda, even when we were younger.** Likewise, most weekend golfers are not Tiger Woods, and most tennis players are not Venus Williams. And just as we don't expect to hit a drive like Tiger or ace a serve like Venus, we shouldn't expect to dazzle men of all ages like Jane did, and still does.

It's pretty much a given, for most women, that while our former sexy self may fade, a newer, wiser, and more confident self will take her place.

"After you hit menopause, you're not considered sexy anymore. You're getting old and that still has negative connotations," says Nancy Avis, the menopause researcher from North Carolina I interviewed by telephone. "Jane Fonda can go through menopause and come out looking great, but most of us didn't look like that premenopause. In our society, there is the notion that a postmenopausal woman no longer has sex appeal. Women may be more respected as they age, but generally speaking, the older a woman gets, the more invisible she becomes," Avis notes.[1]

I figured this out rather belatedly one day, when it struck me that Kippy, my small white Jack Russell terrier, was attracting more stares than I did. I had become an older woman that no one sees, but it had happened so slowly and quietly that I hadn't noticed. I didn't realize how accustomed I was to not being seen until I went out in public with my lovely teenage daughter. It was only then, shopping in a crowded mall one day, that I remembered how it feels to have people pay attention to me, and to really look at me. Or, rather, to look in my direction, if not exactly at me. Suddenly, salesmen were actually asking if I needed help, pedestrians were making way for me, strange men were turning around. This is the kind of special treatment that you take for granted when you are young, mostly because you've always had it. It's only when that attention disappears for good that you realize you attracted it because of your youthful sexual potential, and not for your brilliant wit or your fascinating personality.

Being near that kind of attention again reminded me that I had become the Invisible Midlife Woman, someone to be ignored. A postmenopausal woman is, biologically speaking, no longer capable of reproduction, and therefore unworthy of male stares and smiles.

Thus it's somewhat unfair to get middle-aged women's hopes up by preaching to us about exceptions to the sexual rules. Don't tell us about the Jane Fondas of our generation, because for most of us, "sexy" and "sixty" should not be used in the same sentence. **"Sexy" and "sixty" rarely go together like a horse and carriage,** or like anything else, for that matter. So don't fall for stories in which sexy sixty-year-olds live happily, and sexily, ever after.

Here is one such midlife sexual fairy tale, though I warn you in advance that this story is not about most of us; it is about an outlier, one of those bedazzling and funny outliers who is an exception to the sexual rule.

At fifty-nine, Margie is a lovely blonde, slender and full of energy. Seen from afar, she could easily be in her late thirties; up close, she looks forty-nine. A high-school biology teacher who used to work long hours teaching, grading papers, and doing lesson plans, Margie lives in San Diego, California, in a well-to-do neighborhood, with her second husband, Rick, a successful cardiologist. This is a second marriage for both, and they've been together for only twelve years, so they are relatively lovey-dovey, despite their age and stage of life. Her two children are grown and flown, as are his three children, and they have three grandchildren between them. Their stately house, with five bedrooms and baths, is well maintained, expansive, and empty of offspring.

"My husband just opened his eighth office, and that's good for him, because he needs to be busy every second," Margie says. "If he's not busy, he'll ask me, 'What are we doing next?'"

Not so long ago, Margie was feeling overwhelmed, by the huge house, by her demanding job, and by her husband's constant need for attention, which included a nightly request for sexual activity of one kind or another.

Margie couldn't cope, especially with the sex part.

"I was exhausted because I was working all the time. I'd come home and fall asleep every night at nine o'clock. He wanted me to come home from work and talk to him about his day, and massage his shoulders, and give him sympathy and support, and then, maybe, a blow job," she says with a shake of her artfully dyed blond hair and a honking laugh.

One day, it all became too much, and because she was so fond of him, she burst out with an ultimatum, one that came more from her heart than her head. "You can have a working wife or you can have a concubine, but you can't have both! Which one do you want?" she asked.

Margie posed this choice to her loving husband, a man who could easily afford to support the family in their already affluent lifestyle. She looked him in the eye and he returned her gaze.

There was a long and very pregnant pause. Finally Rick answered, with conviction, "I want the concubine."

He was not joking. So Margie took him at his word.

"I'm retired now, and I just do a little tutoring on the side," Margie says. She considers herself a well-educated, well-aged, and fairly sophisticated concubine, albeit a postmenopausal one.

Unlike, say, a still-fertile woman in her thirties with an adequate supply of estrogen, Margie needs some pharmaceutical aids to get her through her almost daily sexual calisthenics. She needs vaginal lubricants and massage oils and a daily sex pep talk. That's easy, though, since Margie adores her husband, and still feels a deep and thrilling sexual attraction to him. Now that she no longer has to be at work by seven a.m., she has the energy to go out with him at night, to travel to Florida on weekends with him, and to play golf and tennis whenever the mood strikes him. And now that she's somewhat of a professional concubine, she looks forward to their daily sexual activities.

Whenever Margie is feeling "wrinkly or saggy," as she puts it, she gets a little pick-me-up in the form of Restylane, a "dermal filler that restores volume and fullness to the skin," as the manufacturer describes the age-defying drug. Restylane gives Margie that youthful-though-inexpressive face valued by so many Hollywood wives and no-longer-young starlets. Her face does look eerily youthy, certainly a plus for a married, postmenopausal California concubine.

Margie has made her concubine bed, and now she's happy to be sleeping in it.

I tell you the Margie story not to convince you to run out for some Restylane and Rick, but to make you aware that she is the exception to the rule. **Most of us do not, as we age, become even more gorgeous, sexual creatures** whose husbands worship the bed we sleep in. Instead, many of us are tossing and turning in those beds, sweating up a storm at night and cursing our inability to fall asleep, while frantically trying to remember something we were supposed to do that we just can't . . . uh, remember.

Margie is an outlier, and her story is entertaining precisely because she's so *unusual*. Much more typical of female sexuality in midlife is the quiet battle between two powerful and opposing forces, a kind of Star Wars for ladies of a certain age. There is the Dark Side of menopause and biology, a Darth Vader creature of midlife that robs women of estrogen, along with some of their sex drive and desire. And there is the Force of Freedom, which includes being in a stage of life that encourages sexual spontaneity and household nudity once the children are gone.

In this bad news/good news scenario, you can take your pick about which side will win out in the end. On the Dark Side, declining estrogen levels can erode a woman's sensuality and allure. But if the Force is with you, a middle-aged woman and her partner can enjoy a degree of sexual privacy and freedom that they haven't had since before their now-gone teenagers were born. She may even have the luxury of indulging her sexual fantasies, if she can remember what they are.

A friend with two sons in college says she's thrilled that she no longer has to guard her privacy by shutting her bedroom and bathroom doors. She can walk around the house naked, and so can her husband, and they don't have to worry about who will walk in or who will overhear them or who will interrupt them.

She sums up this newfound sense of sexual emancipation with a simple but striking image: "All my doors are open," she says.

She means that literally, but also figuratively, since some of the sexual constraints she felt about making too much noise or being spontaneously sexual are gone with the wind. Or, rather, gone with the children who caused them in the first place.

The Midlife Facts of Life

The bad sex news might be somewhat distressing information for baby boomers, many of whom prefer to think of themselves as forever young and eternally sexy. Members of the boom generation are inclined to deny biological destiny; or at least, we like to think that we can fight it and shape it to our wishes in ways that our mothers never dreamed of doing. We long to believe that we are the exceptions to every rule, that while signs of aging or sexual slippage may have happened to our grandparents and to our parents, we will be able to avoid this fate, because we are special. We are different—a generation of Peter Pans—and we refuse to grow old, in spirit, if not in body.

Our denial of aging works well, at least in part. Our need to feel and look great in midlife has given the world sophisticated forms of cosmetic surgery and Botox injections and hormone therapy and erectile-dysfunction pills. Still, inexorable sexual changes come to all women, with both menopause and aging, whether they accept the fact or not. And although hormone treatments can stave off this transformation, it eventually happens to all of us, sooner or later.

Let's talk about sex after the children leave, the midlife facts of life, if you wish. It's news that your mother certainly never told you, and it's probably news that you haven't read much about, either. The news isn't necessarily bad, it's just a fact, the same as getting your period at the age of thirteen or being in great pain during childbirth or gaining weight after your fortieth birthday. This is biology, so there's no use trying to deny it. It's better, in fact, to confront your biological destiny and learn to deal with it, and perhaps to try to bargain with it a bit.

The midlife sex news is this: **women's sexual desire and sexual pleasure decline with age.**

There is no way to prettify or qualify or hem-and-hawify your way out of this truth.

Having sex and enjoying it gets more difficult for women as they grow older. And, by the way, the same is true for men. Some experts haggle about the reasons for this sexual decline: it's due to the changes wrought by menopause, according to some; others say that it is due to aging. But almost all agree that it happens.

Some wives are adamant that by the time they hit fifty or fifty-five, their sexual spark is mostly gone. It makes them sad, and a bit wistful, but they feel helpless to reignite it.

"I feel heavier than ever, and I certainly don't feel sexier than ever," sighs Danielle, a free spirit with an ex-hippie air who looks a bit like an over-the-hill cheerleader. "I spend a lot of time in front of my mirror, and I don't really like what I see there. My hair looks like shit, because I had it straightened and I don't know how to fix it," she says. "My husband and I have sex less often, and it used to be more exciting than it is. And more frequent. But sex is just not on my mind anymore," Danielle says.

She admits, though, that when a thirty-something guy tried to pick her up at a nearby Home Depot a few months ago, she was completely flattered. "He came up to me and said, 'I'm a sucker for a girl in a cowboy hat. Will you have a drink with me?'" she reports. That was a cheap thrill, but it boosted her spirits for the whole day.

Danielle's friend, Angela, fifty-six, laughs and agrees that she, too, felt the same way when a guy followed her from a gas station to her office and asked her out for a drink, even though he was pretty sleazy looking. "I told him I couldn't, because I was married, and he said, 'So am I,'" Angela says, with a shudder of disgust.

Most of the time, though, Angela agrees with Danielle about her lack of sex appeal. "I feel much less sexy than I used to. I think I look nice, and I like to get dressed up. But I used to think about sex all the time, and now I hardly ever do. When I was in my thirties and forties, I always tried to think of ways to be sexy for my husband, Nate. Now, if I go to bed and Nate is already asleep, I'm just so glad!"

Angela's friends echo this feeling, all of them agreeing that when their husband turns over to go to sleep right away, they breathe a secret sigh of relief.

"I say, 'Whew!'" Angela exclaims.

It's this Whew Factor, the no-sex-tonight feeling of relief, that many midlife women can't ignore or hide. It makes them sad, but they also feel that it's inevitable.

"Aging can certainly impact sexual function for both men and women, because desire or sex drive declines as a function of age and changing hormones," explains clinical psychologist Sheryl Kingsberg in a telephone interview. Kingsberg is an associate professor in reproductive biology at Case Western Reserve University School of Medicine in Cleveland, Ohio.

But sexual desire "also changes as a result of where you are in a relationship. If you're in a brand-new relationship, then your desire will be higher, regardless of how old you are," notes Kingsberg, who studies female sexual dysfunction. When it comes to sex, she says, "there's a big difference between the age of the person and the age of the relationship."[2]

Here's one way to think about it:

Midlife Woman + Long-Term Relationship = Less Sexual Desire

Midlife Woman + New Relationship = More Sexual Desire

In a nutshell, then, wives who have been married for a while have to work harder at maintaining their sexual desire than do single or divorced women with brand-new lovers. It seems to be a potent argument for infidelity, or for serial love affairs, or for late-life remarriage, at least if sex is a priority.

At forty-seven, Gae is a perfect example of a wife who has been sexually recharged by a new relationship. Now in a six-year-old second marriage, Gae refers to her truck-driver husband as "the greatest man on earth. Sometimes I can't believe that life has treated me so well as to bring him into my life." But she doesn't stop there; more gushing follows. "He is everything I ever wanted, dreamed of, but thought I would never experience in a relationship," Gae says. "He brought back adventure and excitement into my life, and I can't imagine how I managed all those years before I met him!"

To put this enthusiasm in perspective, Gae and her husband, who live in Kansas City, have twelve children from both marriages, ranging in age from seventeen to twenty-seven (hers), and twenty-eight to thirty-seven (his), and she says her life had always focused on her children and their lives. Since she remarried, though, she has learned to stop thinking of herself as "so-and-so's mom," and begun to see herself as the adventurous, fun, sex-loving young woman she used to be.

What Gae doesn't realize, perhaps, is that her libido is getting recharged by the novelty of her new love. And because she hasn't hit menopause yet, she hasn't felt the sexual repercussions of reduced estrogen levels.

Almost all women change sexually after the change, at least in terms of their biologically driven levels of desire, according to Kingsberg. This is practically predetermined, she says, since low estrogen levels almost always mean a diminished sex drive.

Still—and here's the good news that qualifies the estrogen let-down—for women, sex is about a lot more than just hormones. Sex, for women, is also about thinking about sex. When it comes to women's sexual enjoyment and pleasure, then, the sensation is not driven just by biology, but by psychology as well. **So it's not just Sex = Hormones, it's also Sex = Emotions.**

After the age of fifty, women's approach to sex is pretty much the same as it was before, just somewhat diminished by biology, agrees Lorraine Dennerstein, an Australian psychologist who has been studying the effect of menopause on women for several decades. Dennerstein says that a woman who has always had a rousing sexual appetite will remain sexually enthused after the change, though she may find that her urges are somewhat subdued. In addition, postmenopausal women's sex lives are also ruled by the presence of a partner and how they feel about that partner. Those without a partner don't have sex, but women who feel affection and attraction for their mates will retain a healthy sex drive, although one that may be slightly diminished.

Thus, women who have always had active and satisfying sex lives, with partners they love, will still feel that way after menopause. It's just that their sexual desire may wane, and they may take a lot longer to achieve orgasm.[3]

A Time of Less

For almost all women in midlife, when it comes to sex, this is a Time of Less. And by this I don't mean that less is more, but that less is simply less.

Here are four ways to describe women's Sexual Time of Less:

Less sex. Sexual activity declines with age. To put it another way, as we age, we do it less. As women and men grow older, on average, they tend to have sexual intercourse less often. This is true in every developed country in which experts have conducted large national studies on sexual behavior, including the United States, Canada, Great Britain, and France.[4]

In a vast study of twenty thousand Americans between the ages of eighteen and fifty-nine, for example, sociologists concluded that age plays a major role in how often adults have sex. Up to the age of forty or so, between 40 and 50 percent of women have sex at least twice a week. But among women in their early fifties, just 20 percent make love as often; among women in their late fifties, only 7 percent have intercourse more than twice a week.

This doesn't mean that women stop having sex, that they go cold turkey once they reach a certain age, the way that most teenagers and young adults assume. It's true that greater proportions of women become sexually inactive as they age: about four in ten women in their late fifties have had no sex at all during the previous year. But that's not necessarily their choice, since women tend to lose sexual partners as they age, due to divorce or death or erectile dysfunction.[5] Although the last is a male problem, it also afflicts the women who love them. When their tango partner can no longer dance, women tend to quit the tango, so to speak.

Kelly, a forty-nine-year-old wife in Springfield, Massachusetts, tells me that she has rediscovered her sexual desire now that her three children are finally gone, but her second husband has lost his desire almost completely. They've been married only two years, she says, which would normally mean that their sex life should blossom like a giant fireworks display. But since Kelly's husband returned from Iraq, where he served with the National Guard, he's had no interest in sex, which leaves her feeling somewhat desperate, she says. She has also become depressed and unhappy, she adds.

Both women and men have sex less often as they get older, and especially when they are getting older together. One way to avoid this problem, as some wealthy and famous men have discovered, is to find a sexual partner who is much younger. That way, the older man joins the younger man sexual-frequency bracket. The same is true, of course, for women who find younger sexual partners. One forty-six-year-old woman from Texas whose twins left home this year explains that her second husband is ten years younger than she is. The two of them, she says, "are looking at each other in a new way, and getting frisky again." She hasn't started menopause yet, so she may have enough estrogen left for high-level friskiness, but surely having a younger man in the sack doesn't hurt either!

Less aroused. Older women have fewer orgasms and fewer sexual fantasies than younger women, according to experts. By implication, then, their interest in sex is also diminished. When researchers asked some one thousand women over the age of twenty how often they think about sex, they find that half of those under thirty-five think of it almost every day, compared to just 23 percent of women over the age of fifty.[6]

For many women thinking about enjoying sex is a large part of actually enjoying the sex, so it's no wonder that older women have more difficulty becoming aroused. Sexual pleasure for women, as I've said, is as much a mental exercise as it is a physical one. About 15 percent of women over the age of forty say that sex is simply not pleasurable, which means that they are not at all aroused sexually.[7]

"I didn't think this was possible, but when I was in my forties, every so often I'd dream that I was having an orgasm, and I'd wake up and it would be true," says Alexandra, now fifty-seven. "But that hasn't happened to me for years, and it makes me sad to think it might never happen again," she adds.

Less lubrication. One of the main reasons that women in midlife may have difficulty becoming aroused is that their lubrication system conks out. Before menopause, any kind of foreplay tends to induce vaginal secretions almost automatically. This lubrication is what greases the sexual wheels for intercourse; it's what makes the whole thing feel good. No lubrication means difficult sex, or even painful sex, which often means less pleasure. The lack of lubrication is due almost entirely to the gradual loss of estrogen. Not only that, but the decline in estrogen also causes a woman's vaginal walls to become thin and inelastic, which means the vagina doesn't stretch as easily during intercourse or during childbirth, either, but that becomes rather beside the point. The vagina itself even shrinks, becoming shorter and less wide, meaning that it can no longer accommodate large objects.

This process is the female body's way of saying it can no longer procreate, so it's shutting down all related systems. As we watch this happen, some of us are yelling, "Wait, wait, we don't want any more babies, but we still want to enjoy sexxxxxxx! Waitttttt!!"

Unfortunately, protesting the change doesn't make much of a difference.

Indeed, a significant minority of midlife women complain about a lack of lubrication during intercourse, according to research. Anywhere between 12 and 31 percent of midlife women suffer from the problem, according to one study. Another study claims that between 16 and 25 percent of women complain of vaginal dryness, and a third reveals that 30 percent of women between the ages of forty and sixty say they suffer from a lack of lubrication.[8]

Lack of lubrication wouldn't be so terrible if it didn't lead to yet another sexual problem, this one a doozy of a pleasure killer. Without natural lubrication, many women find that intercourse is painful. The condition even has an intimidating name: dyspareunia. Again, when researchers question midlife women about pain during intercourse, they find that between 15 and 20 percent cite dyspareunia as a real problem, even if they can't say or spell the word. All they know is that it hurts.[9]

Baby-boom women who have a loving sexual partner will not let a bit of pain or dryness stop them from having sex, however. That's why they buy all kinds of jellies and creams and artificial lubricants to help ease change-of-life insertion problems. They also use estrogen-filled pills and creams that can be inserted vaginally, which trick a woman's sexual organs into believing that she is still premenopausal. This is the method of choice for many women who have become reluctant to take larger doses of hormonal supplements in pill form. In fact, research shows that urogenital atrophy, the shrinking and drying up of a woman's private parts, is dramatically reversed by estrogen supplements, taken either orally or vaginally.[10]

One empty-nest mother from Oregon tells me that she began to dread having sex with her husband of twenty-five years, not because she was sick of him, but because she couldn't face one more painful attempt at intercourse. She tried several different lubricants and creams, and kept three bottles of the stuff in her bedside drawer, but none seemed to reduce the pain and burning she felt. Finally, she asked her gynecologist for a solution and was given a prescription for a pill laced with tiny amounts of estrogen, called Vagifem, to be inserted vaginally, once a day for two weeks, and then a few times a week after that. The change, she says, was dramatic.

"I was much more aroused and I didn't need the K-Y jelly for the first time in years. It was really amazing, especially because I didn't feel pain during intercourse anymore, which had become so embarrassing that I didn't want to tell my husband about it," she says. As a matter of fact, she figures that she might never stop using those teeny pills, so long as she has a shot at some kind of sex life with her husband. "At least as long as his parts are still functioning," she says with a laugh.

Less partners. Through no fault of their own, more midlife women who used to be sexually active find themselves without a partner, or without a sexually capable partner. This cramps their sexual style, at least the kind that doesn't involve solitary activity. When researchers ask women who've had no sex in the prior year why that's so, about two-thirds say either it's because they have no partner or because their partner has erectile problems.[11] It takes two to have sexual intercourse, and very often it's the woman who is ready and able, but not her partner.

Indeed, although men don't suffer from menopause—despite the name, which makes it sound as if they should—the proportion who have trouble becoming erect grows larger as they age. That's not only a pun, it's the simple truth. Some studies estimate that four in ten men have some trouble becoming erect by the time they reach the age of forty, and two out of three have erectile troubles by age seventy.[12]

This reminds me of one of my favorite birthday cards, given to me by my running friends. Seven of us have been running together on weekends, on and off, for almost twenty years. We're slower now, and a few of us are suffering from knee or hip pain, but most of us continue to slog on, and we still insist that it's called "running," even if many observers might call it "walking." Anyway, the card shows an older couple in front of a birthday cake. The wife is blowing out the candles, while the geezer husband asks, "Did you wish you were young and sexy again?"

Open the card, and she answers him. "No, I wished YOU were."

Am I Normal?

In any discussion of sex—whether it's about young singles or harassed new mothers or middle-aged empty nesters—sooner or later, most people really want to know just one thing.

Am I normal?

They want to know if what they do and think and feel about sex is what everybody else is doing and thinking and feeling about sex. One other thing they want to know, too, is if everybody else is doing it more often and having more fun.

What most people don't realize, though, is that **when it comes to sex, there is no such thing as normal.**

Normal sexual behavior ranges the gamut, from the thirty-two-year-old man who has never had sex to the sixty-year-old fellow who has been in love 131 times; from the sixteen-year-old girl who has been pregnant twice to the fifty-year-old woman who has never had an orgasm. And everybody in between.

In the last few decades, we have learned more about sexual behavior than in all the previous millennia combined, thanks to dozens and dozens of large studies on the topic conducted all over the world. From this research, we have gleaned odd nuggets of sexual information, like the fact that educated women and men masturbate more often than the less educated. Or that Americans born after about 1950 are more likely to have engaged in oral sex, both giving and receiving, than those who were born before 1950. Or that 4 percent of American men and 3 percent of American women have never had intercourse.[13]

Still, this doesn't help answer the "Am I normal?" question.

The problem, however, is that there really is no good answer.

"There's a huge range of variation in women's sexuality," says Kingsberg, and experts refuse to call anything wrong or abnormal unless it causes women to feel distress.

"It's important for women to know, for example, that having an orgasm with intercourse is not what happens for the majority of women. They should also know that there's a huge range in what is normal, so if they are talking to their friends or to their sisters or mothers, God forbid, they shouldn't say to themselves, 'If I'm not experiencing sex the way she is, then there's something wrong with me.' Because that simply isn't true," Kingsberg tells me in a telephone interview. "We know that women are situationally orgasmic, which means that under certain circumstances, they will have reliable orgasms, whether it's with oral sex or manual stimulation or a vibrator or something else," she goes on. "Intercourse is usually not one of the most reliable ways to have orgasm."

Unlike men, who almost always reach orgasm once they are aroused, "I don't expect one hundred percent of women to reach orgasm after they are aroused, so I don't have a good definition of normal. There's an infinite variety of sexual responses that would be considered normal and not dysfunctional," Kingsberg says.

There is also no way to define "normal" sex because experts don't agree on what constitutes a sexual dysfunction. So nobody quite knows what it is, exactly, that makes a sexual problem a problem. Men have erectile dysfunction, of course, and women suffer from an inability to achieve orgasm. But what also matters is how much, if at all, these difficulties bother those who suffer from them. Researchers refer to this feeling as "sexual distress," which means that a person is worried or anxious about a sexual dilemma, whatever it may be.

"We don't consider anything a sexual dysfunction unless a woman is distressed about it," says Kingsberg. "If a woman doesn't have much desire, and having sex once every six months is perfectly fine for her, and she's happy with that, we wouldn't diagnose her with dysfunction," she says. But for another woman, such a relatively sexless situation would be terribly distressing and upsetting. In her case, then, it would be considered a dysfunction, Kingsberg points out.

But take a different example. Let's say a woman finds intercourse painful, but she enjoys being sexual and doesn't want to give it up. So she and her partner decide to substitute oral sex or mutual masturbation for intercourse. Voilà, she has no distress, and therefore no dysfunction.

Or let's say a woman has little interest in sex because she rarely achieves orgasm. In addition, her partner has difficulty maintaining an erection. So they don't bother having sex. Voilà, again, no distress and no dysfunction, although both have sexual problems. Finally, a woman I know tells me that her husband has always had a problem with premature ejaculation. But that doesn't bother her now because she's having vaginal dryness and some pain during intercourse. They're a perfect match, precisely because they have beautifully synchronized sexual problems. He doesn't stay erect very long, and she doesn't want him to!

Here's a different example of potential sexual dysfunction. A fifty-year-old wife has intercourse twice a week, which is fairly typical for a woman her age. But what if she's longing to have sex every day, all week long, and her partner is unwilling to do so? She may be sexually distressed, and could even be considered dysfunctional, although she has a comparatively active sex life.

When it comes to sex, then, everything is relative. The proportion of women who are classified as sexually dysfunctional depends on how you define dysfunctional. By one such definition, for instance, about four in ten women between the ages of eighteen and fifty-nine are sexually dysfunctional because they say they have at least one of the following problems. By this definition, about three in ten men in that age range have a similar problem.[14] Here are the seven major sexual-dysfunction issues used in some of this research:

During the past twelve months, did you feel any of the following?
1. A lack of desire for sex
2. Difficulty becoming aroused
3. An inability to climax
4. Anxiety about your performance
5. That you climaxed too quickly
6. Pain during intercourse
7. That sex wasn't pleasurable

By this definition, then, a woman can be dysfunctional for not wanting sex or for being unable to orgasm or for being worried about it or for doing it too quickly, although that's mostly a male problem. These definitions are fairly broad, so they don't pass muster among many experts, some of whom insist that you have to ask women if they actually consider any of these issues to be problems before you term them dysfunctional.

Kingsberg is one expert who rejects this definition of sexual dysfunction as meaningless. "These definitions rely on women's self-report, and they aren't based on any kind of professional diagnosis," she says. So don't take them too seriously.

In fact, she explains, there are really **six types of sexual dysfunction** for women, as defined by the medical profession, and they can be identified only by a physician. They are:

- **Hypoactive sexual desire disorder,** or low sexual desire
- **Arousal disorder,** which is having sexual desire but an inability to feel aroused, as if the body isn't responding to the signals the mind is sending; this is "very common in peri- and postmenopausal women, because there's less lubrication, less sensitivity, and less genital swelling," says Kingsberg
- **Sexual aversion disorder,** which is a phobia about sex resulting in avoidance of it, combined with panic attacks or extreme anxiety about sex
- **Anorgasmia,** an inability to achieve orgasm most of the time
- **Vaginismus,** recurrent or persistent involuntary spasms of the vaginal muscles that interfere with sexual intercourse
- **Dyspareunia,** or pain during intercourse[15]

If we use a much simpler definition of sexual dysfunction—any sexual problem that makes a woman unhappy—then slightly more than two in ten women are sexually distressed, according to several other sex researchers. Thus, **a woman's feelings about sex matter more than her sexual behavior.** Such researchers say that as women age, they find themselves less interested in sex than when they were younger, but this doesn't necessarily bother them all that much.

In one study, researchers asked women a standard list of questions about how often the women had sex, how enjoyable it was, how much the women fantasized about sex, and how sexually attractive the women felt. But they also asked, "How much distress or worry has your sexual relationship caused you during the past four weeks?" and "How much distress or worry has your own sexuality caused you?" If the answers to such questions were "slight" or "none," these researchers say, then sexual problems don't matter. Four in ten women between the ages of twenty and sixty-five had no such distress at all, they found, and three in ten felt slight distress. That leaves three in ten who felt a lot of sexual distress.[16]

Such women—those who suffer over their sexuality—also experience other kinds of emotional woes. They tend to be depressed, to have physical ailments and troubles, to be less educated, and to have troubled relationships with their partners, as well. So sexual distress is very often just one part of an overall package of unhappiness and misery and worry.

Finally, and oddly enough, it's quite normal for women to report a lack of interest in sex, which turns out to be a lifelong issue, according to just about every sex study ever done. About one in three women of all ages says that she has little or no interest in sex, research shows. In my Web survey of empty-nest mothers, too, I find that 34 percent say they have noticed a loss of sexual desire in the past two years.

But one in ten women in my Web survey says she's noticed an increase in sexual desire, so it's possible for the pendulum to swing both ways. Still, it tends to swing more toward the minus side of desire than toward the plus side.

In one large study of women over the age of forty, for example, four in ten women reported a low frequency of sexual desire, even though twice that number, eight in ten, were having sex on a regular basis.[17]

So how do most midlife women feel, sexually speaking? **Midlife women are slightly less interested in sex than before, but they enjoy what's left of it.**

It's also quite common for women to struggle to achieve orgasm, especially younger women. By some estimates, about one in four women has trouble climaxing, and surprisingly, the problem is worst for the youngest women. In a large national study of American sexuality, researchers find that one-quarter of women under forty are unable to reach orgasm, but slightly fewer women over the age of forty are, about 20 percent. That's partly because achieving orgasm, for women, is something that needs to be learned.[18]

Reaching orgasm is just one small part of sexual desire, which is also a longing and aching to become one with a beloved. Indeed, sexual desire is one of the most complicated and mysterious emotions with which human beings have been blessed.

In fact, **sexual desire is composed of three parts,** like a cake with three layers, or a sundae made of ice cream and fudge sauce and whipped cream with a cherry on top.

First, there's **the biological aspect of desire,** which is fueled by hormones and is an inexorable part of the human need for procreation. That's the estrogen and testosterone and all of the other body chemicals that propel the human instinct to Reproduce Right Now.

Second, there's **the social aspect of desire,** which is what we believe is acceptable to desire sexually, in our culture and in our time. A few of the "sexual shoulds" in twenty-first-century America include: You should desire your partner; you should not desire the young guy who lives down the street. You should desire your partner; you should not desire your best friend's husband. You should desire your partner; you can also desire Brad Pitt or George Clooney, but only from afar. If you are divorced or single, you should desire any reasonable man who offers, even more so if he is younger than you.

"If you believe that sex is appropriate and healthy, then when your kids leave home you can have a nice resurgence of sexual interest," Kingsberg points out. "That's because you can have sex anywhere, any place, any time, and you don't have to worry about privacy." On the other hand, she says that if you believe that you are too old for desire of the sexual sort, then your desire will follow your belief, and it will vanish in a puff of smoke. "So age can increase or decrease your desire, depending on your beliefs and values," she tells me.

Take note, because once again, the evidence shows that sexual desire is mostly all in your mind!

Finally, there is **the psychological aspect of sexual desire,** a willingness to be sexual, which is so crucial for women. We have a deep need to feel loved and wanted, and if we feel that way, our lover automatically becomes an object of our passionate desire. While we might fawn over half-naked photographs of New York City firefighters or Chippendales dancers, what we really want is a less-than-hunky guy who will love and adore us, even as our chin sags and our belly protrudes.

"If you're not happy in your relationship, or you are bored, or if you haven't put the effort into maintaining a long-term bond," your sex life will suffer accordingly, says Kingsberg. "You can have all the sex drive in the world, but if you are not happy with your particular partner, you're not going to want to be sexual," she explains. "On the other hand, even if much of your biologic urge is gone, with good connection and other motivators, sex can be really nice."

Or if you are single and you find a new partner, the freshly minted sex can be more than nice; it can be superb.

Maybe that's why *Heading South,* a French movie released in 2006, caused such a sensation among women in their fifties and sixties. The film is set in the 1970s and centers on a group of ladies who vacation at a resort in Haiti, where they hook up with young native boys for randy sexual escapades. The central character, played by sixty-year-old French siren Charlotte Rampling, confesses that "I always told myself that when I'm old, I'd pay young men to love me." But, she continues, "I just didn't think it would happen so fast."

What's even more astonishing than the older-lady-as-sexual-predator plot is the sensation it caused among female moviegoers. A *New York Times* story on the phenomenon was titled "Libidos of a Certain Age" and described the hordes of midlife women who were desperate to see some of their own kind having lots of wild and crazy sex.[19]

Assessing Sex

Researchers figure out how women feel about sex in two ways: they measure by observing actual behavior and they measure by asking.

Some physicians have figured out how to calibrate vaginal and uterine contractions during orgasm, which they use to calculate orgasmic satisfaction. They also study brain activity and skin flushes during orgasm. Others have taken morning blood and urine samples from women, to test for hormone levels. They even developed an objective measure of vaginal atrophy, to figure out how flaccid, thin, or dry the vagina is.

Sex experts have also learned how to ask very detailed and intimate questions about sexuality. When this is done properly, people will offer incredibly honest and accurate answers to all sorts of questions about sexual practices and attitudes and behavior. This is not the kind of survey you could do in, say, Saudi Arabia or Afghanistan, but it works quite well in some of the more open and egalitarian countries, like the United States, Great Britain, Canada, and Australia, for example.

Here are just a few of the questions that researchers have asked in one large research study of Americans' sexual habits:[20]

- ❖ How many times did you have sex with your partner in the last twelve months?
- ❖ When you had sex with your partner, how often did he/she perform oral sex on you?
- ❖ When you and your partner had sex during the past twelve months, did you always, usually, sometimes, rarely, or never have an orgasm—that is, come or come to climax?
- ❖ As far as you know, during the past twelve months has your partner had other sexual partners? If so, were these partners all men, all women, or both?
- ❖ Other than the person you just told me about, who else did you have sex with most recently?
- ❖ Thinking back, since your eighteenth birthday, and during the time before you started living with your partner, how many people, including men and women, did you have sex with, even if only one time?
- ❖ On a scale of 1 to 4, where 1 is very appealing and 4 is not at all appealing, how would you rate each of these activities:
  - ✦ Having sex with more than one person at the same time
  - ✦ Having sex with someone of the same sex
  - ✦ Forcing someone to do something sexual that he/she doesn't want to do

- Being forced into doing something sexual that you don't
  want to do
- Seeing other people doing sexual things
- Having sex with someone you don't personally know

❖ In the last twelve months, did you:
  - Go to nightclubs with nude or seminude dancers?
  - Get a professional massage?
  - Hire a prostitute or pay anyone to have sex with you?
  - Attend a public gathering in which you were nude?
  - Have your picture taken in the nude?

You get the idea: they ask about anything and everything you could imagine, and then a few things you can't. Trained interviewers ask some of these questions in person, face-to-face with the person they are quizzing. Sometimes, though, they ask such questions over the telephone, using a human interviewer or a computer-assisted program. They might also pose such questions in writing, using mail-in surveys. What's most amazing, though, is how willing women and men are to answer such incredibly personal questions about their sexuality. In a way, I think, people find it flattering that scientists are fascinated by what they do and think about sex. So they tell all, and then they tell more than all.

Psychologists have also developed many ways to measure sexual desire, some more successful than others. They devise "sexual desire scales," comprising a series of questions, some with only a few, others that include as many as thirty-six. Here's my version.

THE SEXUAL DESIRE TEST

1. How sexually attractive have you felt recently?
   1. Not at all   2. Somewhat   3. A lot   4. Very
2. How sexually attractive is your partner to you?
   1. Not at all   2. Somewhat   3. A lot   4. Very
3. During the past four weeks, how often did you think about sex with interest or desire, such as having daydreams or fantasies?
   1. Not at all   2. A few times   3. Several times a week
   4. Almost daily

4. How many times during the past four weeks have you masturbated on your own?
   1. Not at all   2. A few times   3. Several times a week
   4. Almost daily

5. How often during sex do you feel aroused or excited?
   1. Not at all   2. Somewhat   3. A lot   4. Very often

6. How often do you enjoy sex?
   1. Not at all   2. Somewhat   3. A lot   4. Very often

7. Over the past four weeks, about how many times have you engaged in sexual activity that led to intercourse?
   1. Not at all   2. A few times   3. Several times a week
   4. Almost daily

8. Over the past four weeks, about how many times have you engaged in sexual activity not leading to intercourse?
   1. Not at all   2. A few times   3. Several times a week
   4. Almost daily

9. When you had sexual activity with your partner, how many times did you experience an orgasm?
   1. Not at all   2. A few times   3. Several times
   4. Almost every time

10. How satisfied are you with how often you have sex?
    1. Not at all   2. Somewhat   3. A lot   4. Very

11. In the past four weeks, how often did you find that your vagina was uncomfortably dry during intercourse?
    1. Almost every time   2. Several times   3. A few times
    4. Not at all

12. In the past four weeks, how often did you feel pain during intercourse?
    1. Almost every time   2. Several times   3. A few times
    4. Not at all

Your score should range between 12, if you answered all 1s, to 48, if you answered all 4s. A score lower than 16 means that you probably have a relatively low level of sexual desire. If your score falls between 16 and 32, you have middling desire. If you scored 33 or higher, your level of sexual desire is among the highest, for women of any age.

What's Your Sex Type?

This do-it-yourself Sexual Desire Test is a quick and easy way for women to begin to think about where they fall on the sexual ladder of desire. Are you up at the top, thrilled to be still at your peak? Are you somewhere in the middle, content to be there or upset by your slippage? Or are you down on a bottom rung, sexed out and sad about it? Or perhaps you're down there, but pleased to have the excuse of menopause and painful intercourse to be done with sex, something you never had much use for in the first place.

There are two crucial facets of sexuality to consider: there's a woman's level of sexual desire, which can be high or medium or low, but there are also her feelings about that desire. Does she view whatever desire she has as a good thing or a bad thing? That's really something only she can judge, and she'll have to look deep into her heart to figure it out. So it's possible that you can feel great about being very sexual, but you might also feel great about being not very sexual. Likewise, being sexual could make you miserable, but so could not being sexual. The mysteries of a woman's heart, and her sexuality, are myriad.

A midlife woman's level of sexual desire is also, of course, a mirror of her marriage, reflecting what's good and bad about that union. After all, sex and marriage go together like an SUV and low gas mileage, but only sometimes. A satisfying sex life is usually accompanied by a good marriage, and a lousy sex life usually implies a not-so-great marriage. In addition, research shows that women who have sex more often, and achieve orgasm more frequently, also tend to be happier than women who rarely have sex and who rarely enjoy it, either.[21]

Here's what my Web survey shows about empty-nest sex. I find that once children leave home, mothers tend to fall into one of three sex types, according to how often they have sex and how much sexual pleasure they feel.

Are You a Sex Bunny?

Since your children left home, how has your sex life changed? Is it better, the same, or worse?

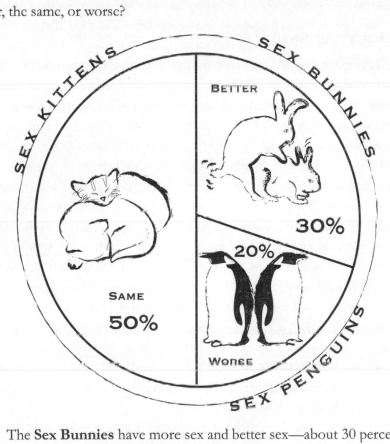

The **Sex Bunnies** have more sex and better sex—about 30 percent of mothers fall into this category. The **Sex Kittens,** about 50 percent of empty-nest moms, say that they have about the same amount of sex as before and they enjoy it as much. Finally, the **Sex Penguins,** about 20 percent of women, are those who have sex less often and find that it is less satisfying than it used to be.

Sex Bunnies

For a happy minority of moms, about 30 percent, sex life actually improves once the children leave home. They say they have sex more often and actually enjoy it more.

There's a chicken-and-egg issue for such women, though. Research shows that women who have sex more often, and who have more frequent orgasms, rate their satisfaction with sex much higher.[22] So the question becomes: does doing it more and doing it better make them happier, or do they do it more and better because they are already happy? There's no way to really know which comes first, the great happiness or the great sex.

But, then, does it really matter?

What's most striking, though, is that single mothers, and those who are divorced, separated, or widowed, are more likely to have more and better sex once the children leave home. They leave wives in the dust when it comes to having a fulfilling sex life. Fully half of single moms have sex more often once the children leave, more than twice the number of married moms. It's as if they've let loose the bonds of well-behaved, unsexy momhood and taken up where they left off when they were young and sensual and single.

Take Barbara, who has been a divorcée for fifteen years and feels mostly relief now that her only child, a son, is gone. "This is my time," she crows. "I feel younger, happier, and sexier than ever before, and I intend to enjoy it!" She's dating whomever she wants, when she wants—mostly men she meets at her gym or at the classes she takes at a local community college. The fact that her son is no longer around to judge her or feel threatened by the other men in her life, she says, is amazingly, unbelievably liberating.

Sex Bunny wives have a similar approach to their child-free sex lives, though their partners may be the same old guy.

Jacklyn, fifty, has been married to Jim for several decades, but now that her two sons are gone, she, too, is a Sex Bunny. She had a hysterectomy at the age of thirty-three, and suffered from surgical menopause, usually a massive roadblock to a great sex life.

But no, she and Jim feel "like we are on our second honeymoon. We come and go as we please, and we never have to worry about being walked in on when we are making love. We can wear as little as we want, or nothing, around the house, and no one cares," she says. Most nights, "I wear sexy lingerie or nothing at all to bed, and that makes me feel twenty-three all over again."

This Sex Bunny confesses that when she and Jim are lying on the couch, watching television, "if the mood strikes us, we start to make out like kids. My husband cops a feel or two, and if we choose to go further, we don't have to go to our room and shut the door."

It's only now that she and her husband have turned up the heat on their sex life, Jacklyn says, that she realizes "how much I put the children first, before Jim, without even realizing it. And he never complained about it, either."

Jacklyn's story is unusual because of her surgical history. In comparing women who reached menopause through surgery, during their forties or fifties, or earlier, during their thirties, researchers find that those who had surgery when young are most likely to have sexual problems. "When we compare women who had surgical menopause young, with those who had surgical menopause later, and with naturally menopausal women, we find the lowest rates of desire among surgically younger women, especially compared to those who reach menopause naturally," Kingsberg tells me.

So Jacklyn clearly beat the odds.

In addition, like most of the Sex Bunnies I've interviewed, Jacklyn says that there's a lot of nakedness at her house. Sex Bunnies often say that either they, or their husbands, or both, are walking around the house either semidressed or completely naked. Think of all those nude baby-boom bodies wandering around America—it's enough to terrify and gross out an entire generation of their grown children.

Sex Kittens

About half of mothers, a neat and clean 50 percent, are not bragging about how great their new sex lives are. Instead, they are continuing to make love at a level that makes them feel comfortable, regardless of whether the children are there or gone.

Here's how Arlene, fifty, describes her freedom with two children gone, leaving her alone with her husband of twenty-six years in their Atlanta home. "We had a great marriage, and we still do. The biggest difference is being able to show affection without offending the kids.

You know, the 'yuck factor.' We always sit close on the sofa, touching each other," Arlene says. "We did that when the kids were home, and we still do. I think it's important for children to see that their parents love and desire each other, so we let them," Arlene explains. "We never stopped being a couple when we became parents," she adds.

Phyllis is also fifty, and surprised by how little she misses her children. As soon as they left, she says, "my husband and I advanced to being parents of adult children and we made a point of trying not to be too intrusive. We still want to be heard, but we just try not to push." Phyllis and her husband have a good marriage, she says, and once they got over the original shock of having both children gone, they were tickled to be on their own. "We're less worried about making noise. We no longer have to wait until we think the kids are asleep, and that lets us be more spontaneous and free," she says.

Sex Penguins

These mothers, about 20 percent, say that their sex lives are worse now that the children are gone. From what they say, I get the distinct impression that their sexual relationships are as icy as a penguin's home, thus their name. But for many of these women, more than just their sex lives have suffered. They're also more likely to feel depressed and unhappy about their situation, and they tend to struggle because they miss their children so desperately.

Deedee, fifty, is an Oklahoma homemaker whose children, twenty-three and twenty-four, are gone. She's also in the Sex Penguin category. "Being a stay-at-home mom, I thought I did a great job raising my children. But now that they're gone, I'm not so sure. I did everything for them, and now I realize that they are lazy and inconsiderate. So in many ways, I feel like a failure," Deedee says. Not only that, but she says she has sex less often, and enjoys it less than before, too. It's not that surprising, then, that she views life without children at home as "empty and lonely as it can be." That's her feeling, in part, because she and her husband don't get along that well, and they are not particularly loving.

On top of it all, Deedee has financial stress, which is almost always an effective way to ruin sexual pleasure. "Along with paying two tuition bills, and my husband's carpentry business taking a turn for the worse, we argue a lot about money," Deedee says. "I have shingles, and I broke my foot, all in the past six months. I have a lot of anxiety about money and about my children."

Another Sex Penguin, a corporate secretary in Washington, D.C., says that she's often depressed and has trouble sleeping. She and her husband, a city worker, live week to week, she says, and "emotionally, I am drained. I feel I can't break away from my sense that I have no control and that there's nothing worthwhile in my life."

Opening Your Own Doors

It's clear that some empty-nest mothers who are Sex Penguins have mired themselves in misery, of which their sexual freeze is only one small part. In such cases, treatment for depression may be warranted.

For others, too, sex is no longer a big deal. In fact, only about one in three women over the age of forty-five says that sex is important to her quality of life, compared to two out of three men.[23] For some women, then, menopause becomes a great excuse to put sex on the back burner, or to take it off the stove completely. And if hubby is having erection troubles, so much the better. Good-bye sex, hello companionship and friendly hugs.

Does this sound like you or not? You'll have to look into your heart and ask yourself if the current state of your sex life is right for you or not. Does the sex life you have right now make you feel:

- ❖ Happy or sad?
- ❖ Content or upset?
- ❖ Thrilled or uneasy?
- ❖ Blameless or guilty?

If you feel mostly positive about your sex life, then you have nothing to work on. But if the bad outweighs the good, and if that disturbs you, then you might consider trying to work yourself up the Sex Bunny ladder. There are at least eight ways to do so.

Eight Ways to Become a Sex Bunny

Find a new partner. One surefire way to improve your sex life, at least if you are single or divorced, is to find yourself a new partner, preferably a younger one (an impractical suggestion for the still married, of course). Thus, you will tap into the increased desire that comes almost automatically with novelty. And you don't have to feel like a cradle robber, since among single women between the ages of forty and sixty-nine, one in three says she prefers to date younger men, about the same number of single men who say they prefer to date younger women. This is from a study of thirty-five hundred single Americans, about six in ten of whom date on a regular basis.[24]

It's not surprising that women and men fantasize about being with someone younger; after all, most of us were awakened to sexual desire when we were young, as were the partners we yearned to possess. Those powerful, first-time sexual stirrings are buried deep within us, tweaked every so often by the sight of a fresh young face or a well-toned, youthful body. It's not that we're perverse, it's just that we learned sexuality based on images of the young and pretty. Although we may admire and respect older men, we may not be aroused by their hairy backs or balding heads or paunchy bellies.

Don't blame us—blame our hormonal memories!

Have patience. Remember that your capacity for arousal is still there, but it will probably take longer than it used to for you to become aroused. Just as you can no longer run a mile in eight or ten minutes, the way you did twenty-five years ago, or work all day on three hours of sleep, you can no longer be aroused after two minutes of foreplay. If you change your expectations about how long it should take you to become aroused, you'll be less worried about it, which may actually make the whole thing go more smoothly.

Don't wait until you are in the mood. Although your biological clock may have ticked its last tock, a woman's sex life is just as much in her head as it is in her hormones. Thus, just because you feel little desire doesn't mean that you won't eventually get in the mood. Just dive into the pool, and don't worry about testing the water or getting your feet wet first.

As Kingsberg points out, many postmenopausal women find that they rarely feel much sexual desire, at least until they are aroused. So don't wait until you feel in the mood to have sex or you may never get there. Instead, follow your mate's urgings, or your own wish to have sex more often, and just go for it. Eventually you will be glad you did.

For men, sexual desire always comes first, followed by arousal and then orgasm, according to Kingsberg. But the path is not nearly so straightforward for women, who may rarely think about sex or whether they want to have it or where or when they want it. This is because low estrogen levels reduce a woman's sexual cravings, though she may be perfectly receptive to the notion once the idea is introduced. In fact, just because women aren't constantly thinking about sex doesn't mean they are not sexual or are incapable of being orgasmic, she tells me, and continues:

> I talk to patients all the time about the idea of going to the gym as an analogy. I have no biologic urge to work out. But I know that once I'm there, once I'm in my workout clothes and once I'm on the treadmill, then I'm happy and I'm glad that I'm there, and I'm enjoying it. That doesn't happen until I'm halfway through my workout, so if I waited for a biologic urge to work out, I would never do it. I don't wait for it, I don't look for it, I don't interpret this as meaning I'm not a healthy person, I just don't expect that I'm going to have an urge to exercise. I can envy those who do, but I don't base my activities on that. If women stop looking for that initial biologic urge for sex, they can actually enjoy the ride, and enjoy the process.

Use it, or . . . you know what. Although it sounds so corny it seems as if it can't possibly be true, the less often midlife women have sex, the more likely they are to suffer from vaginal atrophy. Doctors divided postmenopausal women into two groups, those who had sex at least three times a month and those who had intercourse fewer than ten times a year. They examined the women physically and found that the sexually active women had larger, more flexible vaginas and even higher levels of sex hormones.[25]

Think sexual prime, not genital prime. Biologically speaking, women are at their sexual peak in their twenties and thirties. That's actually a time of genital prime, when the body's sole goal is to reproduce. By the time the children leave, those days are gone, both chronologically and physically. The days of wine and reproduction are over. However, there is still time for sexual prime, which means a woman's ability to achieve emotional intimacy through her sexuality. Although she may not perform as well—taking longer to achieve orgasm and not enjoying it quite so much—she's more fully herself, a complete partner to her partner. This kind of sexual intimacy is one that comes with years and knowledge and familiarity. And though it may not be as photogenic or as prime-time perfect as genital prime, those of us who are in our sexual prime are truly blessed.

Make time for sex time. Once it's just the two of you at home, you can set aside time for sensuality and loving. This doesn't mean, necessarily, having intercourse. It means that you make a point to cuddle and kiss, and touch each other in ways that feel good. You can do massages, either full body or just the feet, say. You can use scented oils or generic skin cream. You are limited only by your imagination, and perhaps by how early you start, so that both of you don't end up falling asleep in the middle.

By the way, this will work only if both partners are gung ho about it. So you may need to spend some time in gentle persuasion.

Have a drink, in moderation. Having one or two drinks a week, either beer or wine or hard liquor, helps reduce the number of hot flashes, according to Jodi Flaws, an epidemiologist at the University of Maryland School of Medicine. She doesn't yet know why, she says, but drinking makes hot flashes less severe and less frequent. On the other hand, though, women who drink too much tend to be less satisfied sexually, she says.[26] So find a happy, in-between medium that will improve the symptoms of menopause but not harm your sexual desire.

Tell your partner what works and what doesn't. "The biggest predictor of a woman's sexual function is how she feels about her partner," says Flaws. If he is loving and supportive, willing to talk and listen, then she is more likely to enjoy sex. It seems obvious, but sometimes couples need to be reminded of the obvious. Also, as I've said before, women's sexual desire is mostly psychological—they need to feel it in their hearts and minds. For men, sexual desire is pure physiology; it's all in the penis. Fix the erection with Viagra, and they're good to go.

"If a man wants a woman to desire him," explains Flaws, "he should help out with chores at home, so it gives her more time to relax." Small gestures like this, which may seem entirely unrelated to sex, will make a huge impact in the bedroom. The most difficult part is convincing a man that this is true.

Ideally, midlife women can master their sexual domain, just as they do nearly everything else—including work and finances and friendships. Read on to find out how empty-nest mothers become mistresses of the rest of their life domains.

CHAPTER EIGHT

Mistress of Work, Princess of Friendship

Midlife women often find that they have mastered almost every aspect of life except for sex. It's as if they begin the Ride of Life way back in the rear passenger cabin, but as the decades pass, they gradually move up front, into the driver's seat. By their fifth or sixth decade, they are in charge of their work and their finances and their friendships.

This take-charge attitude occurs, in part, because the demands of motherhood evaporate when children leave. While women's lives were once filled nearly to the top with mother-related tasks and chores, worries and guilt, affection and disappointment, most of that mother stuff boils away. What's left is a crystallized version of motherhood, one that leaves more room for other roles and responsibilities. For some, it's work; for others, it's friendship and a vibrant social life; for a few more, it's love and marriage; for many others, it's spirituality or a cause or even grandchildren.

There are no standard formulas or prescriptions for the ways in which boomer mothers fill their lives after the departure of their children. In fact, each mom is unique, and so is the path she takes through her fifties and beyond. Those paths are amazingly complicated, full of life's greatest, most thrilling moments, as well as life's most painful and upsetting times. Here's the reason: **later adulthood is a time of life that is more complex than ever before.**

Social scientists say that compared to early adulthood, ages eighteen to thirty-four, late adulthood is much more likely to be filled with challenges. Women in their fifties must deal with changes at work, retirement, moving, altered diet, health problems, taking responsibility for parents, losing one or both parents, watching children move out, watching children move back in, surviving menopause, and becoming a grandmother. Large numbers of midlife women deal with several of these trials all at once, according to a large, national study of Americans. The researchers conclude that life in the fifties is, in fact, "the most complex decade in life."[1]

We are, all of us, heroines of our own complicated comic opera, titled *Your Life: Starring You!* In it, we play the roles of:

❖ Wife or lover
❖ Mother
❖ Daughter
❖ Sister
❖ Worker
❖ Friend

Most of these roles are unpaid, but they have the following features: More stress! More rewards! More responsibility! More wisdom! More irritation! More satisfaction! More aches and pains! More worries! More joy!

People in this stage of life shouldn't be called fifty-something, researchers say, they should be called fifty-anything, because so much in life is changing. Those of us in our fifties are living in the realm of the possible, when nearly everything is up for grabs. It's as if all our doors and windows and portholes are open, to welcome the inevitable changes that enter in the fullness of adulthood.

In a way, **the fifties are a Last-Chance Decade, a nearly final opportunity to improve upon ourselves as parents, as partners, as daughters, as sisters, as friends.**

This is certainly the consensus among a group of New Jersey mothers who gathered at my request one summer evening to discuss their lives in the postmotherhood stage. We meet at Darcy's house, a modest place on a dead-end street, small but completely charming, full of kooky Africanesque sculptures and homemade wooden bowls and planters and gigantic dried bamboo shoots in huge ceramic pots. A low, lacquered Chinese table is covered with tiny bowls of colorful nibbling food, miniature dried soybeans in rainbow colors, salted ghost-white cashews, sesame-sprinkled rice balls with yellow and green dipping sauce, teeny orange and yellow crackers, little chip-like objects, and a long row of perfect, golden nectarines sitting in a wooden tray.

Darcy, fifty-two, has two children in college, and she looks like Mary McDonnell, the actress who played a white woman raised by Indians in the Kevin Costner movie *Dances with Wolves*. She works full-time as an art teacher in a middle school, and her husband owns an employment agency for temporary workers. Darcy went through a few weeks of intense regret and longing when her daughter left home, but she's finished with that now.

"I thought, 'How could it be over? I'm not done yet!'" she says.

But after a while, her regret and her sorrow passed. Now, she's in the glad-to-see-them-come-home and relieved-to-see-them-gone stage. And she's found herself focusing on her own needs and fantasies more than she has in decades. "The fifties are big, very big," she says. "It's a new awakening. It's so intense, I could almost cry."

Then she does, a little bit. After pulling herself together, Darcy continues, clearly filled with intense emotion, most of it uplifting and spiritual, almost as if she's in a kind of dervishlike trance.

"It's a huge privilege to see myself changing. It's so big. My mother died when she was fifty-nine, so I never had the privilege of seeing her grow old. There's a wisdom to it that I feel, but she never got to experience," Darcy continues, crying for real now. "Anyway, I have to embrace this time, because I have no choice."

Her friend Lynette takes over, clearly empathizing with Darcy's heartfelt emotion. "My mother died of lung cancer at forty-nine, so I never saw her grow old, either," Lynette says. At fifty-five, Lynette is tanned and blond, with some black roots showing, and she's muscular, as if she were a former breaststroker gone slightly to seed. She has three sons, and works as a secretary in a mortgage company. Married to a builder, Lynette says that she's had an easy life, since she never had to worry about money or health or feeling loved.

"In my fifties, I'm dealing with health issues for the first time," she says, "mostly because my body is starting to degenerate. Also, I was looking to buy some life insurance, and I had to think, for the first time, 'So how many years do I have left, maybe thirty, max?'"

This stark idea brings the conversation to a standstill, as Lynette and Darcy and their friends contemplate their mortality, a concept that has greater meaning in the fifties than it did in prior decades. Those of us in our fifties are closer to the end than to the beginning, a notion that many baby boomers have trouble wrapping their minds around. But it's a truth that becomes increasingly clear, as many fifty-something mothers begin to deal with their own aging and infirm parents.

Beth, fifty-four, responds by talking about her mother, who died of Alzheimer's less than a year ago. "She was a strong, controlling woman, and I was at her beck and call. I had to step up and take care of her, and I was torn between my teenage twins and my mother. She insisted on moving to Florida, so I had to fly down there every six weeks or so to stay for a few days. I went so often," she says, "they knew me at the airport Hertz counter."

Beth confesses that she doesn't like growing older, so she dyes her hair blond and works out at the gym, and by the way, she can do one thousand crunches at a time, she tells us. This accomplishment shocks her friends into utter silence for a moment, more so than any of the other, more passionate confessions of the night.

"You can?!" they then yell, almost in unison.

Their awe and disbelief are apparent, but Beth insists that she counts to one thousand as she crunches, and that it takes her about twenty minutes to finish ten sets of one hundred. Beth wears white pants and a sleeveless top, and she's a bit puffy around the edges. She doesn't look as if she has the belly of a one-thousand-sit-ups-at-a-time person, which is one reason for her friends' disbelief.

"I like to eat salty stuff," she says in a huff, somewhat defensive about the mistrust her admission has engendered. "My fifties are my transition from caring for my mother and my children to caring for me," Beth says. "Now is my time, and I can finally breathe easier."

Juliana agrees with her, though it's clear that she probably couldn't even do ten sit-ups at a time. At fifty-six, Juliana is a bit chubby, but her highlighted hair is chic, and she's dressed all in black, with a large sequined butterfly brooch on her lapel, and superpointy, high-heeled shoes. A real-estate broker who works sixty or seventy hours a week, Juliana is married to a mostly out-of-work roofing contractor, and she's been the family's main breadwinner for twenty-five years. "My husband is resentful, because I work very long hours, seven days a week, and he wants more time with me," she says. "He's more of a wife than I am; he cooks and shops, and I'm like the man," she adds.

Juliana's daughter is twenty-four, and living at home for a while before moving out on her own. The girl protested when Juliana told her that she was going to meet with other empty-nest mothers, insisting that Juliana's nest was not yet empty because she's still there. "She made such a fuss about my coming here!" Juliana says, with a loud cackling laugh. "But I say she's supposed to be gone, so I *should* have an empty nest. We had a fight because I called her an intruder, and she said, 'How dare you rush me out!'"

As far as Juliana is concerned, "my fifties are enlightening. I've learned a lot about accepting people's faults and their attributes, so I've gotten more sensible. Though I'm sad about getting older, I have to embrace it. I've seen my body go through changes," she says and sighs, "and most of them I don't like. I always had a really nice neck, but now, my neck is sagging."

Juliana is determined, though, to make the most of her fifties, because she finally has the insight to know what matters, a perspective she didn't have in her forties.

"I know now that I need to allot more time to my friends and to enjoying myself," she says. "I have to enjoy life immediately, right now. I don't want to be like my parents, who saved and scrimped on everything. They would never treat themselves, even when they went on vacation. Now, they're in their eighties and they have some money, but they can barely walk to the telephone, and they'll never be able to travel again," she says. "So what was all that saving for?"

Like Juliana, many women view their fifties as a time in which they can finally get their priorities straight and fix the parts of their lives that aren't working. It's a final chance to rewrite and alter our life stories, picking and choosing who we want to be, what work we want to do, and which friends are most important to us.

Women's World of Work

Once children leave home, mothers often reconsider and reevaluate what they do for a living. It's a time of life when they can decide if they want to work for money or for love or both, if possible. Many moms embark on a Mission for More: more satisfying work, more meaningful work, more money for the work.

In fact, a majority of fifties women are in the labor force, about 75 percent, according to recent census figures.[2] In my Web survey, too, about three out of four empty-nest moms work, and after the children leave, a majority say that work is either just as important to them as before or even more so.

Almost all agree, as well, that once the children are gone, they work without guilt. They don't have to rush home to make dinner or to pick up children or to spend quality time. If nothing else, the empty nest becomes a golden opportunity for Guilt Reduction of the Best Kind. They can work late, they can go to the gym on the way home, they can go out for drinks with colleagues, or whatever they used to want to do but couldn't. In fact, their work life begins to resemble what it was when they were much younger and childless. And husbands barely seem to enter the equation.

"I love not worrying about dinner and not having to rush to take care of or to check on everyone," says fifty-one-year-old Shari, a Texas teacher. "I can work late guilt-free, the way I never could when they were home and in school."

Another woman who answered my Web survey instituted a new dinner plan at home, one that she calls "Find it, Eat it." That's when she and her husband rummage around in the refrigerator until they find something edible, and they call whatever they find "dinner." It's a simple method of relaxed meal preparation, because it's no longer her job; it's their job. It's a kind of familial hunting and gathering, one that takes place not on the African savannah, but in the bowels of a midlifer's fridge.

Nonworking mothers, however, don't have this new sense of work-life freedom to enjoy. Indeed, when I analyze my Web survey and compare working and nonworking mothers, I find some surprising and dramatic differences between the two groups. Overall, the **working moms seem to be in much better shape than the non-workers, both emotionally and psychologically, once the children leave home.**

Among working women who answered my survey, full-timers work about forty-one hours a week, and part-timers work about sixteen hours a week. Here are just some of the jobs that women do to fill their days and their wallets. There's a third-grade teacher and a professor of ancient Greek. There's a forensic psychologist, lots of nurses, and at least one ordained minister who is also a psychologist. There are bookkeepers and accountants, attorneys and physicians. There's someone who calls herself a "fiber artist." There's a school superintendent and a woman who runs a candy-making business from her home. There are many real-estate agents and teachers of English as a second language. There are music teachers, librarians, and high-school math teachers. There's a jewelry designer and a teacher's aide in a private Christian school. There are many travel agents, at least one tree- and garden-nursery worker, and several hospice workers. There are receptionists, swimming instructors, and a director of a YMCA. And there's at least one woman who is a factory assembler for motor homes.

Thus, my Web-survey women are white collar, pink collar, blue collar, and every other collar in between. They earn just a few thousand dollars a year to several hundred thousand.

About one-quarter of the women in my Web survey, however, do not work for pay. About three in ten of them say that they have moved recently, which may explain why they are not currently working. Almost all of the nonworkers—nine in ten—are married, so they have partners who are able and willing to support them. In addition, about one in ten had a serious illness recently, another possible reason for lack of work. Also, they are slightly older than the women who still work—nonworkers are about fifty-six years old, on average, compared to fifty-one among full-time workers. It's possible, then, that some of the nonworkers have already retired.

It's fairly clear, I think, that women who don't work for pay tend to be less satisfied and less content with their lot in life. Among nonworking women, for instance, I find that about two in ten say that if they could do it again, they'd be more serious about work this time.

For example, Ginny, forty, doesn't work, and both of her children, ages twenty and seventeen, have moved out. As a result, she's afraid of being on her own. She's aware that "this is a new beginning to my life, that I am starting a new chapter," but she's not sure she's ready for all that newness. "I'm anxious because I put so much of my emotional self into these children, and I'm not sure what to do now that they're gone. I know that they will make mistakes, and that I must let them. But secretly I'm frustrated with their choices. I pretend that I hate being a nag, but it makes me feel needed when they call me for advice and I get to hand out clichés and sound intelligent," Ginny says.

Meanwhile, though, Ginny is stuck in a small town in Georgia, without any kind of work, and wishing that she could go back and redo the last fifteen years of her life, this time making work matter more. "I used to joke about having more free time, that I couldn't wait for it," Ginny says. "But now I'm hesitant to get out there and do anything. I've had to ask questions about myself that I have been avoiding for years about what to do with the rest of my life," she explains.

It is only now that her children are gone and she has no goals for the second half of her life that Ginny realizes that she should have had something other than her children to define her for all those years. "How will people see me now?" she asks, keenly aware that if she'd had a job, or some kind of meaningful volunteer work, she'd have an extra role. Instead, she is simply sitting around and waiting for her children to have a crisis.

"I'm waiting for them to fall, so I can be there to catch them," is how she puts it. "But will I always be 'spotting' them? Who is going to 'spot' me?"

After hearing Ginny's story, it may come as no surprise that more nonworking than working mothers become depressed after their children leave. Also, more of them lose their sexual desire, and more of them gain weight. Not having the engagement and community that work provides, they suffer from a kind of identity crisis once their mother role is sliced apart.

Indeed, when I examine working mothers, seven in ten of whom are married, I find that many more of them say they are excited about their future once the children are gone (50 percent say so, compared to 34 percent of nonworking moms). While just as many of them as nonworking moms think of themselves as a "mother" first, 43 percent also think of themselves as professionals, emphasizing the importance of their work role in how they define themselves.

Compared to nonworking moms, fewer working mothers feel anxious, and fewer have a sense of despair, too. Finally, now that their children are gone, four in ten working women actually feel more involved in their work, and five in ten say they are just as involved as they were before.

Sunny, forty-nine, is a perfect example of a woman who defines herself by her work, as well as by her motherhood. Divorced ten years ago, she is a professor of social work at a private Lutheran college in Washington State. She loves mothering at a distance and calls it "the best part of parenting."

"I am close to my sons, and I often hear about their lives; I see them periodically, and I support their choices," Sunny explains. "But I am shed of the more mundane and less satisfying aspects of being a mom: managing their schedules, deciding when to set limits, worrying about when they come home, cooking their meals, washing their clothes, dealing with the clutter and the mess."

What Sunny loves most, she says, is that her workday is her own, and that she can focus on her students and her teaching with a clear mind. Not only is her time her own, but so is her money. "I am in a better financial position now, after supporting my children all alone for years," Sunny says. "I was recently promoted, so I have more money coming in. I used to think twice about spending more than ten dollars on myself. Now, though, I spend one hundred dollars without giving it a second thought."

Because she's a single mom, all of Sunny's money is Sunny's money. But for working wives, too, bringing in a substantial portion of the family's income is empowering, a major source of self-confidence and mastery. And when couples no longer need to funnel a large portion of their financial resources to the children, that's when moms begin to thrill to the notion of spending their money on themselves, for themselves.

When Amy's sons were in college, she and her husband were working long hours to pay the two hefty tuitions, with no outside help. "We didn't get a new car for seven years, and the house was falling down around our ears," Amy says. But once both boys had graduated, the money was all theirs again, she says.

"That first year, I felt like we had won the lottery!" Amy gushes. "I had all this money, my money, and I could spend it however I wanted! Practically the first thing I did was to get a massage and buy some new clothes for myself," she explains. "It was just a little thing, but it made me feel like queen for a day."

When her sons left home, Amy was working forty-five hours a week as a paralegal, and she didn't have much time or energy to bemoan their departure. Instead, she was deeply involved in her work, and rethinking the ways in which she would combine her work life and her personal life in the future. As it turns out, this is typical of what many professional women do, once the children are gone.

Empty-nest moms tend to create new standards for their work lives by recalibrating their view of what it means to work hard enough and long enough, while still holding on to a rich personal life. A majority of such women begin to redefine success at work, according to one recent study of professional women. They come to believe that they can judge their success using their own personal criteria, and not by using what the boss thinks or what their colleagues believe. For them, success means having a good family life, being fulfilled at work, and doing well according to their own personal standards.[3]

This kind of subtle internal shift is what makes the lives of many working mothers more complex and more satisfying than those of other women. It doesn't mean that their lives are better, but it does mean that their lives may be deeper, and in some ways more rewarding.

In fact, my own research confirms what other social scientists have discovered about women and work. In general, it is this: **the more roles women have, the better, especially if they enjoy those roles.** Women who are wives and mothers and workers, and who are deeply engaged in all three roles, tend to be in better physical and psychological health than women who have just one role or two.

Working mothers tend to have fewer health problems than non-working moms, they are less likely to be depressed, less likely to be anxious and distressed, and they feel happier and better about themselves. The advantage is even greater for women who hold high-status jobs, those with greater-than-average prestige and pay.[4] Thus, women who are well-educated and who have jobs that pay them what they are worth tend to be the happiest and healthiest of all.

The one catch, of course, is that if the work is overly stressful or challenging, then all of this is less likely to be true.

"If the roles fit what a woman wants to be doing, then it's better to have more," agrees Stacy Rogers, a sociologist at Pennsylvania State University who studies women and work. "But it really depends on what she prefers to be doing with her time, and how challenging her job is for her. If she's overchallenged, and faced with stressful situations that are really difficult for her to deal with, then the work role might not be so healthy," Rogers tells me in a telephone interview.[5]

Nevertheless, having a lifelong career can be beneficial for women, both financially and emotionally, experts say. In addition, women who have careers, whose work requires special training and offers higher pay, are much less needy and dependent on others for reassurance than women who have low-level jobs.[6]

Another secret of success for some working women is even more basic: they have a career goal that they have achieved, and that has made all the difference. Having a career goal doesn't mean that you have to be a superachiever, as a neurosurgeon or an astronaut. It doesn't mean you have to accomplish great feats or shatter glass ceilings with the greatest of ease. It simply means that you have a goal, any goal, whether it's to become a kindergarten teacher or a home-schooling mom or an office manager. Then you have to reach that goal.

It turns out that women who set a career goal and achieved it in their thirties are healthier than women who didn't, and they are less likely to be depressed and to feel that they have no purpose in life. Those who fall short of their goals, who don't achieve whatever it was that they wanted, are also more depressed and feel that their lives have little meaning.

These conclusions were drawn from a study of three thousand women in Wisconsin who were interviewed three times: first, as teenagers; second, as thirty-five-year-olds; and finally, when they were in their early fifties. Quite simply, the women who had a career dream when young, whether it was working for pay or volunteering, were protected against feelings of depression and uselessness as they aged.[7]

It's just possible, then, that for many women—although not all—children and grandchildren are not quite enough. For these women, having a dream about a career, and then having the career itself, gives them a sense of meaning and purpose that is nearly as central to their sense of themselves as being a good mother.

I don't mean to imply that every mother has the luxury of choice in the matter of work. When most families need a second income just to pay the bills, that's simply not an issue. But it's true that having a full-time job, or a career, affords some wives the luxury of choice in the matter of staying married or not. Most research shows, in fact, that the more money a wife earns, the more likely she is to divorce. It turns out, though, that working wives aren't simply more eager to leave their marriages. Instead, women whose marriages are already in trouble seek out well-paid work, planning ahead so that they will be financially capable of escape.

In fact, the more money wives earn, both in actual dollars and in the percentage of household income, the happier they are with their marriage and their relationship with their husband. The only exception to this general rule, says Rogers, is when wives earn a lot more money than their husbands. In that situation, wives tend to be less happy with their marriage, and so are husbands.[8]

The number of wives who earn more than their husbands is slowly increasing, at least in the United States. About one in four working couples includes a wife who earns more than her husband, according to recent census figures.[9] Now that so many baby-boom couples are entering their fifties and sixties, more and more of them may include a husband who is winding down his work career, while the wife kicks hers up a notch once the children are gone. In such cases, Rogers points out, there may be a growing disparity in income, with wives earning at least as much or more than their husbands.

With so many wives in the workplace, too, it's clear that "marriage is changing rapidly," Rogers tells me. "That's why more couples tend to live partly independent lives, pursing their own interests and hobbies. They aren't less happy than they used to be," she notes, "but they have less of a sense of obligation than they used to that they should do everything together, all of the time."

Work is also the focus of at least one major crisis in women's lives, according to social scientists. Although most people think of a midlife crisis as more of a man's thing than a woman's, it turns out that just as many women as men have had one. By the age of fifty, 36 percent of women and 34 percent of men say they've experienced such a crisis, according to a major national study. On average, the crisis occurred when they were about forty-six or forty-seven, and it often focused on feeling trapped at work, experiencing a career disaster, or undergoing some kind of psychological calamity.[10]

Another way to think of a midlife crisis is simply as a turning point in life. When researchers asked 724 American women and men to figure out how many major turning points they had experienced during the previous five years, women reported having had more turning points than men did, and half of those turning points involved work. Nearly as many of women's turning points, 47 percent, involved learning something good about themselves, and four in ten had a turning point after fulfilling a dream. Their dreams were often material ones, like buying a new home or a new car, but they also dreamed about sending their children out into the world and about going back to school.[11]

What happens at work that makes women feel they've hit a monumental speed bump in life, something that gives them a sense that they are at an important crossroads of life? Most often, it's when they change careers, by taking a second-act job, or when they try to rearrange their family life to accommodate work.

Second-Act Careers

It's not clear how many midlife women are brave enough and secure enough, as well as willing, ready, and able enough, to flip their lives inside out by starting a new career when their children leave. But a large number certainly do. And they are proud and pleased to talk about the great changes this has wrought in their lives.

In interviews, and in my Web survey, empty-nest mothers extol the glorious changes they've made by switching careers, not quite midstream, but a little beyond that. Once the children are gone, many mothers grab at a chance to rethink, to reimagine, and to reinvent their work lives.

Several of the Argentine mothers I interviewed, for instance, made drastic changes, including the speech therapist who became a sculptor, the English teacher who became a psychotherapist, and the professor who is going back to school to become an expert in handwriting analysis.

In the United States, Rebecca, a mother and wife from Illinois, had been working long, boring, thirty-five-hour weeks as an administrative assistant for almost twenty-five years. Now that her three children are gone, she's fed up. "I'm thinking about finding work that I'd like to do, that would be more fulfilling, instead of work that just pays the tuition bills." She doesn't know yet what that work will be, but she's determined to figure it out.

Hundreds and thousands of empty-nest working moms have the same feeling; it's a sensation that trickles up from deep inside, and comes into consciousness just before sleep or as a waking daydream. It comes when midlife moms realize that they can cure their misery, assuage their boredom, pursue their dream, or intensify their life by working hard for the money but by working at something different.

What's surprising, though, is that **the most psychologically healthy women are the ones who change careers.** In a twenty-year-long study of six hundred men and women, psychologists discovered that the most neurotic women were the ones who stayed in their jobs longest, without ever taking a daring leap into the unknown. The more stable, happier, and healthier women engaged in career shape-shifting, worming their way into new occupations and new trades.[12]

For a history professor who retired as soon as her children graduated from college, that meant opening a bird sanctuary in her home. Along with her second husband, she rescues flying creatures, from owls to sparrows and every other bird in between. With fluff and feathers flying, she has become a bird lady, not of Alcatraz, but of western Oregon, in a new life in which she hopes to live happily ever after.

Or there's Patty, fifty-three, who used to own an executive recruitment firm in Maryland and was accustomed to working long hours to find wealthy men even higher-paying jobs. But after her second child left for college, Patty and her husband moved to California for his work. Patty sold her business and decided that her new career dream would be to learn about apes. She explains:

> My brother and sister-in-law are primatologists. They have study sites in Africa that I've been to, and I love animals. The zoo is really close to my new apartment, and I've joined a team of workers in the Ape House.
>
> I'm a research assistant and I help the on-site scientists do their research on captive primates. We're studying space use now, tracking how the gorillas and chimpanzees use the living areas. It will help zoos around the world design better enclosures for pri-

mates. We check to see how long they are up on the ropes, how long they sit on the ground, how long they rest on the sleeping platforms. I use a tablet computer that tracks them every twenty seconds with an aerial map. I get to know every single one of the seventeen gorillas and eight chimpanzees.

Some women are inspired by their spirituality to begin a second-act career.

Marcy, fifty-two, used to work in human resources for a large corporation in upstate New York. Once her four children were gone, though, that job made her depressed and angry and unhappy about life. Clearly, she says, the children no longer needed her, and she decided that she'd like to merge her work with her notion of motherhood. As a mother to grown children, she now has the option to be "hennish" or not, she says. So, when her children and grandchildren "come to me with their needs and wants and affection, I can give them what they want, or not. I have a choice," she crows, with great delight.

Marcy decided to bestow her motherly attention on everyone who might need it. "My spirituality was way more important to me than the company's health-benefits plan or some guy's need for more vacation days," she realized.

Thus did Marcy quit her job, after twenty-seven years, to enroll in classes at the local seminary. She is now a pastor, as well as a mental-health counselor, being "hennish" with all the little chicks in her church flock. "I felt it was my time to do the things I had put on hold for my family. Once I was back in college, on an education leave from work, my depression lifted," Marcy confesses. "When I finally quit that job, it felt like a miracle! That liberated me!!"

Shannon, fifty-one, made a similar move, though one that was less spiritual in nature. She, too, wanted out from under the demanding teaching job she'd held for fifteen years. Shannon suffers from an inflammatory bowel disease, made worse by stress and anxiety. So she and her husband moved from their suburban home in Connecticut to Maine, where they opened an inn. It was a sitcom-ready, not-so-profitable dream come true, she says.

As the hostess of her inn, Shannon has re-created herself as "übermother," as she puts it. Now that she no longer has to look after her four children, she's got a steady stream of needy guests who are desperate for pampering and chitchat and friendly advice. As if that weren't enough substitute mothering, she also teaches Lamaze classes, ushering flocks of women into motherhood. "My life revolved around my children for years, but now I have work that takes the place of all the mothering I did," she says. "I've forgiven myself for any mistakes I've made with them over the years, and I love, love, love my new jobs!"

For a few women, one major career change isn't enough; they prefer to undergo serial self-reinventions.

Take Nancy, fifty-eight, who lives near Wilmington, Delaware. She raised three children who were gone by the time she was forty-five. A few years before that, she'd gone back to school for an education degree and taught elementary school for ten years. Next, she worked as a researcher for the Franklin Mint, the place in Philadelphia that makes money and produces hundreds of "limited-edition" collectibles. Finally, she decided to get a master's degree, so that she could work at a university library. It's not that she doesn't like what she does, Nancy says, it's just that she keeps noticing new things she'd like to try, as if jobs were ice-cream flavors and she feels the need to taste each one. For her fourth trick, Nancy and her husband are thinking about moving to Texas, so that they can retire and be close to two sons and three grandbabies.

The Money Mystique

Nancy may bounce from job to job like a career kangaroo, but she's typical of a new kind of baby-boom worker. Experts say that, like Nancy, baby boomers are among the first generation of Americans who will not take permanent first-time retirement at any particular age—not at sixty-five or seventy-five. Instead, boomers are likely to take so-called bridge jobs, which are part- or full-time jobs that they find after they finish working at a previous, long-term job. At least half of workers will end up doing bridge jobs, and maybe even as many as two-thirds, researchers say.

Experts note that traditional retirement is passé, out of fashion for many reasons. As Americans live longer, in better health, and with higher expectations for their quality of life, they will refuse to spend time rocking on a front porch or to give up a chance to earn some extra income. And they'll need that money to fund their more active, longer years, allowing them decades more of well-funded semiretirement.[13]

Baby-boom mothers, especially, have grown accustomed to having their own income, and that's not something they are likely to want to give up as they age. Because baby boomers include so many dual-earner couples, they are already better off financially than their parents were at this stage of life, and are also more upwardly mobile. Economists predict, too, that baby boomers will continue to do better as they age into retirement. The only exceptions to this rule are nonwhite families and single mothers, who tend to lag behind the rest of the baby-boom generation in financial well-being.[14]

After parents have finished supporting their children, and helping to pay for college, the vast majority experience a significant boost in income. That's why marketing experts find that empty nesters spend more money than people in any other stage of life on home improvement, on power tools, on travel, on women's clothing, and on dining out.[15]

Once the empty nest is truly empty, then, the credit cards are warmed up and ready for action. They're in the charge mode; first to fix up the nest, and then to escape from the nest.

Many women over the age of fifty also find themselves able to spend more, simply because they are earning more. Midlife women are more likely than midlife men to work as salaried employees and to work part-time. Fewer women than men over the age of fifty are self-employed or own their own business. For this reason, midlife women also tend to earn less than midlife men, but they're also more likely to have health insurance and other fringe benefits. One study shows that midlife women earned an average of thirty-eight thousand dollars a year in 2002, while midlife men earned sixty-nine thousand dollars, a difference that is substantial, but one that shrinks as the years pass.[16]

About four in ten midlife women who are working say that they feel overwhelmed by the amount of work they have to do on the job and by having too many things to do at once. Only about three in ten midlife men feel the same way. But the rest of working women, the majority, in fact, feel they have a great deal of autonomy at work, that they are involved in decision making, that they can trust their boss, and that they receive support from coworkers and supervisors when they do well. The bottom line: six in ten midlife working women say they feel a high level of satisfaction with their work.[17]

Rose, forty-nine, is a perfect example of a hardworking woman who reaps both personal satisfaction and financial benefits from her job. She's a high-school English teacher in a suburb of Atlanta, and because she has worked in the same district for almost twenty-five years, her salary and benefits top six figures. Not only that, but she's happy with her work and feels close to her colleagues.

"My principal supports me when I have trouble with a parent or an out-of-control student," says Rose. "And two of my best friends are teachers here, so when our students do well on the SAT or win awards, we celebrate together, because we feel we played a part in their success."

At the rate she's going, Rose says, she'll be able to retire from teaching, with a decent pension, by the time she's fifty-five. Rose's husband, though, a municipal assessor, will have to work at least another ten years.

"I don't think I'll stop working, I'll just find other things I want to do, and then figure out how to get paid to do them!" Rose says.

The Saving Grace of Girlfriends

Women enjoy their work for many reasons, but one of the most important is that they value their friendships with colleagues and coworkers. Friendships with neighbors and college pals, and of every other kind, develop and stretch once the children are gone. That description makes friendships sound like a pregnant woman's belly during her last trimester, but it's accurate. The children's exodus often leads to a swelling and strengthening of close and closer friendships.

Here's why: **as maternal life shrinks, social life expands**.

Generally speaking, this is a good thing, since having the support and companionship of close friends balances out the losses that come with midlife, when children move out and parents fall ill, become dependent, and eventually die. Real friends stick with you, through hell and high water. They stay to listen and to console and to support. It's true that good friends can also be annoying and demanding and amazingly irritating at times. But they don't judge us, and they make us laugh, so we tolerate their flaws and faults.

Most social scientists agree that women surpass men in the friendship arena. Research shows that women:

- ❖ Are more sociable, and value friendships more than men do
- ❖ Are likely to have a close confidante outside of marriage, but most men name their wives as their closest confidante
- ❖ Disclose more intimate secrets to friends than men do
- ❖ Tend to be the ones who keep in touch with relatives, from both sides of the family; they are known as kin keepers
- ❖ Are more upset by fights and arguments with friends than men are
- ❖ Get together with friends to talk, while men get together with friends to do things
- ❖ Are intimacy experts[18]

Many of these points may seem sexist or outdated, but they are true even now, at the beginning of the twenty-first century. As hard as men may try to achieve a deep and abiding level of intimacy with their friends and family, most of them just aren't as close and well connected to loved ones as women are. That's a real fact of life.

This becomes even more apparent once children leave home, because that's when mothers allow their friendships to blossom. Suddenly, they've got the time and emotional energy to channel into their ties to colleagues and friends and sisters.

"I've gotten to know people I work with on a different level, because I've taken the time to go out with them. I've known them for years, but I just never managed to fit them in before," says Aliza, fifty-two, a first-grade teacher and a mother of three in Arizona. "I resented having my friendships consist of moments on the telephone and getting the husbands to watch the kids so we could see each other," she adds. Now, though, she can meet up with her friends whenever and wherever she wants.

This ability to nurture friendships is yet another newfound freedom of empty-nest motherhood.

My Web survey reveals quite clearly that many midlife moms revel in the ease with which they can enjoy their friendships. I find that almost all empty-nest mothers—95 percent—have a really close friend or a confidante, someone with whom they can share an embarrassing secret. If their husband is having an affair or their son is flunking out of college or they accidentally sent a nasty e-mail to the boss, they can share the mortifying news with at least one great gal pal. About one in ten has a single confidante, 24 percent have two such friends, 23 percent have three intimate friends, and 40 percent have four or more of them.

Darlene, a fifty-year-old secretary in Illinois, says, "I know four women I could say anything to, and they wouldn't judge me. My girlfriends are my saving grace, and I value them very highly." Now that her three children are out of the house, "I have learned to be a better friend to my friends," Darlene says, because before "I was just raising kids and focusing on my marriage. But now I can be there for them in a flash, without having to think about what else I'm supposed to be doing."

"After the age of forty, the best thing about becoming middle-aged is my relationship with other women," Darlene concludes. "The women in my life have become really important to me."

Lisa, forty-five, actually has nine close friends, and that doesn't seem to be an exaggeration. She and her husband own a bookkeeping business and work long hours together, but she's also become much closer to her gang of girlfriends. "I love to spend time with them, and we recently went on a girls-only ski trip to the Sierras and had a great time. I've never done anything like that before, and I hope it will be just the beginning of many more girls-only trips," Lisa says.

For women, this is a new definition of friendship, not only talking to great friends, but actually doing things together, the way men do. It's as if thousands and thousands of midlife moms are singing the chorus of the 1971 James Taylor hit, agreeing in harmony that "it's good to know you've got a friend."

Or two or three friends, actually.

It's especially now, a time of life when mothers no longer put their children first, that they rank friendship much higher on the totem pole of life. In fact, nearly half of the women in my research—45 percent—say that they think of themselves as "friend," right after "mother" and "wife."

But they aren't finished making friends yet, either. It's as if all of the childhood friends, the neighborhood friends, the work friends, and the other friends don't quite fill up their friendship quota. **Nearly half of the moms in my Web survey actually say they hope to make new friends** in the next year or two. In this way, women in midlife resemble the summer campers or college freshmen they once were, still on the prowl for best friends forever.

They're not finished finding friends; they're just beginning.

What is it that makes a woman feel she's found a new midlife friend? And is there a way to take the measure of a friend? Psychologists have been trying to figure out how to test friendship, and they've come up with some fairly reasonable ways. Here's one that I've adapted from recent research.

THE FRIENDSHIP TEST

First, think of one of your closest friends, somebody to whom you would confide a secret, but make sure it's someone other than your husband or your partner. (This is a test of friendship, not of lovers.) Next, answer the following twelve questions with either "true" or "false" about that person. I'm using "she" and "her" here, but if your close friend is a man, feel free to answer these questions about him.

True or false?

1. When my friend is having a hard time, I want to help her.
2. My friend supports me, and she always helps me when I need her.
3. When my friend is happy, I'm happy too.
4. My friend encourages me.
5. My friend would come over and take care of me if I got sick.
6. My friend would lend me money if I asked.
7. My friend would drive me to the hospital at three a.m. if I had an emergency.
8. My friend would listen to me talk for hours if I was really upset about something.
9. My friend makes too many demands on me.
10. My friend gets on my nerves sometimes.
11. My friend tends to be a bit selfish.
12. My friend takes more than she gives.

Give yourself 1 point for each "true" answer you gave for items 1 to 8, and 1 point for each "false" answer you gave for items 9 to 12. Give yourself a 0 for each "false" answer you gave for items 1 to 8, and a 0 for each "true" answer you gave for items 9 to 12. Your score should range between 0 and 12. A score of 9 or more means that your friendship is a strong, solid one. Between 6 and 8 means that your friendship is okay; 5 or fewer means you might want to think about finding a better friend.

There are many other ways to ask about friendship, including one that probes a person's many levels of friendships, known as social networks. Psychologists ask women and men to look at a circle with "YOU" written in the middle and three concentric rings around it. It looks something like the art on the next page.

The Three Circles of Friendship

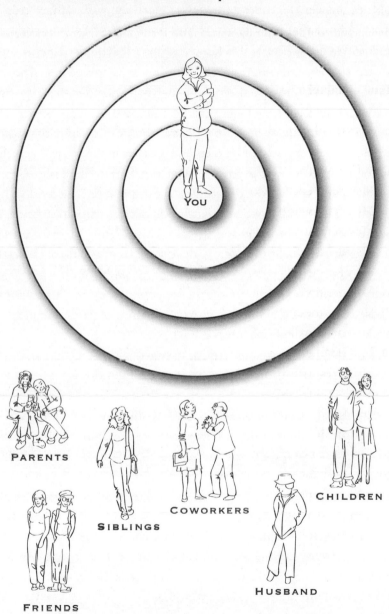

Choose the circles in which you'd place these important people, according to how close they are to you.

The three circles represent layers of closeness to you. The inner circle, the one closest to YOU, is for people to whom you feel closest, the ones without whom you would find it difficult to imagine life. The middle circle is for people to whom you don't feel quite that close, but who are still very important. The outer circle is for people who are close enough and important enough that you consider them friends, but you haven't mentioned them yet.[19]

"Women include their husband and children, their parents, and maybe one best friend, sometimes not, in that inner circle," explains Jennifer E. Lansford, a psychologist at the Duke University Center for Child and Family Policy who uses the triple-circle method in her research. "The middle circle is usually for people who are friends, or other relatives, like brothers and sisters, grandparents, aunts, or uncles. The outer circle usually includes work colleagues, acquaintances, neighbors, or other people you enjoy spending time with. But if you moved or quit your job, you might not see these people anymore. These friends are based on your situation, rather than on bonds of enduring quality," she tells me in a telephone interview.

Using this triple-circle question, psychologists find that "women have more friends in their inner circle than men do, usually at least one more," Lansford says. "Women say that social relationships are more important to them than men do." Women report having about four people in their inner circle and four in their middle circle; men have three in their inner circle, and slightly more in the middle circle.

What's surprising, though, is that women tend to have fewer friends as they get older, although their friendships grow stronger and more solid with age. In a series of studies conducted several decades ago, Lansford and her colleagues found that women over fifty had fewer friends than women in their twenties and thirties, but they were much more satisfied with the friends they did have.[20]

"As people get older," says Lansford, "they selectively narrow their social networks, so they have fewer friends, but the remaining ones are really close."

Indeed, other research shows that women have the most friends at the age of eighteen, but the number decreases at the age of thirty. Yet as women age, they find superficial friendships much less rewarding, so they jettison the ones they feel are not quite worth the effort. It's a matter of less being more.[21]

In fact, many empty-nest moms tell me that the quickie friends they'd made through their children had mostly "faded away," as a woman from California put it. "That's mostly because all we had in common was having kids the same age," she adds.

Valerie, fifty, lives in Chicago and is adamant that since her three children left, "I've definitely cultivated friendships more, and dropped the ones who weren't good for me."

Once the children leave, midlife mothers approach their friendships as if they were weeding a garden, pulling out the pesky troublemakers and keeping the lovely blossoms and the fragrant herbs.

You don't have to be a rocket scientist, or even a social scientist, to know that having friends is a good thing. But it's also possible, on occasion, that friends can be a bad thing. Having confidantes can surely help you get through times of stress and grief and trouble, yet the same friends can sometimes be too needy or too smothering.

"Friends offer emotional support and financial help and caring if you're sick, but there's also the flip side, when friends get on your nerves," says Lansford. "You can have a friend who confides all her troubles, and she calls and talks for an hour about all the bad things in her life. But you might feel, 'I don't have time to listen to this, I've got my own life and my own problems.' And the friendship can become a burden, with too many confidences, and you say, 'Wait! Enough is enough, I've got enough stress to deal with, I can't deal with another person's stress too,'" she explains.

In fact, recent research looks at both the pluses and minuses of having close friends, and confirms that, yes, sometimes even the best of bosom buddies can be really, really annoying. Lansford did a study in which she found that midlife wives say that both their best friends and their husbands sometimes get on their nerves. But she also finds that these women have more patience for their annoying friends than for their obnoxious hubbies.

Women who have a best friend in whom they can confide are depressed less often and are more satisfied with life, according to Lansford's research. And even women whose best friends get on their nerves are more satisfied with their lives than those who have no such friend.[22]

Thus, an annoying friend is better than no friend at all!

Sister Friends

Some midlife moms find themselves going back to their roots, to their actual babyhoods, for friendship, by reconnecting with their sisters, who become the long-lost best friends of midlife.

I examined information collected for the Wisconsin Longitudinal Study, a massive study of 10,317 women and men interviewed many times since 1957, and found that half of these women say they see their siblings at least a few times a month, once a week, or even more often. Even among older women, those between the ages of forty-five and sixty-five, who are less likely than younger women to have living sisters and brothers, 42 percent see their siblings this often.[23]

Arlene, forty-eight, now sees both of her sisters regularly. Although all three live within fifty miles of each other in central Michigan, until their children left they had been too involved with their families to make a concerted effort to hang out together if there wasn't a roasted turkey or a Christmas holiday involved. But now all that has changed, Arlene says. "I've gotten to know my sisters on a deeper basis than before, because we were always so busy with our lives. Now, we make a point to go antiquing one Saturday a month; then we have lunch. It's a good way to strengthen our relationship," Arlene concludes, thrilled by the new feeling of closeness she has with her baby sisters.

Likewise, Dolly has had an on-again, off-again tie to her older sister, Roberta, for years. But it's a friendship she can't imagine living without, she confesses. Dolly is four years younger than Roberta, and she lives in New York, while her sister lives in Florida. But still, they're extremely close. Dolly says of Roberta:

A lot of things drive me crazy about her, but she's an amazing person. She wants everyone in the room to experience what she's experiencing. And that can be terrible. A long time ago, I was having trouble getting pregnant, and I had been trying for four years. Roberta had just had a baby, and I was visiting her. As I was about to leave, she insisted that I smell the baby, because she was so captivated by the way her little baby smelled. But my heart was breaking, and she should have known that. Still, she kept insisting, "You have to smell the baby, just take one smell!" And I kept saying, "I have to go, I have to take a cab." Finally, I gave in and I smelled her baby. Then I left her house, crying.

Despite the smelling fiasco, Dolly and her sister are closer now than ever before, she says, though they have been through some rocky patches together. "When Roberta was going through a divorce, she called me every damn minute. I withstood her divorce," Dolly says, laughing now, but it's clear that she was exasperated with her sister back then.

"My sister knows me very, very well, but I'm still the little sister, and I always will be," she says. What also drives Dolly crazy, she says, is that "if I tell her a problem, she gives me a solution right away, and that's not what I want. I don't want her to solve my problems, because I hate being told what to do. So I sit there going 'La, la, la, la,' so I can't hear what she's saying!"

Proud of her big sister, Dolly is also a bit resentful that the woman "can do anything. She's a great cook. And she painted that picture, from old photographs." Dolly points to a gorgeous, three-foot-tall oil painting of herself and her two children when they were toddlers. It's a view from behind, of three figures wandering on packed wet sand on a deserted beach. The painting is lovely, and Dolly's sister is not a professional painter, she just dabbles. Dolly laughs as she points to the oversized signature in the corner: "ROBERTA, 2003."

"She's not modest," Dolly says and laughs.

These sisters are aging into their friendship, especially now that their own children have been launched.

Weeding Your Garden

Sisters are always sisters, whether they are beloved or resented or actively despised. It's up to us how often we see and talk to them. But the blood tie is a strong one, and so are long-lasting friendships, which grow stronger the older we get, according to some researchers.

Older women have known their closest friends for more than twenty years, according to one study, and they speak of them with great fondness, as being "on my heart," as one woman puts it. For them, the most important parts of friendship are that they can trust each other, they care for each other, and they help each other solve problems. In addition, while women may feel affection for new friends whom they see more often, they feel deep love for long-term friends, even those whom they see only rarely. They consider such long-term friendships sacred.[24]

When our children leave home, and we no longer see the same mothers at soccer games or at school plays or at concerts, we are freed of those mothers-of-the-children's-friends ties that we have taken for granted for ten or twenty years. It's when our children no longer rule so much of our social lives that we have the privilege of selecting our own friends, instead of having them chosen for us, mostly by convenience and car pools.

Robin is only fifty-three, but she has ditched almost all of her friends of convenience by moving. She and her husband decided to sell their dry-cleaning business in Maryland and move to New Hampshire, where they'd spent several summer vacations. She has severed ties with most of her friends in suburban Maryland, except for one couple with whom she and her husband are still very close.

Now, says Robin, "my friends are women of all ages that I meet doing the things that interest me. One of my closest friends is a sixty-five-year-old pottery teacher who gives classes in her home," Robin says. "And my other dear friend is thirty-one, and owns the bakery where I work three days a week doing over-the-counter sales. When my kids were younger, even though I worked in our business, all of my friends were other mothers I knew because of my three kids. It was like they got to rule my social life, but now my social life is finally mine!"

I think the real lesson here is that you are never too old to make new friends, and those friends can never be too old or too young for you.

If you are confused about your friendships, or if you feel cut off from the friends you made through your children, maybe it's time to rethink the ways in which you can connect with potential friends. **Here are eight suggestions for maintaining friendships and finding new ones:**

1. **Keep in touch.** You have to make the effort to call and e-mail and see your friends face-to-face because that's what will strengthen your bonds. Don't wait for her to call you; be the one to make the call. If none of your closest friends live nearby, then maybe it's time to consider finding some "friends of the road." The "friends of the heart" are those you made during childhood or while you were young, and they will always be close to you, but you also need "friends of the road," those you meet along life's journey. Both kinds are valuable, but the road friends are the ones who are right here, right now.

2. **Spend time together.** Make an effort to do things with your friends. Get together on special occasions, like holidays and birthdays, and on every third Friday, too. Go to the movies, go out for coffee, form a book group, take a walk, do stuff! Men forge friendships by planning joint activities—they play golf, they build a deck, they watch football together. Women are more likely to sit around and talk to their friends. But by engaging in both—the doing and the talking—you'll have the best of both worlds, and you'll feel closer to each other.

3. **Introduce your friends to each other.** When social scientists study friendships, they often ask people how many of their friends know each other. If your friends are also friends, that means you have an active social network, one in which everyone is tied in to everyone else. Think of it as a sorority for grown-ups, or a church

of friendship. It really will make you feel as if you have a second family, a family of friends.

4. **If you want to end it, say so.** If you feel that a friendship has run its course—if you no longer have much in common with the mother of one of your child's friends, for instance—then break it off. Don't feel obligated to invest yourself in a dead-end friend.

5. **Work out the problems.** Likewise, if you have a friendship that you value, but one that seems to be rocky, try to figure out what's wrong. Confide your misgivings to your friend and see if she's feeling the same way. Maybe the two of you can find a way to get your friendship back on track.

6. **Tell a secret, hear a secret.** Sometimes women have friends they do things with but don't talk to that much. An almost surefire way to feel closer to someone is to share intimate secrets. And this secret sharing must be a two-way street: to hear one, you have to tell one. The only relationship in which this isn't true would be with a therapist, someone who's getting paid to listen to your secrets, or with a manicurist, who's getting paid to tend to your cuticles. But a friend is someone who listens with sympathy as you tell the worst truth you can imagine, and then tells you one in return.

7. **Be a joiner.** If you are running dry on friendships, then join a group to do something that interests you. This could be anything, from taking a jazz dance class to signing up for introductory Spanish lessons to volunteering to tutor immigrants. If you become engaged in an activity that excites and fascinates you, you will be primed for making a friend who feels the same way you do.

8. **Do Internet research.** You'd be amazed at how many people catch up with old friends by Googling them, or by signing up for classmates.com. Remember that best friend you had in tenth grade but lost touch with? Guess what? You're ten minutes away from finding out that she lives two towns over. If you have any longing to reconnect with old pals, the Internet is the way to go.

Having good work and good friends is the backbone of a healthy midlife for women. But if you are struggling with one or the other, or both, you may need to reflect more deeply on who you are and where you want to go in this next stage of life. Read on to discover how to find yourself in midlife, and what it takes to thrive and survive after your children leave home.

CHAPTER NINE

Coming Into Your Own (Again)

Most of us, at some point, experience a subtle but profound shift of internal gears when our children leave. It happens when we finally understand that the years of intense nurturing are over and we realize that our mostly mother days are mostly over. And after a while, it begins to seem as if that time was part of a fever dream of motherhood, a night vision that has drifted away with the morning haze.

"I feel like I woke up, after years of caring for my children, my house, and my husband," says Jasmine, fifty-three, an out-of-work lawyer. "But I feel more alive than I ever did, too," she adds, "clearer in my vision and my insights about getting older and retiring and being sexual and wondering about the possibilities for my future."

It's only now, after her children are gone, Jasmine says, that she has awakened from her Mother Dream, fully energized and eager to get on with the rest of her life.

"I was happy to be a full-time mother, but I was pushed to move on when my children left," agrees Lydia, fifty-six, of Brewster, New York. She, too, uses the same sleep metaphor that Jasmine does. "Having children now seems like a dream, or like a Beckett play. We come into this world alone and we go out of this world alone, children or no children, and so we had better be the women we wish to be, and lead the lives we feel we need to live," Lydia says.

Moved to similar poetic heights when they describe their situation, many mothers find themselves delighted with the new place in life in which they find themselves.

Lydia is clearly one of those poets. And she's also grateful to be still "madly in love" with her husband, as she puts it. "I'm pleased and relieved that my husband and I are still here and making a go of it," says Lydia, who adds that she always understood that raising children would not be a full-time, lifetime job.

As a mother of two girls who just left home, Betsy agrees it is only now that "I am back to being me, the person I was thirty or forty years ago." At the age of fifty-four, she's been married and divorced and remarried. Betsy's second marriage, though, was to a woman, one with whom she's been living for twenty years. Betsy and her new partner have lived through some dramatic, and traumatic, times—after all, they're lesbians, and they live in Texas. But she says she's never felt so true to herself as she does now.

Other mothers echo Betsy's sentiment.

One says that "I'm a person, not just my children's mother."

Says another, "I'm carving out my own space, one that's not connected to my status as a mother and wife."

For women like these, it seems only natural to realize that motherhood is not the only role that defines them. These women do not give up being Mom; on the contrary, **nearly all of the women in my Web survey insist that they will consider themselves mothers forever.** It's just that they finally feel free to explore other parts of themselves, aspects that have been buried deeply for decades. It's as if they've been living under the sea for years, swimming in the cool blue waters of motherhood, but never raising their heads above water. It's only when they finally decide to swim up to the surface that they notice how much open air lies above.

Evelyn's golden moment came as a realization this simple: "I'm in charge of the life I live now." To Evelyn, this is a gloriously luxurious way to feel. Since she and her husband moved to Vermont from suburban Virginia, her new life consists of "my decisions and doing what I want." Evelyn and her husband downsized their house and their cars and their lives so that they could go mountain biking and tend to their garden and do yoga together. They no longer have to worry about what their children are doing or how they can earn enough money to keep up with the many Joneses in their former upscale neighborhood.

This "I don't care what other people think" attitude is what makes Evelyn feel she has come into her own: her own life, her own love, her own friends, and her own work.

A kinder, gentler way to put this is that life goes on, and we each have to figure out how we will engage ourselves in it, how we plan to start this new chapter in our lives, while still holding on to the chapters that have gone before. It's not that we stop nurturing and being mothers. We just put mothering on pause for a while—at least until we have to fast-forward to grandmothering.

We have arrived at the moment for redrawing our Motherhood Head, by discarding parts of our old self and substituting new ones. If you drew the two, they might look something like this:

Rearranging Your Motherhood Head

OLD YOU

NEW YOU

Your old head was full of child-related minutiae and assorted do-mestic details. But your new head is free of all that, and available to be filled with whatever pleases your fancy.

Another way to think of this process is to imagine your life as a thick book with many chapters. You figure out what the book is called and what's in each chapter, based on the crises and calamities you've suffered, as well as the triumphs and successes you've achieved.

When psychologists in Australia asked women to do just this, they found that women divided their lives into about eight or nine chapters. After the age of forty, most women named at least one chapter about a time they broke out or changed course from a previous path. That transition was often tied into a dramatic change at work. What's especially encouraging, too, is that the older women, those over fifty-five or sixty, were most likely to tell stories with triumphant endings, with a last chapter that emphasized their fulfillment and their achievement of a sense of clarity and closure on life.[1]

When I asked a group of women what they'd call the book of their life, they came up with some insightful titles. The titles women give for their books reveal a great deal about who they are and how they view themselves.

One woman, a stay-at-home mom who started a full-time career the minute her youngest child left home, called her book *The Nicest Person in the Room,* because, she says, "I was always told that if I was nice I would get what I want." Another called her book *It's Good to Be Bad,* because she has always refused to live by the social rules that her mother insisted were the right ones. A third said that her book would be *It's Okay to Be,* because she realized recently that whatever she chooses or decides is fine. Still others called their life books *Lucky Me,* reflecting a blessed existence; *Trying to Get It Right,* for one's who's still striving; and *She Made a Difference,* for one who feels she has mattered.

On the whole, these college-educated, middle-class women are relatively content with their lives, and with themselves, now that their children are mostly gone. (The really nice woman's son has moved back home after graduating from college, and the okay-to-be mom's son is home, too, recovering from a bout of depression.) And, it turns out, their extraordinary level of contentment and security is more the rule than the exception.

Women who have a good love relationship, engrossing work, a decent level of self-esteem, and a network of close and caring friends tend to be happier and to have better mental health than women who don't have these things. That's not so shocking. But here's a surprise: the older a woman is, the higher her level of well-being. It's only after the age of forty or fifty that women have finally built their life to their own specifications, like one of those custom-made teddy bears sold at malls. The only difference is that they have pieced together their lives with love and friends and work, rather than with plastic and plush fabric and satin.

When the children leave home, the nurturing part of women's personality begins to fade, or else it transmutes itself into something entirely different. As women notice this transformation, many are excited and pleased to have moved beyond their need to nurture.

Peggy, a Tennessee paralegal, started having children when she was twenty and didn't stop until she'd had five. Now that she's fifty, all of Peggy's children are finally gone, and she's delighted that she no longer feels she needs to be Mother to the World. "My life is full, and I don't need to nurture to feel fulfillment," she says.

Another woman from my Web survey comments that she realizes that "I am a person, not just my children's mother."

This is an enormous insight for many empty-nest moms, who tell themselves: **I am more than a mother.**

Still, a few mothers can't seem to relinquish their need to nurture, so they redirect that maternal life force elsewhere. Gloria, a forty-nine-year-old mom in North Carolina, says her husband refers to her as "Velcro Mom," because random children keep sticking to her. "We've had two other teenagers live with us for a while, one a friend's child and another a godson, and I still feel a need to have other children in my life," Gloria says.

Gloria doesn't really long to have her almost-grown children back; instead, she yearns for them as they used to be, ten or fifteen years ago. Gloria confesses to missing little ones, the kind who were thrilled when she helped make their Halloween costumes and who thought that going to the movies with her was a treat and not some form of exquisite torture. Gloria figures that this yearning, as well as her Velcro habit, will probably dissipate once she becomes a grandmother.

Another mom reluctant to cut the motherhood cord is Marina, forty-three, an accountant in Colorado. "I don't know how not to be a mom," she complains.

Alicia agrees. Now forty-eight, she says that "I feel less important now that my kids are gone. I need to find something fulfilling to take the place of the nurturing that I used to give my children."

And in what sounds like a keening lament, Christine, forty, wishes that "I had spent more time just on me. I wish I had developed into a person who could just carry on now that she's without children. But what is a mother without her children?"

The problem for some midlife mothers is not that they miss their children, it's that **some women don't know how to function without their primary role as mother.** The social rules for motherhood are clear and well defined, especially when children are young and needy. The job description is clear: a mother cooks and shops for her children, she takes their temperature when they are sick, she helps them with homework, she drives them where they need to go. If and when she can't do some of this, or any of it, she arranges for someone else to do it.

The mother role acts as a kind of boundary line, a high fence that keeps women marching along the narrow path of motherhood. It's only when the fence is cut down or removed that mothers are able to wander and find their own path through life.

Eileen, forty-five, a bookkeeper in Illinois, says that it wasn't until she chose to rid herself of the roles that had defined her, by getting a divorce (wife role) and watching her two children move out (mother role), that she discovered "the woman standing alone was pretty terrific and brave."

Eileen felt brave because she'd never lived as an adult without being a wife or a mother: she realized that she had become her roles, and that she had no other way in which to see herself.

Indeed, standing alone and roleless is a frightening concept for women who feel comfortable only as Mom. Bereft of the mother role, or the wife role, many women find it difficult to figure out what should replace it.

Clara, a divorced college professor in Albuquerque, used to think of herself as "my father's daughter until I was twenty-one, and then my husband's wife until I was thirty-seven, and my children's mother for the next twenty years."

In this way, Clara lived her life rather thoughtlessly, and without much effort, mostly because everything seemed so clear and simple. Now, she says, "I've finally discovered myself as separate person in the world."

But it took her long enough: Clara is sixty-two years old.

Like Clara, some women need decades to be able to view themselves, and their lives, in an objective way. Many of us are so busy living our lives that we have trouble stepping back and asking crucial questions, like **"What's most important to me?"** and **"Who do I want to be?"**

Living with Regret

This kind of stocktaking and self-evaluation can be both challenging and troubling, which is why some women don't try it until the age of forty or fifty, if at all. But performing a life review can be extremely beneficial, because it gives women a clear vision of what they've done wrong, and how to make it right.

In my Web survey, only one out of three midlife moms says she has no regrets after reflecting on her life so far. That leaves two out of three who insist that they'd do at least one thing differently if they could live the last fifteen years of their life over again. Many of these regrets are tied to how they raised their children. Nearly 40 percent of moms say that if they could do it all again, they'd either relax more about their children or they'd appreciate the kids more. Another 20 percent have work regrets, wishing they had taken their career either more seriously or less so. Finally, almost 10 percent have marital regrets, wishing they had stayed in a not-so-bad marriage or had left a not-so-good one.

In several long-term studies of women's lives, psychologists asked women what they'd do differently, if they could. The results were clear: their most common regrets were about not getting more education and about not pursuing a better career. The women didn't necessarily do anything about their regrets, though. In fact, it was especially those who acted on their regrets early, while in their thirties, who had the best mental health later in life, the researchers say.[2]

"When you ask about regrets, every woman has paths not taken or missed opportunities, but few say they have real regrets," says Elizabeth A. Vandewater, an associate professor of human development at the University of Texas in Austin, who conducted this study. "All of this hits you in the face in midlife. I'm forty-three, for example, and I wish I had gone to medical school. But I don't have the time for it now, it's not going to happen, so it's a path not taken. But I don't regret it," she tells me in a telephone interview.

"Regret is a very serious thing to have to carry around with you, because you're clinging to this notion. It's like holding in hostility about something that happened a long time ago," adds Vandewater. "You might say, 'I wish I'd had my children earlier,' or 'I wish I'd had my children later,' but do you regret having your children?" she asks. "No, of course not."

Women who accumulate regrets, like old shoes and torn T-shirts, are sometimes inspired to mend their ways, if not their old clothes. But many also have a "tendency to ruminate," according to Vandewater, which means they are pessimistic about their ability to overcome obstacles.[3]

Ruminators focus on what's bad instead of good, what's hurtful instead of helpful, and they do so in a self-defeating way. They wallow in negativity. If you often feel sorry for yourself, if you are negative, if you make simple things seem complicated, if you are moody and rarely cheerful, then you might be a ruminator. This has nothing to do with chewing your cud, like a cow. It has more to do with predicting your own failure and then living up to, or rather down to, that prophecy. You believe that you will fail, so you do. It's as if you laced up your ice skates, wobbled out onto the ice, and then waited to fall. If you expect to slip and slide, you will.

Julie, forty-nine, answered my Web survey, and I'd say she's definitely a ruminator. Her three children have left home, and there's rarely a moment in which she doesn't feel that someone is getting the better of her, or that she's somehow being cheated. Julie works full-time, as a clerk in a New Jersey insurance office, and she knows that she is being underpaid and overworked. Not only that, Julie believes that most of her coworkers get more interesting assignments than she does, and they take more time off, without penalty.

Julie's mother always favored her younger brother, too, according to Julie, and after the woman died, he got more jewelry and furniture than she did. She feels that wasn't fair, but then she always expected to be cheated out of her inheritance.

It's clear to me from the way in which Julie describes the people she knows that she has no real friends. She'd be uncomfortable asking any of them to take her to a hospital emergency room at two a.m., for example, and if she had an important secret, she wouldn't tell any of them, she says, "because it's not their business."

Julie has become an expert at alienating people, at pushing them away with her negativity and her mood swings. Because she expects people to cheat her and to dislike her, she puts up her defenses early, waiting for the worst to happen. And it usually does. Julie's life is one big bag of regret, more than most people could keep track of in a lifetime.

Many women experience a few twinges of regret, though usually on a much lesser scale than Julie. We regret the guy we didn't marry or the house we didn't buy or the job we never got. When I asked a group of women in rural New York about their regrets, equal numbers insist that they had none, or that they knew precisely how and when they had taken the wrong path, a decision for which they are now sorry.

"I knew that this was my 'road-not-taken' day,'" says Riley, fifty-eight, referring to a trip she took to a judicial conference at which she met a former law-school friend who had been named as a state supreme court judge in Florida. Riley had had a flourishing legal career, but gave it up twenty years ago to raise her twin daughters.

"This hit me viscerally, because I thought, 'This could be me.' I did the fast-track career when I finished law school, and I argued civil rights and gender discrimination cases as a trial attorney," she says. "I had a moment when I thought, 'I took myself off this path,' so I can't regret my choice. But still, it hit me that I had made a very big decision, one that I couldn't go back and change."

Riley is a large, exuberant woman, the kind who sucks all the air out of the room the minute she walks into it. And she's not gorgeous, or even exotic looking, it's just that she is full of life and self-confidence. There's not one whiff of rumination about her. She's the kind of woman who confesses that "I've never felt diminished by anything I did" and makes it seem completely believable.

Riley rid herself of an eighteen-month starter-marriage husband when she was twenty-two, and didn't marry again until she was thirty-two. She didn't have her children, twin girls, until she was thirty-nine, and by then it had taken three years and a series of in-vitro fertilizations for her to get pregnant. When they were born, her girls were ten weeks premature, and "there was no way I was handing them over to a babysitter and going back to work," Riley says.

Riley's friend, Danica, fifty-four, also feels some regret. She regrets "that no one told me I could be anything I wanted to be. I'd have gone to medical school, but nobody pushed me to do it. My mother had two girls, and her goals for my sister and me were that we should go to college and then we should get married," she adds.

Danica did go to college, got married, and had two children. And instead of becoming a doctor, which she didn't even think was in the realm of possibility, she became a high-school English teacher. She's been teaching in an inner-city school in New York for nearly thirty years, in part because that was an acceptable job for a girl.

Riley and Danica's friend Randy, fifty-four, chimes in with her main regret in life. "My mother's only goals for me were that I look pretty and that I find someone to support me," she agrees with a laugh.

Randy has done just that, having two children and being married to a stockbroker for thirty years. She also had a career as an art teacher, but if she had it to do over again, Randy says, she would have gotten a degree in architecture and designed homes and buildings, rather than simply redecorating her own home over and over again.

As I look around Randy's utterly charming house, I can see that she would have been a great designer. Her home is a former carriage house, situated on a tiny sideways plot of land in a small New York village. The place contains only a few rooms, though all are huge. The interiors are brick walls, divided by heavy sliding doors and interrupted by tiny windows, high up. The building was meant to house horses and small carriages for a large estate that used to be nearby, but now the place is a cozy, comfortable, and unique modern home. Randy's collection of antique signs covers the brick walls, giving a look of authenticity to all of its rough edges. The lighting fixtures blend into the high ceilings, and the home feels as if it has been transported here in a time machine, directly from the mid-nineteenth century.

Randy's friend Iris, fifty-two, insists that she, too, has one major regret, although she's had a successful career as a mathematics professor at a local community college. Iris wears bright red shoes and a little white miniskirt, and with her crazy curly dark hair and her red tube top, she almost looks as if she were thirty-something and ready to go to a disco.

"I was living on my own in New York City, and the chairman of my department told me that he would admit me to the PhD program in math education. There was a catch, though. All I had to do was to go to Chile with him, where he was going to translate textbooks. I thought he wanted me to be his helper, like a research assistant. I was close to running off with him, until I realized that the offer involved me being his mistress," Iris confesses. "So I didn't pursue it. The issue became important recently, when I changed jobs and was told I would be fired because I didn't have a doctorate. Now I regret that I didn't say to the guy, 'I want the degree part, but not the mistress part,'" she concludes.

Iris isn't devastated by regret, but she's peeved that she hadn't been more assertive with her lecherous professor. Women like Iris, who are able to overcome regret, or who never have much of it in the first place, eventually find themselves achieving a sense of well-being. This trait— call it happiness or life satisfaction or mental health or contentment—is difficult to measure. But it fascinates psychologists, who are desperate to figure out not only *who* has the highest level of well-being, but *why* they do.

Finding Well-Being

What is well-being?

It's happiness and contentment and satisfaction; it's having more good feelings than bad ones. But well-being is not one specific thing— there's no single well-being number, the way there's a number that reveals your cholesterol level or your blood pressure. If you've got what experts call "subjective well-being," you feel cheerful and optimistic; you are lacking hopelessness, anxiety, and nervous fidgets. If you've got "psychological well-being," then you are overflowing with feelings of self-acceptance, of mastery, and of purpose in life. You also feel positive about your relationships with other people, you have a sense of independence, and a sense of personal growth.[4]

With these aspects of well-being in mind, social scientists asked a large group of Americans dozens of questions about themselves and their feelings. At one extreme, the experts found that a small number of people were Flourishing. The Flourishing are psychologically and socially healthy, they often feel positive emotions, and they rarely feel negative ones. **About 17 percent of Americans, or almost one in five people, are Flourishing.**

To be considered in the Flourishing category, people had to say that all or most of the time during the past thirty days they had felt cheerful, in good spirits, extremely happy, calm and peaceful, satisfied, and full of life. In addition, when asked to rate their life these days, from 0, the worst possible life overall, to 10, the best possible life, they put themselves close to the 10 end. But that's not all. Those who are Flourishing also agree that they like most parts of their personality; that their lives have been a constant process of learning, change, and growth; that they felt a sense of purpose in life; and that they are adept at managing the responsibilities of daily life.[5]

Two groups fall at the other extreme—**12 percent are Languishing and 14 percent are Depressed.** The Languishing are in poor emotional and psychological health, and they tend to lose workdays and limit their activities due to physical problems. The seriously Depressed are even worse off, getting no pleasure out of life, often feeling despair and hopelessness and suffering from insomnia, and their activities are seriously limited by their emotional paralysis. The Languishing may also be Depressed, but not all of them are.

Finally, there's the great unwashed middle, where most of the rest of us fall. **Moderates** are those who are neither at the peak of mental health nor at its very bottom: **about 57 percent of Americans are in the Moderate range of mental health,** according to this research.

Most of us are not as deliriously chipper as the Flourishing folks, nor are we as deeply miserable as the Languishing or the Depressed. If you want to get a general idea of where you might fit in, answer the following questions.

THE WELL-BEING TEST

This is a very rough measure, vastly oversimplified, but it will give you a best guess of how happy you are, in case you don't already know.

During the past thirty days, how often did you feel the following? Use this scale to answer the first four questions.

1=Almost every day   2=A few times a week   3=Once a week   4=A few times   5=Almost never

1.	Anxious, nervous	1	2	3	4	5
2.	Hopeless	1	2	3	4	5
3.	Sad, depressed	1	2	3	4	5
4.	Worthless	1	2	3	4	5

Use this scale to answer the next four questions.

1 = Almost never   2 = A few times   3 = Once a week   4 = A few times a week   5=Almost every day

5.	Cheerful	1	2	3	4	5

6. Happy	1	2	3	4	5
7. Full of life	1	2	3	4	5
8. Filled with a sense of purpose	1	2	3	4	5

Your score should range from 8, if you answered all 1s, to 40, if you answered all 5s. If you scored between 8 and 18, you may be either Languishing or Depressed. Between 19 and 28, you are likely in the Moderate group. And if you scored 29 or higher, you may be among the Flourishing.

What most women don't realize, though, is that their well-being is influenced by several factors that are out of their control. As we age, for instance, we tend to feel more positive feelings and fewer negative ones.

Here are five of the most important social factors that influence well-being and general all-around cheerfulness—some are a lot more obvious than others.

- ❖ Education: more educated people are less likely to be depressed
- ❖ Work: those with jobs are less depressed than the unemployed
- ❖ Being satisfied with finances: leads to lower levels of depression
- ❖ Being married: the married have lower levels of distress than the never married and divorced
- ❖ Age: sixty-three is the optimum age for happiness, lack of distress or depression, and contentment with life[6]

The sociologists who conducted this study say that the fifties and sixties are an "optimum age" for psychological well-being. **They also found that levels of depression and distress decline with age.** Thus, by the age of sixty-three, Americans have reached a peak of maturity, emotional health, career and financial success, and physical vigor and they have launched their children into the world, which means they are liberated from many parental duties. **It's almost as if sixty-three is the age of the last good time.**

Other social scientists agree that midlife signals a kind of halcyon period, when women and men ease into themselves and into their lives, so that they feel better about pretty much everything. As they age, Americans say that they feel relatively content with their family relationships, as well as with their work, their finances, and their life. The only aspects of life that get worse with age are people's health and their satisfaction with their sexuality. That's probably because their health is actually getting worse, and they are having sex less often than before.[7]

In one study of satisfaction and well-being, researchers divided adult life into three parts: young adulthood, which lasts from the ages of twenty-five to thirty-four; middle adulthood, which stretches from age thirty-five to sixty-four; and older adulthood, which begins at age sixty-five and ends at age seventy-four. (They considered seventy-five or more to be old age.) The researchers found that feelings of psychological distress and misery are actually highest among young adults and lowest among older adults. Not only that, but young adults feel positive emotions least often, while those in middle and older age experience positive feelings most often.[8]

So, **OLDER = BETTER, at least as far as being happy goes.**

The reason for so much youthful misery, according to some psychologists, is that young people tend to feel all of their emotions much more intensely, so that their suffering is more extreme. Maybe that's why young people are so much more unhappy than everyone else—they just feel everything more deeply. According to this approach, older adults have tamped down their feelings to the point that they aren't ever really in despair, but neither are they ever filled with unimaginable joy. It's an "only the young can be wild and crazy" hypothesis, with a notion that only the young are truly passionate.

To that, I say: baloney.

And so do other psychologists, many of whom, like me, also have graying hair (or we would, if we didn't color it!).

Among these skeptics is a group of researchers who decided to try and figure out if people really do become less emotional as they age. They gave pagers to a large group of adults of all ages, and then paged them randomly five times a day, every day, for a week. The people had to note which emotions they were feeling at the precise moment the pager went off. So instead of asking adults about *memories* of feelings, they asked about *actual* feelings.

This clever research found that, indeed, **older folks feel negative emotions least often,** while those between the ages of eighteen and thirty-four feel bad most often. Not only that, but **older men and women feel positive for much longer periods than do younger ones.** This is not to say, however, that older people's feelings are any less intense than those of younger people. Rather, these psychologists conclude that people's emotions become deeper and more complex as they age.[9]

Thus, women are like good red wine, improving over time as they rest on the wine rack of life.

The positive feelings that improve with age include being cheerful, being in good spirits, feeling extremely happy, being calm and peaceful, feeling satisfied, being full of life, feeling excitement, being amused, being interested, feeling proud, and feeling a sense of accomplishment. That just about covers everything and anything having to do with feeling fabulous.

The feelings strongest among younger adults are feeling so sad that nothing can cheer you up, being nervous, feeling restless or fidgety, feeling hopeless, feeling that everything is an effort, feeling worthless, feeling embarrassed, feeling ashamed, feeling irritated, feeling guilty, feeling disgusted, feeling afraid, feeling frustrated, and feeling bored. That pretty much covers the waterfront of lousy sentiments.

Simply put, then, being young is emotionally difficult. **Though looking young may be everybody's goal, feeling young means being in pain, anxious, and often miserable.**

It's older folks who are happiest, agrees Margie Lachman, a professor of psychology at Brandeis University, in Waltham, Massachusetts. "Well-being increases right on up to age seventy or seventy-five, and only then does it stop," she tells me in a telephone interview. "It's only after the age of seventy-five or eighty that we see a decline in well-being, when the loss of function and illness take over," adds Lachman, who specializes in the study of adult development and aging.[10]

In trying to figure out why older seems better, another group of psychologists interviewed one thousand Americans every day for a week and asked them about every single bit of stress in their lives, including things that had happened to a close friend or relative. They asked this question, in particular, because women tend to view their friends' problems as their own problems: it's a "your problem is my problem" view. Men tend to have an opposing point of view, however, which is usually "your problem is your problem."

This study revealed that four in ten Americans say they have at least one stressor every day, and one in ten has several stressors each day. Also, women do, in fact, report having more stress than men, things like too much work, tension, and fights with coworkers and friends, as well as problems suffered by friends. Finally, in what could be viewed as a lesson in Modern Life and Modern Aging 101, younger people, those between the ages of twenty-five and thirty-nine, also report having the most daily stress, while those between the ages of sixty and seventy-four feel the least stress.[11]

Age is not the only factor that determines how we feel about life, of course. The way our parents raised us also plays a major role in determining how happy we are, even decades after we've left the nest. A team of British doctors claims that a woman's original family has a powerful and surprising influence on her happiness in midlife. They studied a large group of British women, all of whom were born in 1946, and interviewed these women dozens of times over the years, including six times when the women were between forty-seven and fifty-two years old. The doctors classified women as being psychologically distressed if they often felt the following symptoms: anxiety and depression, irritability, fearfulness, and feelings of panic.

They found that women who grew up poor were much more psychologically distressed, many years later, as adults. In addition, women whose parents divorced when they were young felt more distress in midlife, and that distress was even worse if they themselves had also divorced. Heavy smokers and the overweight were also most distressed, as were those who admitted that they had no one to turn to in a time of crisis.[12]

Does this mean that once you are born into your family, your fate and your personality are signed, sealed, and delivered?

Thankfully, no.

We all make our own destiny, and while it can be difficult to leap across social and economic barriers, many women do. Not only that, but psychologists are embroiled in a decades-long debate over whether personality changes during adulthood. On one side are those who believe that personality is pretty much set in stone after the age of thirty or so. They believe that no matter what happens, you are who you are, and the only thing that really changes is your hair color and your waist size. Other psychologists, though, are convinced that personality can undergo any number of significant transformations throughout adult life, just like, say, skin tone and belly fat. Not only that, but they believe that these changes can be incredibly dramatic.

Does Personality Change?

So which experts are right?

Is it the ones who say we are doomed to be whatever our genes and our parents made us, never to alter our own path through life? According to these fatalists, women will be happy or miserable, cheerful or gloomy, talkative or shy based on the personality they were born with and the way they developed during childhood.

Or are the psychologists who feel we can remake ourselves in whatever image we choose the ones who are right? They'd say that a woman who is mean and nasty, a friendless Wicked Witch of the West, can transform herself, over time, into Glinda the Good, can become a lovable do-gooder, if she wills it so.

Personally, I'm a firm believer in the Wizard of Oz personality-can-change point of view, because it seems more fair and less fatalistic, less defeated-before-you-begin. If we all have the potential for change, then we can do something about all the parts of us that we don't like or we think have room for improvement. And it's during midlife that we are best able to see ourselves clearly and make a dramatic and sincere attempt to reconfigure ourselves.

It seems that many midlife moms agree with me. Two out of three women in my Web survey say they often feel a desire to reinvent themselves. So they, too, hold on to a fervent belief in the transformative power of personality: if you will yourself to change, you will change! Think of the process as *Extreme Makeover: My Edition,* only there's no surgery or drastic home renovation involved. Instead, it's a quiet, ongoing revolution that happens mostly on the inside.

It's especially true that when children leave, women have the energy and the time and the motivation to engage in re-creating themselves. Women reach midlife as if they have been worked in clay and then fired in a kiln. In their twenties, they entered the oven of life as unfinished, raw clay. When they emerge, years later, they are hard baked and strong—with the skin to prove it!

But in every woman's raw material are quirks and traits that make her who she is, that were encoded in her genes since before she was born. Along with whatever kind of pushing and prodding she got, or didn't get, from her parents, a few of these special traits become as comfortable and familiar as an old pair of jeans. Think of these as standard-issue, basic personality traits, like the package of accessories that comes with a new car.

The basic personality package is simple, and consists of traits that psychologists refer to as "the Big Five," or NEO, in honor of the first three. They are:

- ❖ **Neuroticism:** the tendency to be anxious and fearful, with frequent mood swings, or not
- ❖ **Extroversion:** being outgoing and sociable, or shy and self-conscious
- ❖ **Openness to experience:** being creative and willing to try what's new, or preferring the stick-to-the-familiar approach
- ❖ **Agreeableness:** being friendly and easy to get along with, like Glinda, say, or being more ill-tempered, like that other witch
- ❖ **Conscientiousness:** being practical and organized, or being a disorganized mess

Some psychologists believe that these traits are fixed by the age of thirty because they are the basic building blocks of human personality. But other experts insist that even these attributes can change gradually throughout adult life, finally becoming stable only after the age of fifty or so. That's according to researchers who combined all the evidence from 152 different studies of personality change over time that had been conducted during the last several decades. Examining this mountain of research, all of it about whether personality changes or not, they concluded that the Big Five are not set in stone, but bend and change as women and men mature into their middle years.[13]

Other experts agree that people become more conscientious as they age, and more agreeable, and that they hit a peak of practicality and friendliness in midlife. In addition, they say, people tend to become less neurotic and more open as they age.

Maybe the real answer is this: nobody really knows how fixed or flexible personality is. But we can act as if we believe in our own ability to change, because that way we will feel in charge of our own path to self-improvement.

And then we can try mightily to walk that line.

Margie Lachman is one of those who believes that a few aspects of personality don't change, but nearly everything else does. "If you include other things in personality, like self-esteem, self-confidence, having a sense of purpose in life, and a sense of control, then I think these things do change, based on your experience and the natural growth process," she tells me. "The broader view of personality is that it isn't just black and white," Lachman continues. Instead, it's much more complex, and much more fascinating.

Worried About Growing Older

Personality can include any trait, from how shy you are, to how compulsive you are, to how often you become grumpy and irritable. It can even include specific anxieties, such as how worried you are about growing older. And guess what? Concern about aging is one aspect of personality that changes over time, according to some experts.[14] It's obviously an issue that becomes more central to women as they advance in years. And, of course, it makes sense that women are more worried about getting older as they actually get older. Four in ten of the mothers in my Web survey admit they are afraid of growing old, for example. In addition, about two in ten have already had some kind of major health problem.

I interviewed so many women who made jokes about falling apart before their own eyes that it became one of my standard questions. I'd ask every woman the same thing: "What's the most upsetting part of watching yourself age?"

Their answers tended to be loud and full of self-mocking good humor.

The litany of women's worries about aging is endless. They fret about everything, from top to bottom. They worry about their graying and thinning hair, their sagging eyelids, their deep smile and forehead lines, their melting jawline. They agonize over their crepelike neck, their freckled shoulders, their puffy middle, their droopy derriere, their thickening thighs, their heavy calves, their rough and swollen feet. They notice every single aging cell on their aging bodies, with grief and laughter, and with a special blend of acceptance and defiance.

And while nearly all women have had at least one thought or passing whimsical notion about cosmetic surgery, very few, only 4 percent, say they've actually had surgical intervention to look younger.

Finally, a major aspect of concern about aging is that many women are afraid of becoming their mother. They fear looking like her and also becoming like her.

MaryJo is fifty-one and gets that horrified worry every time she looks in a mirror. "Lately, I feel that when I look in the mirror, I actually get scared," she says. "I start thinking of my mom and what she was like at my age with all of us out of the house." MaryJo is actually nothing like her mother, because she works full-time and her mother never worked for pay. MaryJo also has her own life, taking several vacations a year, going to the movies or out for a drink with friends several times a month, a living-it-up life that her mother never, ever had.

But these facts don't prevent MaryJo from inner shudders over the I-Am-Becoming-My-Mother terror. "It is so hard, because even though I am physically aging—I'm gaining weight, I have wrinkles here and there, and age spots everywhere—my mind still thinks I'm twenty-one!" MaryJo says with a moan.

It's hard to think of yourself as a twenty-something if you look a lot more like a fifty-something, a problem tailor made for the baby-boom generation, a group of the eternally young (in their own minds, at least), who once thought that being old meant being over thirty. Ha! Now that we're over fifty, we're rethinking the meaning of wrinkles and love handles and saggy skin.

"I'm really trying to wrap my mind around the idea that my puffy eyes and the lines around my mouth don't look old, they just look mature," says Claudia, a baby boomer who just turned fifty-seven. "But then I look at my elbows, and, like, they don't even look human anymore, the skin isn't even skinlike," she says. "So I try to avoid mirrors most of the time, because I look better in my mind than I do in the glass," Claudia admits with a laugh.

Anyway, she adds, "I never thought that I'd say this, but fifty seems really young to me now, and I don't think I look much over fifty."

Claudia is among the many midlife women who feel they need to fight the aging battle, in part by redefining what old looks like, while also being slightly appalled by what's happening to their faces and their bodies. But some women the same age have overcome a life-threatening disease, and their view of looking and being old is radically different—and much more forgiving.

Roxy is fifty-two, but she's convinced that she looks fine. Roxy developed breast cancer when she was thirty-nine, so she is just grateful to be alive. After chemotherapy, radiation, and surgery, Roxy is glad that she can still look in a mirror and see herself at all. Now that her three children are no longer at home and she lives with a loving husband, she has found a new sense of exhilaration and freedom.

"I had forgotten what it feels like to be responsible only for me," Roxy says. "I have the luxury of taking care of only me, and I'm becoming selfish with my time. I say 'No' more often, and I don't let people push me around anymore. It has taken me fifty years to feel this way, but I am finally liberated. I don't know if it has so much to do with the children leaving or just being happy that I'm still alive. Cancer will do that to you," she concludes rather cheerfully.

Who's in Control?

Beating cancer is a surefire way to feel that you have control over your own life and fate. And it turns out that having a sense of control is a key personality trait, one that almost certainly changes over time. Researchers define control as having a sense of mastery over life and getting what you want. It's a matter of whether you believe that you are in charge of your fate, or if you think that what happens to you is mostly due to luck or random acts of the universe. Psychologists call this having a sense of control, or not.

Lachman has conducted several studies about control, and she has figured out how to measure a woman's sense of mastery and constraint. You probably feel a sense of mastery if you agree with the following statements:

- ❖ "I can do just about anything I really set my mind to."
- ❖ "When I really want to do something, I usually find a way to succeed at it."
- ❖ "What happens to me in the future mostly depends on me."

On the other hand, if you feel there are limits to your ability to control your fate, you might be more likely to agree with statements like these:

- ❖ "Other people determine most of what I can and cannot do."
- ❖ "What happens in my life is often beyond my control."
- ❖ "I often feel helpless in dealing with the problems of life."[15]

Lachman's research shows that the more money people earn, the greater their sense of mastery and the lower their feelings of constraint. Having enough money, or more than enough, can make you feel like a female master of the universe. Likewise, she finds that those with better health score higher on mastery and lower on constraint. As long as you haven't been stricken by breast cancer or arthritis or any other debilitating illness, you're more likely to say that you're in charge of your own life. And you are, in a sense, at least until something goes wrong.

Lachman found dramatic differences between adults who feel a sense of control and those who do not. Those who feel in control of their lives have a greater sense of well-being, they have higher self-esteem, they have lower levels of stress hormones, and they actually exercise more and eat a healthier diet. It's difficult to know, though, which comes first, since control and happiness are the major chicken-and-egg problem of modern psychology.

Do you feel happy and good about yourself because you feel a sense of control, or does having a sense of control make you feel that way?

Nobody really knows the answer to this question.

When Lachman looked at how people's sense of control changes as they get older, she found that midlife women feel more control over their work, their finances, and their marriage as they age. But they feel less control over their children and their sex lives, mostly because their children don't listen and they're having sex less often than they used to.[16]

"The feeling of control that changes most," she says, "is control over children, which decreases significantly over time. It probably makes sense, since the older children are, the less control we really do have over them." Once the children leave home, though, mothers and fathers start to feel a greater sense of control over the rest of their lives, she adds. "That makes sense, because if you have no control over children, your lives become more flexible once they leave, and you are no longer trying to control something that you really can't control," she tells me.

Thrivers and Survivors

In my Web survey, I asked women a simple question about how their sense of control changed after their children left home. Do they feel they have more control, less control, or about the same amount of control? Their answers, it turns out, are quite revealing.

The **Thrivers,** 60 percent of mothers, say that they have more control over their lives.

The **Survivors,** 20 percent of mothers, say they have noticed no real change in their sense of control.

And the **Stuck and Out of Luck,** also 20 percent, say they have less control, as if they have retreated into a shell and refused to emerge.

Thrivers

These women take charge of their lives when their children leave, feeling more in control of their lives, their time, their money, themselves. The largest number of Thrivers, about seven in ten, felt happy when their children left. That's because they don't need their children around to feel whole or complete.

Rosemary is a Thriver, and she's content because she realizes that she no longer controls her children "and the paths they have chosen or the life problems they encounter." She is clear-sighted about the fact that her children's lives are their own, "and I cannot control the direction they take in life. They have to make their own lives, their own mistakes, and their own successes, and they have to face their own fears."

By giving up the need to control her children's lives, Rosemary has actually gained a greater sense of control over her own life.

It's a wonderful paradox: cede control to get control.

In fact, Rosemary feels that she has more control over her finances, "which is extremely liberating and stress relieving." Now fifty-four, Rosemary works full-time as a hospital administrator in Dallas, Texas. She had her two children when she was in her early twenties, so they've been gone for a while. Rosemary loves to see her kids when they visit, but admits that after about a week, "we begin to get on each other's nerves."

Merry, too, is a Thriver, although by all rights she should feel much less control over her life. After all, her husband, Hal, recently had surgery for heart disease and is now suffering from severe depression. Not only that, but he is impotent, and Merry is a certified sex educator, "so it is ironic that I am experiencing this sexual blight," she says.

Despite the bad-health hailstorm that has descended on her family, Merry feels that she is "less a victim of irrational and meaningless circumstances, and I'm able to make choices more freely and independently."

At fifty-nine, Merry is remarkably resilient. A mother of four, she lives in a small town near Rochester, New York. She is pleased that her children are gone, she insists. Still, she describes her nineteen-year-old daughter as "a ray of sunshine, full of contagious exuberance and a zest for life," and when the girl comes home and leaves again, Merry admits that she cries. She says:

> It takes me a couple of days to adjust, and to surmount my feelings of loss. But I adapt pretty quickly, and then I feel a renewed sense of happiness, and I look forward to hearing about her adventures.
>
> Now that I am no longer a dedicated caregiver for everybody else, I am beginning to take care of me. I have tried to shun the "shoulds" and examine instead the possibilities for new horizons. One of my realizations is that my life will end, so I am determined to immerse myself in joyous moments, rather than settling for being a senseless robot. I don't equate the end of direct mothering with the end of life, but my arrival into this new phase has made me more aware of the quick passage of years and the inevitability of aging and death. Still, I feel I have the tools I need to jump into this stage of my life with ardor and joyful anticipation.

Survivors

These are the two out of ten mothers who feel no change in their feelings of control once the children leave.

Survivors seem a bit more ambivalent than Thrivers about where they are in life, which may be why they see no change in their sense of control. Patty, sixty-one, is a Survivor who is divorced with two sons. She's also a professional translator, transforming books written in French into books written in English, but she is having some difficulty transforming her own life.

"I realize that living with my children allowed me to put off facing all of the big, existential questions by focusing exclusively on the concrete problems at hand. Those questions never go away, of course, and are just waiting for us when the children leave. I now understand that my children have been safeguarding me, and not vice versa," Patty says.

It wasn't until her youngest left home a few years ago, she says, "that I went into a tailspin, suddenly facing my solitude and the fact that I had nothing to look forward to except my work," Patty adds. It doesn't help matters that both sons are now living in Paris, far from her home in Baltimore.

Corey, fifty-six, is also a Survivor, from Illinois, just outside of Chicago. She has one daughter and is deciding whether to continue as a full-time office manager or to become a part-time consultant. Meanwhile, she visits her homeland in the Philippines several times a year, to see her family and to figure out if she and her husband should buy a home there.

"My level of control varies," she says, "because sometimes I feel like I have more control, but at other times I have less, and I have to listen to what's happening and make whatever choices are available to me."

Corey's eyes are wide open to the fact that her daughter has her own life to live, "so it becomes even more important for me and my husband to make our own life choices," she says. "While I am proud of my daughter, and I believe her successes are of her own making as well as partly ours, I do not mark my life's success based on hers. We don't live in each other's shadow," says Corey.

Stuck and Out of Luck

Mothers who feel they have less control once their children leave home, about two in ten, are least likely to be happy about the kids' departure. In part, this is because so many of them gained their sense of identity and competence from their children. Once the kids are gone, though, they are like Humpty Dumpty; they've fallen and don't know how to put themselves back together again.

"I was surprised at my level of sadness after all three of my children had gone," says Stacey, fifty-five. "I felt without worth, and saddened by the loss of punctuation marks in the days and weeks and months that children and their school schedules provide," she explains. "It has been hard for me to discover another sense of purpose as great as being a mother, one that carries the same built-in sense of importance," Stacey says with regret.

Other Stuck and Out of Luck women seem to retreat from a sense of feeling in charge after being struck by medical or other disasters. Married thirty years, Katie is fifty-six and raised two children and a niece in her Iowa home. Katie's husband was just diagnosed with stage four stomach cancer. She has developed diabetes, and she is unhappy about being thirty-five pounds overweight. Not only that, but she has to care for her ninety-year-old mother-in-law, who moved to the neighborhood from Florida. And Katie's own parents and her father-in-law all died last year.

"My life is not as much fun as it was before I had children, probably because I wish I had done a better job with each of them, in different ways," she says. "My oldest is self-contained and goal driven, but we have no emotional connection. My second had learning and behavior problems all his life that have led me to distance myself from him, and now he is very angry with me, permanently," she says. "I look at other families and wonder what we did wrong, that we are not closer and happier," Katie mourns. "Maybe it's because we stopped taking true family vacations; that was a mistake."

Katie knows that she has retreated from life, but she has no idea how to get herself back on track.

Rowena, fifty-three, also falls into the Stuck and Out of Luck group, which she attributes to the fact that her husband has controlled her life for thirty-two years. She works full-time as a secretary in her Arkansas town, but sees herself only as a mother, not as a wife or a worker or a sister. "I have allowed another person, my husband, to control my future way too much," she says, and admits that she doesn't know if her marriage will survive much longer.

Finally, there's Lena, fifty-five, an administrator for a law office in New York City. She feels less in control of her life, especially over her two sons. Her youngest just told her that he's gay, a development that shocked Lena to her bones.

"I just had no idea at all," she says, her voice shaky. "I know I don't have much say in his life now, but along with my aging, needy parents, and bad stuff going on at work, I feel like I can't handle this right now," she adds. Lena feels lonely most of the time, with both boys in college, and although she lives with her husband, "the house feels too quiet," she says. "I am trying to accept having less control, and I've gotten into yoga. This has made me more contemplative, and I'm trying to look at things in new ways," Lena says.

Giving Back

One of the secrets of overcoming the Stuck and Out of Luck feeling is to devote yourself to causes and beliefs that go above and beyond your own family. Unfortunately, women who feel that they have lost control of their lives are often in no position, emotionally or in any other way, to focus on how to help other people.

That's too bad, since generativity is one of the major hallmarks of healthy personality in midlife.

Being a mother is one form of generativity, but that's not what I'm talking about, since all empty-nest mothers have experienced that kind of nurturing. Instead, I'm talking about what happens to women's need to nurture after their children leave home. It is when family is no longer the driving force of women's purpose in life that some women decide it's time to give back to other people, those unrelated by blood or marriage. This is generativity, a strong motivation to pass on wisdom and to help people outside of family. It's a yearning to leave a legacy, no matter how small. It's not about being the next Mother Teresa or the next Madame Curie, single-handedly trying to save the world's poor or discovering radioactivity, it's about helping out in whatever way possible in one tiny place on the planet.

The mothers in my Web survey, for example, volunteer an average of about two hours a week, helping other people. Their level of involvement in volunteering varies, however, from no time at all to eighty hours a week.

There's a woman in New Jersey who volunteers at a shelter for battered women about ten hours a week. Another, in New Mexico, teaches at two literacy programs, one for adults and another for teenagers, about fifteen hours a week. An Illinois mom rocks infants at an adoption agency and teaches English as a second language. There are women who do counseling at crisis-pregnancy centers, others who are math tutors for underprivileged children, one who leads a Bible study class at the county jail, and another who gives tours at the Art Institute in Chicago. A woman in Maine serves as a member of the town council, an elected position that requires about twenty hours of unpaid service each week.

All of these women are acting on their desire for generativity, which has less to do with feeling in control and more to do with spiritual union and empathy. This is a powerful and mysterious force, one that a group of psychologists recently tried to study. They found that the benefits of generativity were more of the heart than of the mind, more emotional than practical. Having generativity, the researchers say, is a sense of having done some good, of being of service to others.[17]

Many mothers act on their need for generativity while their children are still home, but only if it's for their children's benefit. Thus, they volunteer to be soccer-team coach or to bake cookies for a school fund-raiser or to serve on a committee to help organize the junior prom. In this way, their sense of social responsibility is turned inward, to family.

Eventually, though, many women feel a shift in their sense of social responsibility, turning it outward, to projects that don't involve their own children. This is especially true of women who have a college education, according to researchers. In one study of Americans between the ages of twenty-five and seventy-four, sociologist Alice Rossi found that parents with young children spend more of their time giving emotional support to family and friends. Parents of older children, though, feel less obliged to family and develop a greater sense of civic obligation and altruism. This is especially true among the college educated, more so than among than those with only a high-school degree, she found.

Indeed, women's sense of generativity peaks in the fifties, and gradually declines in the sixties and seventies, according to Rossi. Those who are more religious also give more time and more money to charitable causes, she says. Again, as in other studies, those with only a high-school education or less defined their well-being mainly by family, and not by how they fit into a larger social fabric. Indeed, high-school graduates are less likely to volunteer their time than are college graduates.[18]

Although you probably won't win a Nobel Prize for your volunteer work, your spirit of generativity is alive and well if you spend some time every week or month volunteering your time. If, during the past year, you have you done any of the following, then you probably have a greater gift for generativity and altruism than you realize.

Have you:

1. Served on a jury?
2. Donated blood?
3. Taught children who are not related to you for no pay?
4. Taken care of children who are not related to you for no pay?
5. Been elected to a local office or named to a board of directors?
6. Done any kind of fund-raising?
7. Been active in a religious group?
8. Helped to feed or care for the homeless?
9. Volunteered at a food pantry?
10. Served as a mentor or role model?

Spreading Your Wings

Many women have difficulty figuring out their place in the larger world. Sometimes it's for the simple reason that we're so busy and distracted that we can't ask essential questions like "Why?" and "What's it all for?"

In life, as in everything else, your view depends on your point of view. When you sit back and evaluate your life so far, the way you see your past depends on your level of generativity, how wise you are, and how resilient you are.

People high in generativity, for example, tend to see their lives in terms of commitment, and they are sensitive to the suffering of others, according to psychologists. What's most important, though, is that such people have developed an ability to transform what is upsetting and troubling into what is comforting and soothing. They cope with adversity simply by redefining their illness or trauma or bereavement into a chance to overcome and triumph. It's not that they don't suffer, it's just that the highly generative tend to be less depressed, more satisfied with life, and more confident about themselves. As a result, they are much more likely to tell their life story in terms of redemption. When they face suffering, they turn it into a change for the better, in themselves, in their relationships, or in their spiritual beliefs.[19]

May, a resilient sixty-year-old widowed office worker in Texas, illustrates a story of redemption. Both of May's sons, ages twenty-five and twenty three, have left home, but the youngest returned recently to save money for college.

"My husband died when my children were in high school, and I worried about how I would deal with their leaving," May says. "I worried about how they would resolve their grief, and I worried about my finances. Just when my youngest son left home, my mother and my mother-in-law died in a two-month period. Then came September 11, and I was in a real low mental state. But since that time, I have turned things around. I lost weight and I started therapy to work through my grief and anger about my husband dying. I started to travel, I started dating, and I can't believe it, but I fell in love again. I even blossomed in my career, and I started in a new job," says May.

May has transformed her sorrow and fear, refashioning both into a different kind of victory. She will never let go of her sadness over her husband's tragically early death, but she has moved past her grief so it won't destroy her life.

Likewise, Noreen, a mother of three in Bloomington, Indiana, is aware of her own capacity for redemption. "I have been capable of weathering terrific storms and surviving. Just after my three children left home, my husband's parents came to live nearby because both had Alzheimer's, and that took all my spare time every day after work. Then one of my children suffered from severe depression, I got fired from my job, my husband had his second heart attack, and my best friend died," she says.

So many problems and tragedies, one after the other, could defeat even the strongest of women. But not Noreen.

"It was tough, but I hung in there, and pretty soon I got another job, and my children and husband recovered," Noreen says. It may seem unbelievable, but Noreen says that she is at peace with herself in a way that she has never been in her life so far.

"My husband and I are still together, I volunteer teaching autistic children a few hours a day, and two of my children are married. I continue to have the opportunity to learn and grow in so many ways, and I'm grateful that I can still travel and participate in the lives of those I love," Noreen concludes.

Noreen is grateful for what she has, not bitter about what she doesn't.

It's almost as if Noreen, and other women like her, were born with a special "I-shall-overcome gene," one that allows them to triumph over adversity. Imagine if doctors could transplant that gene into anybody who wanted one; it would be as popular as Advil at a headache convention.

Rosie, fifty-seven, seems as if she's had a magic gene transplant. Married to a man who is blind and partly paralyzed, she has three children, one of whom is a severely disabled daughter, due to a childbirth injury. "I could afford to stay home because we won a lawsuit over my daughter's disability, and it would have been hard for me to find a job in the rural, poor area where we live in Wisconsin," she adds. They live in the boonies, she says, "because my husband likes it here." So for twenty-five years, Rosie has had to care for her three children and her husband, too.

"I was the chief transporter, homemaker, yard person, cook, and cleaner," she says. "My husband was a teacher and fund-raiser and on a number of state-level committees, so I had to make trip arrangements for his quarterly meetings, getting him there, along with all three of our children."

A few years ago, a short while after two of Rosie's children had left home, her disabled daughter died suddenly at the age of twenty. "I felt my job had been snatched from me, although the money continued to come in," Rosie says. But instead of taking a well-deserved rest, Rosie now spends her time caring for other disabled children, using the skills she learned from taking care of her daughter to help other parents with seriously ill children, all for no pay.

"It's somewhat sad and quiet around the house," Rosie says, "but I have started drawing again, which gives me great pleasure. And I feel that I am giving a break to other moms like me, who have an enormous caretaking burden placed on them."

A key to learning generativity and resilience, I think, is achieving a level of wisdom about what matters in life, as Rosie has. But unfortunately women don't automatically gain wisdom with age as easily as they gain flab and wrinkles.

While it's fairly difficult to pin down the concept of wisdom and maturity, a group of psychologists concluded that mature, happy people are those who remember their lives based on what helped them grow, not on what they bought or achieved or won. By this definition, the researchers concluded that **mature and wise people are those who value doing things for themselves, and not for the approval of others.** Those who live a wise life, they say, are those who recall their lives in terms of deeper understanding, new perspectives, and lessons learned. The ones who remember their lives based on the fancy car they bought, or the beach house they owned, or the day they got a huge bonus at work turn out to be less happy with life and, ultimately, less wise and less mature.[20]

So even as we grow older, not all of us are growing wiser, according to Lachman, who feels strongly that "wisdom is not necessarily something that comes with age, as most people think."

Wisdom has three parts, she tells me. To be wise, you need some basic intelligence, as well as an emotionally even temperament, and you have to have the right personality, which includes the ability to care for and about people other than your own family, according to Lachman. "Wisdom is also being able to make good decisions and good choices about complex, complicated domains of life. You have to be able to look at multiple perspectives, and to see complex issues in a way that's adaptive and helpful," she adds.[21]

Wisdom is kind of like pornography, then. It's difficult to define, but you know it when you see it.

Another piece of the Great Life Puzzle, along with generativity and wisdom, is being resilient in the face of pain and despair, which includes the ability to find redemption in even the worst-case scenarios.

In my Web survey, I listened to the voices of hundreds of women, many of whom were able to grow and thrive in the face of disaster.

There's Tiffany, forty-five, a mother of three in a small town in Utah. Her son joined the army after high school and was sent to Iraq soon after. She also has a twenty-year-old daughter with Down syndrome, a girl who will never leave home.

"I had to go to work every day, stocking shelves, but every minute I was home I was glued to the television to find out about the war," Tiffany says. "I didn't hear from my son for four months, and that was the worst." Still, Tiffany says her life is wonderful, and she is proud that her son is serving his country, although she worries about him every minute of every day.

Or take Cara, fifty-six, an Arizona mother of two who had a benign tumor on her spinal cord. It was removed a year ago, but she has lingering pain, muscle problems, and trouble balancing when she walks. Because her mother died fourteen years ago, she was responsible for her father, who needed a great deal of care during the past few years, until his recent death. On top of it all, Cara works full-time as a customer-service representative, and has to deal with people yelling and screaming at her every day about the lousy electrical or gas service they get from her utility-company employer.

Cara is counting the days until she can retire, so that she and her husband can relax, exercise more, travel, and volunteer at a local cancer ward more than just a few hours a week, the way she does now. Still, she is thankful that she is alive, that the tumor wasn't malignant, and that her daughters are doing well.

"I realized that I had to appreciate what I have, because I've seen people with a lot less who are a lot worse off than I am," Cara says.

So many mothers, like Rosie and Tiffany and Cara, are amazingly, incredibly resilient. They bounce back like a SuperBall, no matter what fate befalls them. What's most astonishing is that in the face of loss and trauma, life-threatening situations and death, many people are much more resilient than you can imagine.

Being Resilient

Psychologists who study this phenomenon believe that not everybody falls apart in the face of grief, and not everyone needs to "work through" their losses. Almost half of the population feel only low levels of distress after a loss, and many never experience a delayed form of grief. The ones who suffer most after bereavement may actually be ruminators, people who lean toward pessimism and depression even in normal times. They're the ones who suffer most, because they tend to focus on what is most upsetting and horrible about their bereavement.

In a study of 253 adults who had recently lost a close relative, psychologists found that ruminators were much more pessimistic about the future than others, both one month and six months after their loss. It's as if their natural predisposition for morose self-pity and gloom is confirmed by their suffering, either major, like bereavement, or minor, like everyday distress. They expect to feel bad, so they do.[22]

Ruminators simply don't have what psychologist George Bonanno calls "genuine resilience in the face of loss." He says that resilient people are those who have a great many friends or relatives they can count on for help. They also tend to be intelligent and have more than a high-school education. Resilient nonruminators usually have had no previous psychological problems and they have another special personality trait called hardiness.[23]

You have a hardy personality if:
* You are determined to find meaning and purpose in life
* You believe you have control over your surroundings and what happens to you
* You believe that you can grow from your experiences, both the good and the bad

Likewise, you are resilient if you have a great deal of self-confidence, almost to the point at which your view of yourself might be unrealistically, absurdly positive. It's easier to be resilient, of course, if you've gotten through life avoiding major tragedies and bereavement, if you've never really been put to the test of staying positive despite personal disaster.

Those who repress their feelings somewhat, who deny the worst, also seem to cope better. That's probably because they are also Deniers, members of the Ridiculously Optimistic Club. Thus, a small degree of denial is actually useful. Finally, being able to laugh through adversity helps people to be resilient.

With the right combination of generativity, wisdom, resilience, and hardiness, a majority of mothers will find themselves living happily ever after when the children leave home.

Where Do You Go from Here?

Now that your children are grown and flown—and you are aged and uncaged—it's really up to you whether you spread your wings and fly or huddle deeper in your nest and wait for winter.

Some psychologists call this stage of adult development the "afternoon of life." But most of us baby boomers would probably prefer to think of ourselves as being just past noon—at, say, one p.m. rather than four or five p.m. And even if we are moving toward late afternoon, we'd like to think that it's the afternoon of a long summer day, when twilight won't arrive until late in the evening. That's because, as baby boomers, many of us have been obsessed by youth since we were young. Although we no longer look young, we believe that we can always think and feel young in our hearts. We still like loud rock-and-roll music, dancing, good food, and partying with friends. We work on keeping our passion alive for experimentation and adventure, by taking risks and living for the moment.

We'd all like to imitate Babette, from Pennsylvania, who was widowed young and then remarried her high-school sweetheart at the age of fifty-nine, after renewing their flame on the Internet all these years later. They found each other again forty-five years after their first date, and it was as if almost no time had passed, Babette says. "We knew right away that we were destined to spend the rest of our lives together," she adds, admitting that she hates to sound so corny, but it's the truth.

Babette believes in love.

Or we might want to be as strong as Gayla, a criminal-defense attorney in San Francisco who never remarried after an early divorce. She's had several serious boyfriends, but no long-term lover. Instead, she runs a blog for incensed divorcées, and sells T-shirts of her own design, with messages like "Denial—Not Just a River in Egypt" and "Check His Wallet."

Gayla has faith in herself.

Or we might try to emulate the strength of Ilene's convictions. She too is divorced, but she's also deliberately celibate, having given herself over to Jesus, as a born-again Christian. "This time alone has afforded me the opportunity to learn who I am as person," she says. "I have grown in my relationship with God, friends, and family, and I have learned not to be ashamed of myself. I have learned to walk in God's ordinances and seek his will and purpose for my life," she explains.

Ilene has faith in her devotion.

If that's not your cup of tea, you might try to emulate Wendy, a weaver in California, who believes that she is now in her third chapter of life. First she was a student. Next a mother. Now she's an artist, she says. She sells her textiles and wearable art on a Web site, where she describes herself, and her work, as "sensual, jubilant, with colors reminiscent of a childhood surrounded by desert spaces."

Wendy's life revolves around "teams of people who love to do what I love," she explains. That includes her theater group and her art-projects group, friends "who are the best substitute for the closeness you feel in a family."

Wendy has faith in her newly invented family.

Whatever and however you choose to expand and enlarge your life after the children are gone, it is almost certain that you will have to do less juggling. You won't need to figure out how to fulfill all of your responsibilities at work while also juggling the needs of your children and your husband. Instead, to follow through on the circus metaphor, you might find yourself more focused on shooting yourself out of a cannon.

You will need to search for your own brand of faith in whatever you decide to do.

What's most important is that you appreciate being given the gift of choice. If you can choose where and when and what kind of work you do, you are blessed. If you can choose where to live and how to live, you are blessed. If you can choose with whom you live and who you love, you are blessed.

These gifts are given only to some, most often to those with financial means and to those who feel that they are in control of their own lives. So if you have these blessings, please remember to appreciate them.

Regardless of how much choice mothers have once they grow beyond the mommy years, most of us are united in our rebellion against outdated expressions for who we are.

Don't call us seniors or elders or golden girls. We are mothers still, though our children may not live at home. We are wives and lovers still. We are workers and volunteers and friends and neighbors and sisters. But please remember, we are not yet old.

Finally, there is one word that best describes what we want from the rest of our lives. It is "more."

We want more fun, more travel, more life, more passion, more friends, more interests, more of everything.

More.

Acknowledgments

The following women were kind enough to allow me to interview them at length. I am indebted to them for their insights, humor, and honesty. Teri Levine, Beth Zolkind, Janice Landrum, Patti Lancaster, Jennefer Schifman, Josie Drinane, Kathy St. Vincent, Diane Trifiletti, Sandra Striker, Adrian Kalikow, Kathy Goltzman, Emie Barnes, Barbara Brandfon, Carol Mayefsky, Marla Schechner, Karen Norton, Helen Liberatore, Paula Bernard, Carol Denberg, Harriet Chertok, Susan Claster, Melissa Spitalnick, Berta Balkan, Maxine Leeds, Amy McNamara, Debby Horan, Yona Gelfand, Eleanor Latimer, Phyllis Kochavi, Cheryl T. Hornyan, Amy Hubbard, Merrily Williams, Barbara Coleman, Jennifer Brinton Roblkin, Debbie Ravacon, Val Wood, Nancy Eshelman, Barbara Dowdall, Helen Harkness, Teresa Nall, Andrea Edelstein, Susan Lovejoy, Claudia Briones, Bea Hirsch de Baumann, Carla Frank, Silvia Heyman, Delia Rubens, Monica Soffer, Annette Vanore, Cookie Woltz, Carol Shaw, Andi Klausner, Francine Nagin, Deborah Richman, Robin Drucker, Karen Bonheim, Diane Gross, Georgann Wilensky, Ellen Schifrin, Laurie Brown-Nagin, Adrienne Ottenberg-Hartman, Betty Robbins, Ronnie Grosbard, Sally Koslow, Laurel Palladino, Turkan Senturk, Louis Troubh, Lori Fife, Susan Levitin, Sara Fleischman, Debbie Konner, Lorraine Gelardi, Susan Reed, Susy Glasgall, Leslie Morgenthal, Robyn Kaplan, Renee Shamosh, Doreen Spector, Donna Hess, Linda Casper, Ronda Ballig, Chris Wood, and many others who asked to remain anonymous.

The following groups and organizations helped publicize my survey, for which I am truly grateful. Jessica Papatolicas at Tufts University, Stacey Coleman-Litterer at Mount Holyoke College, Jane Garrett at Wellesley College, Mary Routh Yoe at the University of Chicago, Jim Roberts at Cornell University, John McMillan at Smith College, Denise Witmer, the parenting teens guide on about.com, the folks at college confidential.com, Peggy Northrup and Barbara Jones at *More* magazine, and Heather Perram at Meredith Interactive.

In addition, I could not have written this book without the Internet savvy of Mark Watkins of txworld.com. He's the wizard behind the curtain at www.drcarin.com. So is George Sharrard, the wonderful wizard of data analysis. Thanks to Lloyd Ellman, Ron Bucalo, Adrienne Hartman, and my sister, Joann Neufeld, who helped with drawings and encouragement and her group of Philadelphia friends.

Thanks to my mother, Trudy Rubenstein, my late father, Alvin Rubenstein, and my brother, Steven Rubenstein. Also, a hearty hug of thanks to Ken Neufeld, Laura Spitzer, Harriet Fier, Kay Brown Grala, Sarah Kahn, Kate Stone Lombardi, Susan Carpenter, Paola Raffo, Penelope Cassar, Julia Anello, Jeanne Silverman, Marion Fischer, Deborah Doyle, Carol Silverman, and Sue O'Connell.

I must thank my agent, Neeti Madan, a doubly great literary agent worth twice her weight in gold; and my editor, Karen Murgolo, whose idea this was in the first place.

Finally, I have to thank my husband, David Glickhouse, and my children, Rachel Glickhouse and Jonathan Glickhouse, for their patience and support and for leaving home at the right time. And thanks to Kippy, too.

Notes

Chapter One: There Is No Empty-Nest Syndrome

1. Liz Seymour, "Inviting anarchy into my home," *New York Times*, March 9, 2006.
2. Ronald C. Kessler, Robert L. DuPont, Patricia Bergland, and Hans-Ulrich Wittchen, "Impairment in pure and comorbid generalized anxiety disorder and major depression at 12 months in two national surveys," *American Journal of Psychiatry*, December 1999, Vol. 156 (12), 1915–1923.
3. Norval D. Glenn, "Psychological well-being in the postparental stage: Some evidence from national surveys," *Journal of Marriage and the Family*, February 1975, Vol. 37 (1), 105–110.
4. L. Dennerstein, E. Dudley, and J. Guthrie, "Empty nest or revolving door? A prospective study of women's quality of life in midlife during the phase of children leaving and re-entering the home," *Psychological Medicine*, 2002, Vol. 32, 545–550.
5. Sharon McQuaide, "Women at midlife," *Social Work*, January 1998, Vol. 43 (1), 21–31.
6. Valory Mitchell and Ravenna Helson, "Women's prime of life: Is it the 50's?" *Psychology of Women Quarterly*, 1990, Vol. 14, 451–470.
7. Leonard Steinhorn, *The Greater Generation: In Defense of the Baby Boom Legacy* (New York: St. Martin's Press, 2006).
8. Barbara J. Crowley, Bert Hayslip, and Juliann Hobdy, "Psychological hardiness and adjustment to life events in adulthood," *Journal of Adult Development*, October 2003, Vol. 10 (4), 237–248.
9. Abigail J. Stewart and Joan M. Ostrove, "Women's personality in middle age: Gender, history, and midcourse corrections," *American Psychologist*, November 1998, Vol. 53 (11), 1185–1194.
10. Bernice L. Neugarten, Joan W. Moore, and John C. Lower, "Age norms, age constraints, and adult socialization," *The American Journal of Sociology*, May 1965, Vol. 70 (6), 710–717.
11. Quotes drawn from telephone interview with Abigail Stewart, March 30, 2006.
12. John R. Logan, Russell Ward, and Glenna Spitze, "As old as you feel: Age identity in middle and later life," *Social Forces*, December 1992, 71 (2), 451–467.
13. Dolores Cabic Borland, "A cohort analysis approach to the empty-nest syndrome

307

among three ethnic groups of women: A theoretical position," *Journal of Marriage and the Family,* February 1982, Vol. 44 (1), 117–129.

14. Frances Goldscheider, "Why study young adult living arrangements: A view of the second demographic transition," presented at the Max Planck Institute for Demographic Research, Rostock, Germany, September 2000. Quotes are drawn from telephone interview with Frances Goldscheider, February 28, 2006.

15. U.S. Census Bureau, "Projected life expectancy at birth by race and Hispanic origin, 1999 to 2100," retrieved from www.census.gov/population/documentation/twps0038/tabC.txt, July 2006.

16. Frances K. Goldscheider, Arland Thornton, and Li-Shou Yang, "Helping out the kids: Expectations about parental support in young adulthood," *Journal of Marriage and Family,* August 2001, Vol. 63, 727–740.

17. Richard A. Settersten, Jr., "A time to leave home and a time never to return? Age constraints on the living arrangements of young adults," *Social Forces,* June 1998, 76 (4), 1373–1400; and "The salience of age in the life course," *Human Development,* September/October 1997, Vol. 40 (5), 257–281.

18. Settersten, "A time to leave home," 1394.

19. Richard A. Settersten, Jr., and Gunhild O. Hagestad, "What's the latest? Cultural age deadlines for family transitions," *Gerontologist,* April 1996, Vol. 36 (2), 178–188.

20. Richard A. Settersten, Jr., and Gunhild O. Hagestad, "What's the latest? II Cultural age deadlines for educational and work transitions," *Gerontologist,* October 1996, Vol. 36 (5), 602–613.

21. Frances Goldscheider and Calvin Goldscheider, "Whose nest? A two-generational view of leaving home during the 1980's," *Journal of Marriage and the Family,* November 1993, Vol. 55 (4), 851–862. See also Shengming Tang, "The timing of home leaving: A comparison of early, on-time, and late home leavers," *Journal of Youth and Adolescence,* February 1997, Vol. 26 (1), 13–23.

22. William S. Aquilino, "Family structure and home leaving: A further specification of the relationship," *Journal of Marriage and the Family,* November 1991, Vol. 53 (4), 999–1010.

23. Lynn White, "Coresidence and leaving home: Young adults and their parents," *Annual Review of Sociology,* 1994, Vol. 20, 81–102.

24. Frances Goldscheider, Arland Thornton, and Linda Young-DeMarco, "A portrait of the nest-leaving process in early adulthood," *Demography,* November 1993, Vol. 30 (4), 683–699.

25. Richard A. Settersten, Jr., Frank F. Furstenberg, Jr., and Ruben G. Rumbaut, eds., *On the Frontier of Adulthood: Theory, Research, and Public Policy* (Chicago: University of Chicago Press, 2005).

26. Roger Avery, Frances Goldscheider, and Alden Speare, Jr., "Feathered nest/Gilded cage: Parental income and leaving home in the transition to adulthood," *Demography,* August 1992, Vol. 29 (3), 375–388.

27. White, "Coresidence and leaving home."

28. William S. Aquilino, "The likelihood of parent-adult child coresidence: Effects of

family structure and parental characteristics," *Journal of Marriage and the Family*, May 1990, Vol. 52 (2), 405–419.

29. Mike Murphy and Duolao Wang, "Family and sociodemographic influences on patterns of leaving home in postwar Britain," *Demography*, August 1998, Vol. 35 (3), 293–305; Jenny DeJong Gierveld, Aart C. Liefbroer, and Erik Beekink, "The effect of parental resources on patterns of leaving home among young adults in the Netherlands," *European Sociological Review*, May 1991, Vol. 7 (1), 55–71.

30. Fumie Kumagai, "The life cycle of the Japanese family," *Journal of Marriage and the Family*, February 1984, Vol. 46 (1), 191–204.

31. Maggie Jones, "Shutting themselves in," *New York Times Magazine*, January 15, 2006.

32. Juan Antonio Fernández Cordón, "Youth residential independence and autonomy: A comparative study," *Journal of Family Issues*, November 1997, Vol. 18 (6), 576–607.

33. Susan De Vos, "Leaving the parental home: Patterns in six Latin American countries," *Journal of Marriage and the Family*, August 1989, Vol. 51 (3), 615–626.

34. Telephone interview with Claudia Briones, April 7, 2006.

35. Nicholas Buck and Jacqueline Scott, "She's leaving home. But why? An analysis of young people leaving the parental home," *Journal of Marriage and the Family*, November 1993, Vol. 55 (4), 863–874.

36. Telephone interview with Abigail Stewart, March 30, 2006.

37. Sue Monk Kidd, *The Mermaid Chair* (New York: Viking Penguin, 2005), 309.

Chapter Two: The Countdown Year

1. Figures are for 2004, from the National Center for Education Statistics, retrieved August 2006 from http://nces.ed.gov/programs/digest/d05/tables/dt05_182.asp.

2. Etienne van de Walle and Nadra Franklin, "Sexual initiation and the transmission of reproductive knowledge," *Health Transition Review*, Supplement 6, 1996, 61–68.

3. Alan Morinis, "The ritual experience," *Ethos*, Summer 1985, Vol. 13 (2), 150–174.

4. College Parents of America, 2006. Retrieved May 18, 2006, from www.collegeparents.org/cpa/about-press.html.

5. Janet Kenney and Anu Bhattacharjee, "Interactive model of women's stressors, personality traits and health problems," *Journal of Advanced Nursing*, July 2000, Vol. 32 (1), 249–258.

6. Janet Kenney, "Women's 'inner-balance': A comparison of stressors, personality traits and health problems by age groups," *Journal of Advanced Nursing*, March 2000, Vol. 31 (3), 639–650.

7. K. S. Kendler, R. C. Kessler, A. C. Heath, M. C. Neale, and L. J. Eaves, "Coping: A genetic epidemiological investigation," *Psychological Medicine*, May 1991, Vol. 21 (2), 337–346.

8. Quiz adapted from John A. Fleishman, "Personality characteristics and coping patterns," *Journal of Health and Social Behavior*, June 1984, Vol. 25 (2), 229–244.

9. Andreas Busjahn, Hans-Dieter Faulhaber, Kristina Freier, and Friedrich Luft, "Genetic and environmental influences on coping styles: A twin study," *Psychosomatic Medicine*, July/August 1999, Vol. 61 (4), 469–475. See also Beata Kozak, Jan Strelau, and Jeremy

Miles, "Genetic determinants of individual differences in coping styles," *Anxiety, Stress, & Coping,* March 2005, Vol. 18 (1), 1–15.

10. David A. Karp, Lynda Lytle Homstrom, and Paul S. Gray, "Of roots and wings: Letting go of the college-bound child," *Symbolic Interaction,* 2004, Vol. 27 (3), 357–382.

11. Quotes drawn from telephone interview with David Karp, April 3, 2006.

12. Anita Ilta Garey and Terry Arendell, "Children, work and family: Some thoughts on 'mother blame,'" April 1999, Working Paper No. 4, Center for Working Families, University of California, Berkeley.

13. Terry Arendell, "Conceiving and investigating motherhood: The decade's scholarship," *Journal of Marriage and the Family,* November 2000, Vol. 62 (4), 1192–1207.

14. Katherine A. DeVet and Henry T. Ireys, "Psychometric properties of the maternal worry scale for children with chronic illness," *Journal of Pediatric Psychology,* August 1998, Vol. 23 (4), 257–266.

15. Ben Shpigel, "Milledge family follows the sun," *New York Times,* March 7, 2006.

16. Alexa Albert and Kris Bulcroft, "Pets, families and the life course," *Journal of Marriage and the Family,* May 1988, Vol. 50 (2), 543–552.

Chapter Three: Three Stages of MotherLaunch

1. Lynn White and John N. Edwards, "Emptying the nest and parental well-being: An analysis of national panel data," *American Sociological Review,* April 1990, Vol. 55 (2), 235–242.

2. Barbara Kantrowitz and Peg Tyre, "The fine art of letting go," *Newsweek,* May 22, 2006.

3. Liana C. Sayer, Suzanne M. Bianchi, and John P. Robinson, "Are parents investing less in children? Trends in mothers' and fathers' time with children," *American Journal of Sociology,* July 2004, Vol. 110 (1), 1–43.

4. U.S. Department of Labor, Bureau of Labor Statistics Time Use Survey, 2003. Retrieved April 2006 from http://www.bls.gov/tus/.

5. Ronald C. Kessler, Patricia Berglund, Olga Cemler, Robert Jin, Doreen Koretz, Kathleen R. Merikangas, A. John Rush, Ellen E. Walters, and Philip S. Wang, "The epidemiology of major depressive disorder," *Journal of the American Medical Association,* June 18, 2003, Vol. 289 (23), 3095–3105.

6. Regina A. Shih, Pamela L. Belmonte, and Peter P. Zandi, "A review of the evidence from family, twin and adoption studies for a genetic contribution to adult psychiatric disorders," *International Review of Psychiatry,* November 2004, Vol. 16 (4), 260–283.

7. Douglas A. Raynor, Michael F. Pogue-Geile, Thomas W. Kamarck, Jeanne M. McCaffery, and Stephen B. Manuck, "Covariation of psychosocial characteristics associated with cardiovascular disease: Genetic and environmental influences," *Psychosomatic Medicine,* March/April 2002, Vol. 64 (2), 191–203.

8. Richard Wiseman, *The Luck Factor* (New York: Hyperion, 2003).

9. Nadine F. Marks, Larry L. Bumpass, and Heyjung Jun, "Family roles and well-being during the middle life course," in *How Healthy Are We? A National Study of Well-Being at Midlife,* Orville Gilbert Brim, Carol D. Ryff, and Ronald C. Kessler, eds. (Chicago: University of Chicago Press, 2004).

10. Laurie Stenberg Nichols and Virginia W. Junk, "The sandwich generation: Dependency, proximity, and task assistance needs of parents," *Journal of Family and Economic Issues,* Fall 1997, Vol. 18 (3), 299–326.

11. Russell A. Ward and Glenna Spitze, "Sandwiched marriages: The implications of child and parent relations for marital quality in midlife," *Social Forces,* December 1998, Vol. 77 (2), 647–663.

12. Valerie A. LaSorsa and Iris G. Fodor, "Adolescent daughter/Midlife mother dyad: A new look at separation and self-definition," *Psychology of Women Quarterly,* December 1990, Vol. 14 (4), 593–606.

13. Lucy Rose Fischer, "Transitions in the mother-daughter relationship," *Journal of Marriage and the Family,* August 1981, Vol. 43 (3), 613–622.

Chapter Four: Back to Stage Zero

1. Lynn White, "Coresidence and leaving home: Young adults and their parents," *Annual Review of Psychology,* 1994, vol. 20, 81–102.

2. Harry Blatterer, "New adulthood: Personal or social transition?" Center for Social Change Research, Queensland University of Technology, October 2005.

3. Telephone interview with Frances Goldscheider, February 28, 2006.

4. James Gorman, "In some bird species, little chance for an empty nest," *New York Times,* October 29, 2002.

5. P. Byrnes, *New Yorker,* April 10, 2006, 36.

6. Robin W. Weinick, "Sharing a home: The experiences of American women and their parents over the twentieth century," *Demography,* May 1995, Vol. 32 (2), 281–297.

7. Frances Goldscheider, Calvin Goldscheider, Patricia St. Clair, and James Hodges, "Changes in returning home in the United States, 1925–1985," *Social Forces,* December 1999, Vol. 78 (2), 695–728.

8. U.S. Census Bureau, "Estimated median age at first marriage, by sex: 1890 to the present," retrieved from www.census.gov/population/socdemo/hh-fam/ms2.pdf, May 2006.

9. Sarah Harper, "Changing families as European societies age," *European Journal of Sociology,* 2003, Vol. 44 (2), 155–184.

10. T. J. Mathews and Brady E. Hamilton, "Mean age of mother, 1970–2000," *National Vital Statistics Reports,* Vol. 51 (1), 2002.

11. Harper, "Changing families."

12. U.S. Census Bureau, "School enrollment surpasses 1970 baby boom crest," June 2005.

13. Michael S. Clune, Anne-Marie Nunez, and Susan P. Choy, "Competing choices: Men's and women's paths after earning a bachelor's degree," National Center for Education Statistics, *Statistical Analysis Report,* March 2001.

14. Frank F. Furstenberg, Jr., Sheela Kennedy, Vonnie C. McCloyd, Ruben G. Rumbaut, and Richard A. Settersten, Jr., "Between adolescence and adulthood: Expectations about the timing of adulthood," Research Network Working Paper No. 1, July 2003; retrieved February 2007 from http://www.transad.pop.upenn.edu/downloads/between.pdf.

15. William S. Aquilino, "Impact of family structure on parental attitudes toward the economic support of adult children over the transition to adulthood," *Journal of Family Issues,* March 2005, Vol. 26 (2), 143–167.

16. Quotes drawn from telephone interview with William Aquilino, May 18, 2006.

17. Furstenberg et al., "Between adolescence and adulthood."

18. Timothy M. Smeeding and Katherin Ross Phillips, "Cross-national differences in employment and economic sufficiency," *Annals of the American Academy of Political and Social Science,* March 2002, Vol. 580 (1), 103–133.

19. Nancy Gibbs, "Parents behaving badly," *Time,* February 21, 2005; Barbara Kantrowitz and Peg Tyre, "The fine art of letting go," *Newsweek,* May 22, 2006; "helicopter parent" in Wikipedia, The Free Encyclopedia, retrieved May 2006 from http://en.wikipedia. org/w/index.php?title=Helicopter_parent&oldid=51945225.

20. See http://www.collegeboard.com/parents/plan/getting-ready/50129.html, retrieved May 2006.

21. Partly adapted from www.dickinson.edu/parent/guide/guide2.html#3, retrieved May 2006.

22. Jon Reidel, "(Re)orientation," *View,* retrieved May 2006 from http://www.uvm.edu/ theview/article.php?id=1682.

23. "Being the parent of a college student," Dickinson College, retrieved May 2006 from http://www.dickinson.edu/parent/guide/guide2.html#3.

24. Mel Levine, "College graduates aren't ready for the real world," *Chronicle of Higher Education,* February 18, 2005, Vol. 51 (24), B11.

25. Ibid.

26. Jeffrey Jensen Arnett, "Emerging adulthood: A theory of development from the late teens through the twenties," *American Psychologist,* May 2000, Vol. 55 (5), 469–480.

27. Jeffrey Jensen Arnett, "Conceptions of the transition to adulthood: Perspectives from adolescence through midlife," *Journal of Adult Development,* April 2001, Vol. 8 (1), 133–143.

28. Karl Pillemer and J. Jill Suitor, "Explaining mothers' ambivalence toward their adult children," *Journal of Marriage and the Family,* August 2002, Vol. 64 (3), 602–613.

29. William S. Aquilino, "From adolescent to young adult: A prospective study of parent-children relations during the transition to adulthood," *Journal of Marriage and the Family,* August 1997, Vol. 59 (3), 670–686.

30. William S. Aquilino and Khalil R. Supple, "Parent-child relations and parent's satisfaction with living arrangements when adult children live at home," *Journal of Marriage and the Family,* February 1991, Vol. 53 (1), 13–27.

31. Lynn K. White and Stacy J. Rogers, "Strong support but uneasy relationships: Coresidence and adult children's relationships with their parents," *Journal of Marriage and the Family,* February 1997, Vol. 59 (1), 62–76.

32. Frances K. Goldscheider and Leora Lawton, "Family experiences and the erosion of support for intergenerational coresidence," *Journal of Marriage and the Family,* August 1998, Vol. 60 (3), 623–632.

33. Russell Ward, John Logan, and Glenna Spitze, "The influence of parent and child

needs on coresidence in middle and later life," *Journal of Marriage and the Family,* February 1992, Vol. 54 (1), 209–221.

34. Russell A. Ward and Glenna Spitze, "Gender differences in parent-child coresidence experiences," *Journal of Marriage and the Family,* August 1996, Vol. 58 (3), 718–725.

35. Lynn White and Naomi Lacy, "The effects of age at home leaving and pathways from home on educational attainment," *Journal of Marriage and the Family,* November 1997, Vol. 59 (4), 982–995.

36. Linda J. Waite, Frances Kobrin Goldscheider, and Christina Witsberger, "Nonfamily living and the erosion of traditional family orientations among young adults," *American Sociological Review,* August 1986, Vol. 51 (4), 541–554.

37. Telephone interview with Abigail Stewart, March 30, 2006.

38. Barbara A. Mitchell, Andrew V. Wister, and Ellen M. Gee, "The ethnic and family nexus of homeleaving and returning among Canadian young adults," *Canadian Journal of Sociology,* Fall 2004, Vol. 29 (4), 543–575.

39. White, "Coresidence and leaving home."

40. Barbara A. Mitchell and Ellen M. Gee, "Boomerang kids and midlife parental marital satisfaction," *Family Relations,* October 1996, Vol. 45 (4), 442-448.

41. L. Dennerstein, E. Dudley, and J. Guthrie, "Empty nest or revolving door? A prospective study of women's quality of life in midlife during the phase of children leaving and re-entering the home," *Psychological Medicine,* April 2002, Vol. 32 (3), 545–550.

42. Russell A. Ward and Glenna D. Spitze, "Marital implications of parent-adult child coresidence: A longitudinal view," *Journals of Gerontology: Series B Psychological Sciences and Social Sciences,* January 2004, Vol. 59 (1), S2–S8.

43. Frieder R. Lang and Yvonne Schütze, "Adult children's supportive behaviors and older parents' subjective well-being—A developmental perspective on intergenerational relationships," *Journal of Social Issues,* Winter 2002, Vol. 58 (4), 661–680.

Chapter Five: The Great Changes in Change of Life

1. Nancy E. Avis and Sybil Crawford, "Menopause," in Sherry L. Willis and Susan Krauss Whitebourne, eds., *Baby Boomers Grow Up: Contemporary Perspectives on Midlife* (Mahwah, NJ: Lawrence Erlbaum, 2006). Quotes drawn from telephone interview with Nancy Avis, June 8, 2006.

2. Nancy E. Avis, Rebecca Stellato, Sybil Crawford, Joyce Bromberger, Patricia Ganz, Virginia Cain, and Marjorie Kagawa-Singer, "Is there a menopausal syndrome? Menopausal status and symptoms across racial/ethnic groups," *Social Science and Medicine,* February 2001, 52 (3), 345–356.

3. WHO Scientific Group, "Research on the menopause in the 1990s," in WHO Technical Report Series, 866 (Geneva: World Health Organization, 1996).

4. Department of the Interior, Census Office, "Report on the Insane, Feeble-Minded, Deaf and Dumb, and Blind in the United States at the Eleventh Census: 1890" (Washington, D.C.: Government Printing Office, 1895).

5. Mary Scharlieb, *The Seven Ages of Woman: A Consideration of the Successive Phases of Woman's Life* (London: Cassell and Company, 1915). Quotes are from pp. 264–269.

6. Carroll Smith-Rosenberg, "Puberty to menopause: The cycle of femininity in nineteenth-century America," *Feminist Studies,* Winter–Spring 1973, Vol. 1 (3/4), 58–72. Quote is from p. 67.

7. Nancy E. Avis, "Women's perceptions of the menopause," *European Menopause Journal,* October 1996, Vol. 3 (2), 80–84. Quotes from telephone interview with Nancy Avis, June 8, 2006.

8. Frederic Thomas, François Renaud, Eric Benefice, Thierry de Meeus, and Jean-François Guegan, "International variability of ages at menarche and menopause: Patterns and main determinants," *Human Biology,* April 2001, Vol. 73 (2), 271–290.

9. Ibid.

10. Ann Kinney, Jennie Kline, and Bruce Levin, "Alcohol, caffeine and smoking in relation to age at menopause," *Maturitas,* April 2006, Vol. 54 (1), 27–38.

11. Debbie A. Lawlor, Shah Ebrahim, and George Davey Smith, "The association of socio-economic position across the life course and age at menopause: The British women's heart and health study," *BJOG: An International Journal of Obstetrics and Gynaecology,* December 2003, Vol. 110 (12), 1078–1087.

12. Ming-Huei Cheng, Shuu-Jiun Wang, Peng-Hui Wang, and Jong-Ling Fuh, "Attitudes toward menopause among middle-aged women: A community survey in an island of Taiwan," *Maturitas,* November/December 2005, Vol. 52 (3/4), 348–355.

13. Foo-Hoe Loh, Lay-Wai Khin, Seang-Mei Saw, Jeannette J.M. Lee, and Ken Gu, "The age of menopause and the menopause transition in a multiracial population: A nation-wide Singapore study," *Maturitas,* November/December 2005, Vol. 52 (3/4), 169–180.

14. Melissa K. Melby, "Factor analysis of climacteric symptoms in Japan," *Maturitas,* November/December 2005, Vol. 52 (3/4), 205–222.

15. S. Kaur, I. Walia, and A. Singh, "How menopause affects the lives of women in suburban Chandigarh, India," *Climacteric,* June 2004, Vol. 7 (2), 175–180.

16. Z. Dilek Aydin, Bircan Erbas, Nesibe Karakus, Osman Aydin, and Sule K-Ozkan, "Sun exposure and age at natural menopause: A cross-sectional study in Turkish women," *Maturitas,* November/December 2005, Vol. 52 (3/4), 235–248.

17. Lotte Hvas, "Menopausal women's positive experience of growing older," *Maturitas,* June 2006, Vol. 54 (3), 245–251.

18. Gabriele Nagel, Hans-Peter Altenburg, Alexandra Nieters, Paolo Boffetta, and Jakob Linseisen, "Reproductive and dietary determinants of the age at menopause in EPIC-Heidelberg," *Maturitas,* November/December 2005, Vol. 52 (3/4), 337–347.

19. Joanna L. Michel, Gail B. Mahady, Mario Veliz, Doel D. Soejarto, and Armando Caceres, "Symptoms, attitudes and treatment choices surrounding menopause among the Q'eqchi Maya of Livingston, Guatemala," *Social Science and Medicine,* August 2006, Vol. 63 (3), 737–742.

20. Susan R. Miller, Lisa M. Gallicchio, Lynn M. Lewis, Janice K. Babus, Patricia Langenberg, Howard A. Zacur, and Jodi A. Flaws, "Association between race and hot flashes in midlife women," *Maturitas,* June 2006, Vol. 54 (3), 260–269.

21. Avis et al., "Is there a menopausal syndrome?"

22. Daniel Kadlec, "The marathon generation," *Time,* June 26, 2006.

23. C. N. Soares, "Insomnia in women: An overlooked epidemic?" *Archives of Women's Mental Health,* November 2005, Vol. 8 (4), 205–213.

24. Arthur J. Barsky, John D. Goodson, Richard S. Lane, and Paul D. Cleary, "The amplification of somatic symptoms," *Psychosomatic Medicine,* September/October 1988, Vol. 50 (5), 510–519.

25. Sandra P. Thomas, "Psychosocial correlates of women's self-rated physical health in middle adulthood," in Margie E. Lachman and Jacquelyn Boone James, eds., *Multiple Paths of Midlife Development.* (Chicago: University of Chicago Press, 1997).

26. Ibid.

27. Y. Netz, S. Zach, L. Dennerstein, and J. R. Guthrie, "The menopausal transition: Does it induce women's worries about aging?" *Climacteric,* December 2005, Vol. 8 (4), 333–341.

28. Ellen S. Mitchell and Nancy F. Woods, "Symptom experiences of midlife women: Observations from the Seattle midlife women's health study," *Maturitas,* August 1996, Vol. 25 (1), 1–10.

29. Joyce T. Bromberger, Susan F. Assmann, Nancy E. Avis, Miriam Schocken, Howard M. Kravitz, and Adriana Cordal, "Persistent mood symptoms in a multiethnic community cohort of pre- and perimenopausal women," *American Journal of Epidemiology,* August 2003, Vol. 158 (4), 347–356.

30. Nancy E. Avis, "Depression during the menopausal transition," *Psychology of Women Quarterly,* June 2003, Vol. 27 (2), 91–100. Again, quotes are from telephone interview with Nancy Avis, June 8, 2006.

31. Gita Mishra and Diana Kuh, "Perceived change in quality of life during the menopause," *Social Science & Medicine,* January 2006, Vol. 62 (1), 93–102.

32. Steriani Elavsky and Edward McAuley, "Physical activity, symptoms, esteem, and life satisfaction during the menopause," *Maturitas,* November/December 2005, Vol. 52 (3/4), 374–385.

Chapter Six: Making or Breaking Marriage

1. Lynn White and John N. Edwards, "Emptying the nest and parental well-being: An analysis of national panel data," *American Sociological Review,* April 1990, Vol. 55 (1), 235–242.

2. Thomas N. Bradbury and Benjamin R. Karney, "Understanding and altering the longitudinal course of marriage," *Journal of Marriage and the Family,* November 2004, Vol. 66 (4), 862–880.

3. Jody VanLaningham, David R. Johnson, and Paul Amato, "Marital happiness, marital duration, and the U-shaped curve: Evidence from a five wave panel study," *Social Forces,* June 2001, Vol. 78 (4), 1313–1341.

4. Quotes drawn from telephone interview with Debra Umberson, June 20, 2006.

5. VanLaningham, Johnson, and Amato, "Marital happiness."

6. Debra Umberson, Kristi Williams, Daniel A. Powers, Meichu D. Chen, and Anna M. Campbell, "As good as it gets? A life course perspective on marital quality," *Social Forces,*

September 2005, Vol. 84 (1), 493–511. Additional quotes from telephone interview with Debra Umberson, June 20, 2006.

7. Phyllis Moen, Jungmeen E. Kim, and Heather Hofmeister, "Couples' work/retirement transitions, gender, and marital quality," *Social Psychology Quarterly,* March 2001, Vol. 64 (1), 55–71.

8. Laura L. Carstensen, John M. Gottman, and Robert W. Levenson, "Emotional behavior in long-term marriage," *Psychology and Aging,* March 1995, Vol. 10 (1), 140–149.

9. Catherine E. Ross and Marieke Van Willigen, "Gender, parenthood, and anger," *Journal of Marriage and the Family,* August 1996, Vol. 58 (3), 572–584.

10. David R. Johnson, Teodora O. Amoloza, and Alan Booth, "Stability and developmental change in marital quality: A three-wave panel analysis," *Journal of Marriage and the Family,* August 1992, Vol. 54 (3), 582–594.

11. Russell A. Ward, "Marital happiness and household equity in later life," *Journal of Marriage and the Family,* May 1993, Vol. 55 (2), 427–438.

12. Kristi Williams, "Has the future of marriage arrived? A contemporary examination of gender, marriage, and psychological well-being," *Journal of Health and Social Behavior,* December 2003, Vol. 44 (4), 470–487. Quotes are drawn from telephone interview with Kristi Williams, June 23, 2006.

13. Peter Uhlenberg, Teresa Coohey, and Robert Boyd, "Divorce for women after midlife," *Journal of Gerontology: Social Sciences,* January 1990, Vol. 45 (1), S3–S11.

14. Bridget Heidemann, Olga Suhomlinova, and Angela M. O'Rand, "Economic independence, economic status, and empty nest in midlife marital disruption," *Journal of Marriage and the Family,* February 1998, Vol. 60 (1), 219–231.

15. Nadine F. Marks, "Flying solo at midlife: Gender, marital status, and psychological well-being," *Journal of Marriage and the Family,* November 1996, Vol. 58 (4), 917–932.

16. Kristi Williams and Alexandra Dunne-Bryant, "Divorce and adult psychological well-being: Clarifying the role of gender and age of child," *Journal of Marriage and the Family,* December 2006, Vol. 68 (5), 1178–1197. Quotes from telephone interview with Kristi Williams, June 23, 2006.

17. Marks, "Flying solo at midlife."

18. Kristi Williams and Debra Umberson, "Marital status, marital transitions, and health: A gendered life course perspective," *Journal of Health and Social Behavior,* March 2004, Vol. 45 (1), 81–98.

19. Williams, "Has the future of marriage arrived?"

20. John Mordechai Gottman, "A theory of marital dissolution and stability," *Journal of Family Psychology,* June 1993, Vol. 7 (1), 57–75.

21. Ibid.

Chapter Seven: Sexuality: All My Doors Are Open

1. Telephone interview with Nancy Avis, June 8, 2006.

2. Quotes drawn from telephone interview with Sheryl Kingsberg, July 6, 2006.

3. Lorraine Dennerstein, Philippe Lehert, Henry Burger, and Janet Guthrie, "Sexuality," *American Journal of Medicine,* December 19, 2005, Vol. 118 (12B), 59S–63S.

4. Julie Fraser, Eleanor Maticka-Tyndale, and Lisa Smylie, "Sexuality of Canadian women at midlife," *Canadian Journal of Human Sexuality*, Fall/Winter 2004, Vol. 13 (3/4), 171–187.

5. Edward O. Laumann, John H. Gagnon, Robert T. Michael, and Stuart Michaels, *The Social Organization of Sexuality: Sexual Practices in the United States* (Chicago: University of Chicago Press, 1994).

6. John Bancroft, Jeni Loftus, and J. Scott Long, "Distress about sex: A national survey of women in heterosexual relationships," *Archives of Sexual Behavior*, June 2003, Vol. 32 (3), 193–208.

7. Laumann et al., *Social Organization*.

8. Ibid.; Bancroft et al., "Distress about sex"; Laumann et al., *Social Organization*; and D. Tomic, L. Gallicchio, M. K. Whiteman, L. M. Lewis, P. Langenberg, and J. A. Flaws, "Factors associated with determinants of sexual functioning in midlife women," *Maturitas*, January 2006, Vol. 53 (2), 144–157.

9. Virginia S. Cain, Catherine B. Johannes, Nancy E. Avis, Beth Mohr, Miriam Schocken, Joan Skurnick, and Marcia Ory, "Sexual functioning and practices in a multi-ethnic study of midlife women: Baseline results from SWAN," *Journal of Sex Research*, August 2003, Vol. 40 (3), 266–276.

10. Linda Cardozo, Gloria Bachmann, Donna McClish, David Fonda, and Lars Birgerson, "Meta-analysis of estrogen therapy in the management of urogenital atrophy in postmenopausal women: Second report of the Hormones and Urogenital Committee," *Obstetrics & Gynecology*, October 1998, Vol. 92 (4), 722–727.

11. Cain et al., "Sexual functioning."

12. Sheryl A. Kingsberg, "The impact of aging on sexual function in women and their partners," *Archives of Sexual Behavior*, October 2002, Vol. 31 (5), 431–437.

13. Laumann et al., *Sexual Organization*.

14. Edward O. Laumann, Anthony Paik, and Raymond C. Rosen, "Sexual dysfunction in the United States: Prevalence and predictors," *Journal of the American Medical Association*, 10 February 1999, Vol. 281 (6), 537–544.

15. List and quotes drawn from personal interview with Sheryl Kingsberg, July 6, 2006.

16. Bancroft et al., "Distress about sex"; Fraser, Maticka-Tyndale, and Smylie, "Sexuality of Canadian women."

17. Cain et al., "Sexual functioning."

18. Laumann et al., *Sexual Organization*.

19. Elizabeth Hayt, "Libidos of a certain age," *New York Times*, July 16, 2006.

20. Laumann et al., *Sexual Organization*.

21. Ibid.

22. Linda J. Waite and Kara Joyner, "Emotional satisfaction and physical pleasure in sexual unions: Time horizon, sexual behavior, and sexual exclusivity," *Journal of Marriage and the Family*, February 2001, Vol. 63 (1), 247–264.

23. "Sexuality at Midlife and Beyond," from http://assets.aarp.org/rgcenter/general/2004_sexuality.pdf, retrieved July 2006.

24. Sarah Mahoney, "Seeking love," *AARP: The Magazine*, November/December

2003, retrieved from http://www.aarpmagazine.org/lifestyle/Articles/a2003-09-23-seekinglove.html, July 2006.

25. S. Leiblum, G. Bachmann, E. Kemmann, D. Colburn, and L. Swartzman, "Vaginal atrophy in the postmenopausal woman. The importance of sexual activity and hormones," *Journal of the American Medical Association,* April 22, 1983, Vol. 249 (16), 2195–2198.

26. Quotes drawn from telephone interview with Jodi Flaws, July 14, 2006.

Chapter Eight: Mistress of Work, Princess of Friendship

1. Cary Silvers, "Smashing old stereotypes of 50-plus America," *Journal of Consumer Marketing,* 1997, Vol. 14 (4), 303–309.

2. From www.census.gov/prod/2005pubs/censr-20.pdf, retrieved June 2006.

3. Judith R. Gordon, Joy E. Beatty, and Karen S. Whelan Berry, "The midlife transition of professional women with children," *Women in Management Review,* 2002, Vol. 17 (7), 328–341.

4. Rosalind C. Barnett, "Gender, employment, and psychological well-being: Historical life course perspectives," in Margie E. Lachman and Jacquelyn Boone James, eds., *Multiple Paths of Midlife Development* (Chicago: University of Chicago Press, 1997).

5. Telephone interview with Stacy Rogers, July 18, 2006.

6. Elizabeth A. Vandewater and Abigail J. Stewart, "Women's career commitment patterns and personality development," in Margie E. Lachman and Jacquelyn Boone James, eds., *Multiple Paths of Midlife Development* (Chicago: University of Chicago Press, 1997).

7. Deborah Carr, "The fulfillment of career dreams at midlife: Does it matter for women's mental health?" *Journal of Health and Social Behavior,* December 1997, Vol. 38 (4), 331–344.

8. Stacy J. Rogers and Danelle D. DeBoer, "Changes in wives' income: Effects on marital happiness, psychological well-being, and the risk of divorce," *Journal of Marriage and the Family,* May 2001, Vol. 63, 458–472.

9. From www.census.gov/hhes/www/income/histinc/f22.html, retrieved July 2006.

10. Elaine Wethington, "Expecting stress: Americans and the 'midlife crisis,'" *Motivation and Emotion,* June 2000, Vol. 24 (2), 85–103.

11. Elaine Wethington, Ronald C. Kessler, and Joy E. Pixley, "Turning points in adulthood," in Orville Gilbert Brim, Carol D. Ryff, and Ronald C. Kessler, eds., *How Healthy Are We? A National Study of Well-Being at Midlife* (Chicago: University of Chicago Press, 2004).

12. Frederick T. L. Leong and Kristin A. Boyle, "An individual differences approach to midlife career adjustment: An exploratory study," in Margie E. Lachman and Jacquelyn Boone James, eds., *Multiple Paths of Midlife Development* (Chicago: University of Chicago Press, 1997).

13. Kevin E. Cahill, Michael D. Giandrea, and Joseph F. Quinn, "Are traditional retirements a thing of the past? New evidence on retirement patterns and bridge jobs," September 2005, retrieved from http://agingandwork.bc.edu/documents/bridge_jobs_post_002.pdf, July 2006.

14. Lisa A. Keister and Natalia Deeb Sossa, "Are baby boomers richer than their parents? Intergenerational patterns of wealth ownership in the United States," *Journal of Marriage and the Family,* May 2001, Vol. 63 (2), 569–580.

15. Robert E. Wilkes, "Household life-cycle stages, transitions, and product expenditures," *Journal of Consumer Research,* June 1995, Vol. 22 (1), 27–42.

16. James T. Bond, Ellen M. Galinsky, Marcie Pitt-Catsouphes, and Michael A. Smyer, "The diverse employment experiences of older men and women in the workforce," November 2005, retrieved from http://agingandwork.bc.edu/documents/Center_on_Aging_and_Work_Highlight_Two.pdf, July 2006.

17. Ibid.

18. Toni C. Antonucci, Hiroko Akiyama, and Jennifer E. Lansford, "Negative effects of close social relations," *Family Relations,* October 1998, Vol. 47 (4), 379–384.

19. Ibid. Also, Antonucci was the first to use this method. See Toni C. Antonucci, "Hierarchical mapping techniques," *Generations,* 1986, Vol. 10, 10–12.

20. Jennifer E. Lansford, Aurora M. Sherman, and Toni C. Antonucci, "Satisfaction with social networks: An examination of socioemotional selectivity theory across cohorts," *Psychology and Aging,* December 1998, Vol. 13 (4), 544–552. Quotes drawn from telephone interview with Jennifer Lansford, July 19, 2006.

21. Laura L. Carstensen, "Social and emotional patterns in adulthood: Support for socioemotional selectivity theory," *Psychology and Aging,* September 1992, Vol. 7 (3), 331–338.

22. Toni C. Antonucci, Jennifer E. Lansford, and Hiroko Akiyama, "Impact of positive and negative aspects of marital relationships and friendships on well-being of older adults," *Applied Developmental Science,* 2001, Vol. 5 (2), 68–75.

23. From my own analysis of the Wisconsin Longitudinal Study, Wave 2 data set, 1992–1994, available online at http://www.ssc.wisc.edu/wlsresearch/.

24. Rosemary Blieszner, "'She'll be on my heart': Intimacy among friends," *Generations,* Summer 2001, Vol. 25 (2), 48–54.

Chapter Nine: Coming Into Your Own (Again)

1. Alisa Burns and Rosemary Leonard, "Chapters of our lives: life narratives of midlife and older Australian women," *Sex Roles,* March 2005, Vol. 52 (5/6), 269–277.

2. Abigail J. Stewart and Elizabeth A. Vandewater, "'If I had it to do over again . . .': Midlife review, midcourse corrections, and women's well-being in midlife," *Journal of Personality and Social Psychology,* February 1999, Vol. 76 (2), 270–283.

3. Quotes are drawn from a telephone interview with Elizabeth Vandewater, August 2, 2006.

4. Corey L. M. Keyes, Dov Shmotkin, and Carol D. Ryff, "Optimizing well-being: The empirical encounter of two traditions," *Journal of Personality and Social Psychology,* June 2002, Vol. 82 (6), 1007–1022.

5. Corey L. M. Keyes, "The mental health continuum: From languishing to flourishing in life," *Journal of Health and Social Behavior,* June 2002, Vol. 43 (2), 207–222.

6. Scott Schieman, Karen Van Gundy, and John Taylor, "Status, role, and resource

explanations for age patterns in psychological distress," *Journal of Health and Social Behavior,* March 2001, Vol. 42 (1), 80–96.

7. William Fleeson, "The quality of American life at the end of the century," in Orville Gilbert Brim, Carol D. Ryff, and Ronald C. Kessler, eds., *How Healthy Are We? A National Study of Well-Being at Midlife* (Chicago: University of Chicago Press, 2004).

8. Daniel K. Mroczek, "Positive and negative affect at midlife," in Orville Gilbert Brim, Carol D. Ryff, and Ronald C. Kessler, eds., *How Healthy Are We? A National Study of Well-Being at Midlife* (Chicago: University of Chicago Press, 2004).

9. Laura L. Carstensen, Monisha Pasupathi, Ulrich Mayr, and John R. Nesselroade, "Emotional experience in everyday life across the adult life span," *Journal of Personality and Social Psychology,* October 2000, Vol. 79 (4), 644–655.

10. Telephone interview with Margie Lachman, July 31, 2006.

11. David M. Almeida and Melanie C. Horn, "Is daily life more stressful during middle adulthood?" in Orville Gilbert Brim, Carol D. Ryff, and Ronald C. Kessler, eds., *How Healthy Are We? A National Study of Well-Being at Midlife* (Chicago: University of Chicago Press, 2004).

12. Diana Kuh, Rebecca Hardy, Bryan Rodgers, and Michael E. J. Wadsworth, "Lifetime risk factors for women's psychological distress in midlife," *Social Science and Medicine,* December 2002, Vol. 55 (11), 1957–1973.

13. Brent W. Roberts and Wendy F. DelVecchio, "The rank-order consistency of personality traits from childhood to old age: A quantitative review of longitudinal studies," *Psychological Bulletin,* January 2000, Vol. 126 (1), 3–25.

14. Alyssa N. Zucker, Joan M. Ostrove, and Abigail J. Stewart, "College-educated women's personality development in adulthood: Perceptions and age differences," *Psychology and Aging,* June 2002, Vol. 17 (2), 236–244.

15. Margie E. Lachman and Suzanne L. Weaver, "The sense of control as a moderator of social class differences in health and well-being," *Journal of Personality and Social Psychology,* March 1998, Vol. 74 (3), 763–773.

16. Margie E. Lachman and Kimberly M. Prenda Firth, "The adaptive value of feeling in control during midlife," in Orville Gilbert Brim, Carol D. Ryff, and Ronald C. Kessler, eds., *How Healthy Are We? A National Study of Well-Being at Midlife* (Chicago: University of Chicago Press, 2004). Quotes from telephone interview with Margie Lachman, July 31, 2006.

17. Elizabeth D. Mansfield and Dan P. McAdams, "Generativity and themes of agency and communion in adult autobiography," *Personality and Social Psychology Bulletin,* July 1996, Vol. 22 (7), 721–731.

18. Alice S. Rossi, "Social responsibility to family and community," in Orville Gilbert Brim, Carol D. Ryff, and Ronald C. Kessler, eds., *How Healthy Are We? A National Study of Well-Being at Midlife* (Chicago: University of Chicago Press, 2004).

19. Dan P. McAdams, Jeffrey Reynolds, Martha Lewis, Allison H. Patten, and Phillip J. Bowman, "When bad things turn good and good things turn bad: Sequences of redemption and contamination in life narrative and their relation to psychosocial adaptation in midlife adults and in students," *Personality and Social Psychology Bulletin,* April 2001, Vol. 27 (4), 474–485.

20. Jack J. Bauer, Dan P. McAdams, and April Sakaeda, "Interpreting the good life: Growth memories in the lives of mature, happy people," *Journal of Personality and Social Psychology,* January 2005, Vol. 88 (1), 203–217.

21. Quotes drawn from telephone interview with Margie Lachman, July 31, 2006.

22. Susan Nolen-Hoeksema, Louise E. Parker, and Judith Larson, "Ruminative coping with depressed mood following loss," *Journal of Personality and Social Psychology,* July 1994, Vol. 67 (1), 92–104.

23. George A. Bonanno, "Loss, trauma and human resilience," *American Psychologist,* January 2004, Vol. 59 (1), 20–28.

Index

About the Author

Carin Rubenstein, PhD, is the author of *The Sacrificial Mother: Escaping the Trap of Self-Denial* and has written for the *New York Times* and other national publications. She lives in Sleepy Hollow, New York, with her husband, David Glickhouse, and has two children, Rachel and Jonathan, and a dog, Kippy.